WEALTH AND PROGRESS

WEALTH AND PROGRESS

A CRITICAL EXAMINATION OF
THE LABOR PROBLEM

THE NATURAL BASIS FOR INDUSTRIAL REFORM
OR HOW TO INCREASE WAGES
WITHOUT REDUCING PROFITS OR LOWERING RENTS:
THE ECONOMIC PHILOSOPHY OF THE
EIGHT HOUR MOVEMENT

BY
GEORGE GUNTON

"No remedies for low wages have the smallest chance of being efficacious, which do not operate on and through the minds and habits of the people."
—JOHN STUART MILL.

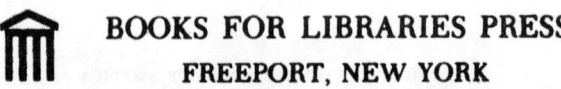

BOOKS FOR LIBRARIES PRESS
FREEPORT, NEW YORK

First Published 1887
Reprinted 1970

INTERNATIONAL STANDARD BOOK NUMBER:
0-8369-5522-6

LIBRARY OF CONGRESS CATALOG CARD NUMBER:
71-130549

PRINTED IN THE UNITED STATES OF AMERICA

TO

PARKE GODWIN,

WHO TO A PROFOUND KNOWLEDGE OF ECONOMIC SCIENCE

ADDS THE BROADEST HUMAN SYMPATHIES,

THIS BOOK

IS RESPECTFULLY INSCRIBED

BY THE AUTHOR.

PREFACE.

IN submitting this book to the public, duty to the dead requires that its origin be told. The central thought contained in the following pages and the first effort at its statement belongs to Ira Steward, of Boston, the history of whose life is the history of the labor movement in Massachusetts. For more than twenty years he was the real leader and inspirer of the labor movement in that State; and to him, more than to any other person, we are indebted for the Massachusetts Labor Bureau—the first, and to-day the best, institution of its kind in the world.

He was the pioneer of the short-hour movement in this country, and after years devoted to the furtherance of its claims, he decided to write what he termed " a statement of the labor question." While thus engaged, the present writer made his acquaintance, from which grew a friendship ripening into a complete unity of thought and purpose.

But Mr. Steward's work was not destined to completion at his hands. After a protracted illness he died, March 13, 1883. When it became evident that he could not recover, he made a special request, strongly re-enforced by his friends, that I should complete his unfinished task.

In accepting this responsibility, however, it was with the expectation that the work was far advanced toward completion. But, to my surprise, and that of

his friends, his papers when examined were found to consist of disconnected matter, made up of more or less extended notes, none of which were in a condition to be used. Hence it became necessary for me to work out the whole subject anew.

Accordingly, while the central thought presented in this book belongs to Ira Steward, its development and presentation is the work of the present writer. By the central thought I mean the idea that the standard of living is the basis of wages, and that social opportunity, or more leisure for the masses, as expressed in *less hours of labor*, is the natural means for increasing wages and promoting progress. But this thought was not developed into any theory of wages or progress, nor was it formulated at all ; neither had he collected any historical or statistical data. Indeed, his contribution was conveyed to the writer by verbal statement rather than by anything found in his writings.

I make this explanation here, that Mr. Steward may not be held responsible for the defects of my work. Whatever there is of value in the original thought I reverently lay at his feet, and all the imperfections of its presentation I take to myself.

Although my practical experience with industrial affairs has been very extensive, and my opportunities for observation have been exceptionally good both in Europe and in this country, and although I have for twenty years been a close student of economic questions, it was not until I undertook this task that I began to see the subtlety, complexity, and vastness of the industrial problem.

In order to treat the subject inductively, I made an extensive investigation into the rise and development of the wages system, and I soon found that the labor

question is not a simple detached subject that can be arbitrarily settled by statutory enactments fixing wages, profits, interest, money, etc., but that it is an integral part of the science of social economics; and that all consideration of the subject by English and continental writers, as well as American, has hitherto failed to recognize the true economic relation the material condition of the masses sustains to industrial and social progress; and also that the question of wages has been very superficially and often flippantly treated.

Therefore it became clear to me that no adequate treatment of the labor problem is possible without a review of the entire question, and in many respects a reconstruction of the accepted doctrines of economics. This task I found myself logically forced to undertake, the results of which I am now ready to submit to the public.

At this point I met with a new difficulty: I have what will make a seven or eight hundred page book— too large for one volume. But it is naturally divided into two parts, both of which are complete regarding the subjects to which they relate. One is devoted to the much-misunderstood question of wages and its economic and practical relation to social reform. The other, to a presentation of the principles of social economics. It gives me great pleasure to acknowledge that it was by the suggestion of Parke Godwin, LL.D., with whose invaluable assistance and criticism I have been favored throughout this work, that I have decided to publish it in two books in the following order.

The first—the present volume—deals with the burning question of the day upon the basis of broad economic principles and in a direct, practical manner that can be

understood and appreciated by the laboring classes. In this work I trust the reader will find a statement of the labor problem as founded upon the eternal principles that underlie and the laws which govern human progress not only through the wages system, where eight hours are practicable and feasible, but the laws which govern social evolution in all its stages, from savagery to the highest phases of civilization.

The second will be more of a text-book for students, devoted to the consideration of the general principles of social progress, of production, of exchange value, the cost of production and its relation to price ; of profits, interest, and rent ; of money, taxation, the duty of the State, etc., which will present the philosophical basis for the present one, and will immediately follow it.

NEW YORK, October, 1887.

CONTENTS.

INTRODUCTION.

	PAGE
Problem of the hour...................................	1
Poverty more dangerous than formerly..................	1
The laborer helpless when discharged..................	2
Laborer's social character changed....................	3
Poverty dangerous to the wealthy classes..............	4
Popular remedies for poverty..........................	5
True basis for social reform..........................	5
Production and distribution, erroneous views regarding.	6
Economically inseparable..............................	7
Productive wealth and consumable wealth...............	7
Concentration of the former...........................	8
Implies wide distribution of the latter...............	9
High wages induce large production....................	9
A chief cause of confusion............................	10
The practical problem stated..........................	11
Object of present work................................	11
Outline of Part I.....................................	12
Outline of Part II....................................	13
Outline of Part III...................................	14

PART I.

INCREASING PRODUCTION: ITS LAW AND CAUSE.

CHAPTER I.

THE RELATION OF LABOR TO PRODUCTION.

Labor and the creation of wealth.......................	15
Fallacy of popular idea concerning.....................	16
Capital not "stored-up labor" labor defined............	17
The perishablenesss of labor...........................	18

The laborer's share of the product............................ 19
Capital does not rob labor, but aids it 20
Capitals the largest where wages are the highest................ 21
Society progresses as human labor is lessened.................. 22

CHAPTER II.

INCREASED CONSUMPTION BY THE MASSES THE REAL CAUSE OF IMPROVED MACHINERY.

False view of the employing class............................. 23
The laborer's prosperity the basis of the capitalist's success...... 24
Capital used only when cheaper than labor..................... 25
Cheaper only when it yields increasing returns................. 26
Low wages mean hand labor and dear products. 27
High wages promote the use of machinery and lowers prices.... 28
No use for capital in low-wage countries....................... 29
High wages stimulate the use of machinery in two ways......... 30
Arbitrary rise of real wages impossible 31
Natural rise of wages always gradual.......................... 31
Effect of rising wages upon profits............................ 32
No permanent disadvantage to the employer................... 33
Rise of real wages the basis of social progress.................. 34

PART II.

THE LAW OF WAGES STATED AND HISTORICALLY ESTABLISHED.

CHAPTER I.

POPULAR THEORIES OF WAGES CONSIDERE

SECTION I.—*The Wages-Fund Theory.*

The doctrine stated.. 35
Generally accepted in the United States........................ 36
It is the doctrine of low wages................................ 37
Necessary part of the theory that " profits rise as wages fall".... 37
Accepted by both laborers and employers...................... 38
Monopolies, tariffs, and strikes all based upon it................ 38
Thornton's attacks and Mill's conversion...................... 39
Professor Cairnes reaffirms and defends the doctrine............ 40

	PAGE
Cairnes's defence considered	41
A learned effort at twisting terms	43
The theory at best only a truism	44
Wages not paid from capital	45
More paid in wages than any wages-fund contains	46
Wages are paid out of present product	47
Labor always furnished on credit	48
The doctrine inadequate if true	49
Wages not governed by supply and demand	50
The facts all against the theory	51
The failure of the doctrine	52

Section II.—*Francis A. Walker's Theory.*

His theory stated	53
Wages the leavings of rent, interest, and profits	54
Wages paid before profits and rent	55
Destroyed by self-contradiction	56
Production not the measure of wages	57
Why production is increased	58
Less complete and more inconsistent than the English theory	59

Section III.—*Henry George's Theory.*

His theory stated in his own words	60
Its logical sequence	61
Necessary part of his scheme	62
Wages always the lowest where land is free	63
The doctrine everywhere controverted by facts	65
A delusive presentation of the case	66
Wages not fixed by the margin of cultivation	67
Shown by the facts in every industry	68
The theory historically baseless	69
Wages nowhere obey Mr. George's so-called law	70

CHAPTER II.

WAGES AND THE LAW OF WAGES.

Section I.—*Wages Defined.*

Scientific tests of the true law of wages	71
Popular definitions of wages	72
The true definition	73

Section II.—*Real and Nominal Wages.*

	PAGE
Real wages and nominal wages defined	74
Social well-being indicated only by real wages	75

Section III.—*The Economic Law of Wages.*

Three industrial states: savagery, slavery, and wages	76
The similarity of the slavery and wages systems	77
The difference in the two systems	78
Labor subject to the law of prices	79
The economic law of prices	80
The law of prices illustrated	81
It fully explains the phenomena	82
The law of prices applied to labor	83
The order of economic movement	84
Arbitrary rise of real wages impossible	85
Mr. Brassey's experience in India	86
Mistaken view of high wages by employing class	87

Section IV.—*Standard of Living.*

Standard of living defined. The family constitutes the basis	88
The true theory of wages	89
The "iron law" of wages fallacy	90
Mistaken view of Lassalle and others regarding	91
Inversion of economic relations	92
Wages fixed by the dearest laborers	93
Why foreigners can save money here and not at home	94
Using and not saving wealth promotes progress	95

Section V.—*The Cost of Living.*

How the cost of living is determined	96
Prices affect nominal not real wages	97
The law as universal as wage-paying conditions	98

CHAPTER III.

SIMILARITY OF WAGES IN ASIA AND EUROPE IN THE THIRTEENTH CENTURY.

Standard and cost of living in India	100
The rate of wages in India	101
Buchanan and Brassey's experience	102

	PAGE
Mode of living in China	103
Wages in India and China eight and ten cents per day	104
Style of living in Asia and England	105
Habitation of English laborer in the thirteenth century	106
Wages in England nine cents per day	107
Difference in the progress in England and Asia since 1300	108
Both governed by the same law	109

CHAPTER IV.

THE RISE OF REAL WAGES IN ENGLAND IN THE FOURTEENTH CENTURY.

SECTION I.—*Why Real Wages Rose after the Famine in 1315-21.*

The first rise of wages in England, errors regarding	110
Inferring facts to sustain a bad theory	111
Supply and demand fail to explain the phenomena	112
Thorold Rogers's deductions controverted by his own data	113
Unemployed labor and increased wages not incompatible	113
The phenomena easily explained by the true theory of wages	114
Why wages did not fall with the fall of prices after 1321	115
Rise of real wages result of social causes	116
Social power of the free cities	117
Their influence in obtaining the "*Magna Charta*"	118
Change in the laborer's social condition	119
Effect upon his wants and character	120
Transformed the rise of nominal into a rise of real wages	120

SECTION II.—*Black Death not the Real Cause of the Rise of Wages.*

The black death pestilence in 1349	121
Real wages not promoted by famines and pestilence	122
Failure of the "scarcity of labor" theory	123
Why wages only rose to fivepence a day in 1350-51	124
Rise of wages in 1350 due to the same causes as in 1321	125
Increase of the laborer's wants—chimneys, glass windows, etc.	126
The new demand made higher wages necessary	127
Efforts of Parliament to prevent the rise of wages	128
The "Statute of Laborers"	129
Its failure to stop the rise of wages	130

CHAPTER V.

THE RISE OF REAL WAGES ARRESTED BEFORE 1450. HOW IT WAS BROUGHT ABOUT.

	PAGE
Statute of laborers not enforced, increased penalties	132
Statutes of 1360 and 1363 fixing the diet and apparel	133
Law limiting social mobility, fatal blow to social opportunity	135
The law of 1388 rigidly enforced	136
Means for cutting off social opportunity completed (1406)	137
The rise of real wages arrested before 1444	138
Wages as fixed by the statutes of 1444, 1496–1514	139
Price of wheat in 1444, 1496–1514	140
Decline of chartered towns, growth of the open towns	141
Abolition of the guilds. The act of settlement	142
True cause overlooked by historians and economists	143
Blunders of Henry VIII. merely the incident	144

CHAPTER VI.

MOVEMENT OF WAGES FROM THE FIFTEENTH TO THE NINETEENTH CENTURY.

SECTION I.—*Why Nominal Wages do not Rise and Fall with the Rise and Fall of Prices.*

Rise in nominal but not in real wages	145
Perishableness of labor. Sellers of, numerous and necessitous	146
Wages move slower than prices. The last to rise or fall	147

SECTION II.—*Wages and Prices in the Sixteenth Century—Effect of Henry VIII.'s Depreciation of the Currency.*

Necessity of large generalizations	148
Rogers's pessimism the cause of much error	149
Comparison of special dates misleading	150
General averages the only reliable data	151
Full table of prices and wages 1520–82	152
Average price of wheat and labor 1520–82	153
Wages rose twenty-seven and wheat twenty-eight per cent	154
Wages fixed according to the price of bread—"gallon loaf" the basis	155
Cost of living the final standard	156

SECTION III.—*Wages and Prices during the Seventeenth, Eighteenth, and Nineteenth Centuries.*

	PAGE
Average price of wheat for the seventeenth century	156
Rate of wages and price of wheat for the eighteenth century	157
Dawn of the factory system. Increased social intercourse	159
Real wages of artisans began to rise again	159
Why agricultural wages did not rise in the same ratio	160

CHAPTER VII.

UNIVERSALITY OF THE LAW OF WAGES.

SECTION I.—*Wages and the Cost of Living in Different Countries.*

Causes that affect the cost of living	162
Wages higher in large than in small towns. The law universal	163
Trades-union prices unconsciously based upon it	164
Wages and cost of living in different countries	165
Wages in different industries. Why vary in the same locality	167

SECTION II.—*The Income of the Family not Increased by the Wages of the Wife and Children.*

The man's wages fall as the earnings of wife and children increase	168
Wages of men lower in factories than in other industries	169
Wage-earners and cost of living in 65 industries compared	170
Women's wages fixed by the same law	172
Why they are lower than men's	173
Wages and cost of living of women	174

SECTION III.—*The Theory Further Sustained by Dr. Engel's Law of Expenditures.*

Dr. Engel's law of expenditures stated	175
Its logical sequence. Wants and wages in different countries	176
Wages the highest where social wants are the largest	177
The evidence ample and conclusive	178

CHAPTER VIII.

WAGES UNDER PIECE-WORK.

"Piece-work" a delusive expression	179
"Day-work" wages the basis of "piece-work" prices	181

	PAGE
Historical basis of the law	182
"Piece-work" prices higher in large cities	183
"Piece-work" prices fall, day wages rise as machinery is improved.	184
Sliding scale of "piece-work" prices	185
"Piece-work" prices and "day-work" wages obey the same law.	186

CHAPTER IX.

ULTIMATE ANALYSES OF THE LAW OF WAGES.

SECTION I.—*How the Standard of Living is Determined.*

Standard of living, wants the basis of	187
Economic wants defined	188
Man's economic wants the incentive to all productive effort	189
Production governed by consumption	190

SECTION II.—*Social Wants, How Determined.*

Man, a twofold being, has physical wants and social wants	190
The power of habit universal	191
It affects all classes on all lines	192
Social influence of custom. Observed by economists	193
True regulating principle in the law of wages	194
True test of economic soundness	195

SECTION III.—*The Influences which Determine Social Character.*

Man's state at birth	195
His inherent and acquired wants	196
Internal and external forces—influence of	197
Easy to do as others do	198
Social influences irresistible. The power of ostracism	199
Fixity of habit the guaranty of social permanence	200
How new wants are created	201
Social intercourse the basis of new wants	202
Social wants the basis of character	203
Social character the basis of wages	203

PART III.

PRINCIPLES AND METHODS OF SOCIAL REFORM.

CHAPTER I.

POPULAR REMEDIES FOR SOCIAL EVILS.

SECTION I.—*Industrial Progress the Cause not the Consequence of Political Freedom.*

	PAGE
Political freedom the effect of industrial progress	205
Popular inversion of the order of progress	206
The economic condition of woman	207
Her social disadvantages the cause of her low wages	208
Drunkenness a social disease	209
The saloon competes with the home	210
The saloon recedes as the home improves	211

SECTION II.—*Rent, Profit, Tax, and Money Reforms.*

Basic error of these reforms	212
The economic function of money. Scientific basis necessary	213
Currency reform, not a basic social question	214

SECTION III.—*Inadequacy of Socialistic Methods.*

The true function of the social philosopher	215
The mistake of idealizing. Social law the true basis of reform	216
Socialistic industry impracticable—History of	217
Profit-sharing enterprises. Godin's and Leclaire's success	218
If general, it would reduce wages	219
By same law that children's earnings reduce men's wages	220
Claims of the State Socialist	221
The post-office experiment not a financial success	222
Its successful features not due to State control	223
Specialists required to conduct complex industries	224
Public officials seldom experts	225
Socialistic reforms based upon a mistaken premise	226
Sound sense of the trades-unionists	227
Poverty not due to distribution	228
Greater production the only remedy for poverty	229

CHAPTER II.

HOW TO ENLARGE THE SOCIAL OPPORTUNITIES OF THE MASSES.

	PAGE
The first question to be settled	230
Social opportunity defined	231
The true economic fulcrum	232
The basic principle of social reform	233
More leisure for the masses the first condition	234
Leisure and idleness explained and defined	235
Enforced idleness dangerous to society	236
Helplessness of the discharged laborer	237
Cause of enforced idleness	239

CHAPTER III.

ECONOMIC EFFECT OF REDUCING THE HOURS OF LABOR.

SECTION I.—*The General Situation Stated and the Line of Opposition Indicated.*

Reduction of the hours of labor the first step	240
Employers' opposition due to inverted economics	241
The attitude of the press	242

SECTION II.—*The Principles which should Govern the Reduction of the Hours of Labor.*

Less hours sought for uneconomic reasons	244
The social basis for reducing the hours of labor	245
The principle stated	246
Absurd objections. Recapitulation of the arguments	247
Principle must be scientifically applied	248

SECTION III.—*How much can the Hours of Labor be Safely and Wisely Reduced?*

Application of the principle under wage-conditions	249
Hours of labor in different countries	250
Average working day in those countries	251

SECTION IV.—*Direct and Immediate Effect of an Eight-Hour System.*

Number working for wages in the United States	252
Effect of an eight-hour system on enforced idleness	253
Number of unemployed in the United States (1886)	254

CONTENTS.

	PAGE
Unemployed in European countries	255
Effect upon wages if adopted only in this country	256
Its adoption in England, France, and Germany also	256
Number of working children under fifteen years of age	257
Its effect on the general market	258

SECTION V.—*The Permanent Economic Effects.*

The permanent effect the important one	259
The social opportunity eight hours will create	260
Its influence upon the social character of the masses	260
Variation in wages—sphere of their oscillations	261
Influence of less hours upon children	262
Social effect of half-time schools	263
High wages and large productions mean low prices	264
Less hours mean higher wages	265

CHAPTER IV.

THE EFFECT OF AN EIGHT-HOUR LAW UPON PROFITS.

Evil influence of the popular theory	266
A plausible error	267
Fall of wages not a rise of profits	269
A rise of wages beneficial to all classes	270
Short hours not injurious to capital	271
The adoption of the measure should be general	272
It should be gradual. Duty of employers	273

CHAPTER V.

WHAT WOULD BE ITS EFFECT UPON RENT?

Rent subject to the same law as profits	274
Poverty of the poor not due to the wealth of the rich	275
Military and industrial states of society	276
Rome an uneconomic state	277
Rising rents incompatible with falling wages	278
High rents always imply high wages	279
This principle universal	280
Movement of rent in England since 1689	281
Land-owners richer and products cheaper with high wages	282
Redistribution is not reform. Progress must include all classes	283
Less hours beneficial to all classes	284

CHAPTER VI.

FEASIBILITY OF SHORT-HOUR LEGISLATION.

SECTION I.—*History of Factory Legislation in England from 1800 to 1840.*

	PAGE
Short-hour legislation not an untried experiment	285
England the cradle of the factory system	286
Condition of factory operatives in 1800	287
Worked fourteen hours a day and Sundays	288
The first factory bill in 1802	288
Opposition of the manufacturers	289
The use of steam as motive power	290
It enabled the "masters" to evade the law	291
Twelve-hour law for all under sixteen years, 1819	292
Eleven and a half hour law, 1825—eleven-hour law, 1831	293
Bitter opposition of employers—their doleful prophecies	294
Child-labor law of 1835 provided two hours a day schooling	295
Efforts to repeal the law and counter-movement to extend it	296
Victory for the operatives in 1839	297

SECTION II.—*History of the Half-Time Law of 1844 and the Ten-Hour Law of 1847.*

Lord Ashley's leadership in Parliament	297
Demand for a ten-hour law. A government compromise in 1843	298
Resulted in a half-time school law	299
Its social and educational influence. Ten-hour bill again pushed	300
Increasing opposition of the manufacturers	300
Bitter opposition of John Bright and Free-traders	301
Lord Ashley's great speech	302
The ten-hour bill adopted in 1847	303

CHAPTER VII.

PHENOMENAL EFFECT OF THE TEN-HOUR LAW AND HALF-TIME SCHOOLS IN ENGLAND.

SECTION I.—*The Striking Success of these Laws Converted Sir James Graham, Mr. Roebuck, and Other Opponents.*

Effect of this *opportunity-creating* legislation	304
Improved condition of the laboring classes	305
Increased wages, improved health, and greater intelligence	306

	PAGE
Testimony of Chief Factory Inspector Baker	306
Conversion of Mr. Roebuck	307
His speech announcing it in the House of Commons	308
Sir James Graham's conversion	308
His candid recantation in Parliament. Mr. Gladstone's testimony	309
Its economic soundness admitted by economists	310
The nine and a half hour law	311

SECTION II.—*Social Progress Shown by the Rise of Wages, the Fall of Prices, and the Diminution of Illiteracy, Pauperism, and Crime.*

Social well-being of the masses, how indicated	311
Percentages not a safe basis for wages comparisons	312
Rise of wages in England since 1850. Mr. Giffin's estimates	313
Manchester Chamber of Commerce returns	314
Leone Levi's estimates	315
Mulhall's calculations—Average rise since 1850 $2.10 per week	316
Fall of prices since 1850	317
Progress of intelligence among the masses	318
Decrease of crime since 1850	319
Decrease in the consumption of alcoholic drinks	320
Decrease in the use of beer among the laborers	321
Decrease of pauperism	323
The improvement not due to free trade	324
Its good influence not confined to England	325
How it prevented the government from siding with the South	326
Ten-hour law in Massachusetts	327
More wages for less hours than in any other State	328

CHAPTER VIII.

RELATIVE INDUSTRIAL PROGRESS IN ENGLAND AND OTHER COUNTRIES SINCE 1850.

SECTION I.—*England and Continental Countries Compared.*

How much of England's progress is due to short hours	329
Actual increase in wages in the various countries	330
Rise of wages in France and Germany since 1850	331
Rise of wages in England, France, and Germany compared	332
Movement of prices in the various countries	333
Fall greater in England than in other countries	334

CONTENTS.

	PAGE
Agricultural wages in different countries	335
Use of steam, wages, and the cost of labor in various countries	336
Productive power of various nations	337
Increase of the income per capita in different countries	338
Superiority of in England	339
Cost in labor of food, clothes, rent, and taxes in various countries	340
Increase in education of children compared	341
Number of letters sent through mails per capita	341
Crime in different countries	342
Pauperism in various countries	343
Progress of political freedom	344

SECTION II.—*Industrial Progress in England and the United States Compared.*

Political institutions not proof against poverty	344
Industrial depressions	345
Rise of real wages in England and this country	346
Prices in the United States since 1850	347
Estimates of Mulhall, Wright, and United States census	348
Use of aggregates misleading	349
Income per capita the only safe basis	350
Increased earnings per capita in England and America	351
School attendance in the two countries	352
Crime in England and America	353
Growth of political freedom	354

CHAPTER IX.

SOCIAL AND POLITICAL NECESSITY OF AN EIGHT-HOUR AND HALF-TIME SYSTEM.

The proposition feasible	355
Lack of progress not due to our political institutions	355
Social character the barometer of progress	356
The wages system favorable to progress	357
Misconception of the law of wages	358
Mistaken industrial policy	359
Its tendency to limit social opportunity	360
Our foreign population indifferent to education	361
Children driven into the mills. They miss the common school	362
The per cent of foreigners in the various occupations	363

	PAGE
Seventy per cent of all outside of agriculture..................	364
Not opposed to immigration. More social opportunities needed..	365
High social character our only protection.....................	366
Long hours and unwholesome hovels prevent it.................	366
The truck system...	367
Operatives' homes indescribable.............................	368
Condition as stated in official reports........................	369
Owned by corporations—Operatives compelled to live in them ..	370
City tenement-houses..	371
Make social and moral development impossible.	372
Cheap voters furnish an excuse for despotism.................	373
Lamentable lack of statesmanship—mainly political quackery....	374
Social character must rise, or the Republic will fall............	375
More social opportunity for the masses our only safety..........	376
Leisure the basis for social opportunity.....................	376
Less hours of labor the first step toward leisure................	376
Eight hours and half-time schools a social and political necessity.	377
Summary and Conclusion.....................................	378

INTRODUCTION.

By common consent the industrial question has become the problem of the hour. There never was a time when the demands of the labor question were so urgent nor when the failure to adequately meet those demands by a scientific solution involved so much danger to the well-being and progress of society as it does to-day. Not because there is more poverty or worse degrees of it in the world than in former times, but because it is more intense in kind and dangerous in character.

That the material and social condition of the masses has been greatly improved with the progress of society, especially since the phenomenal increase in the production of wealth by the use of machinery, no one will deny who is acquainted with industrial history, notwithstanding the cry raised by those who have essayed the task of social reform that "the poor are growing poorer," and that the laborer is no better off than he was in the middle ages.

But while it is not true that "the poor are growing poorer," nor that the economic condition of the laborer is worse than it was in the middle ages or at any previous time, it is unquestionably true that poverty is more inimical to society to-day, more dangerous to social order, freedom, and democratic institutions than ever before.

Nor is the reason for this difficult to understand if we remember the changed social condition of the workingman. In the middle ages he was a serf, inseparable from the lord's estate ; his wants were few and meagre, being practically limited to his physical necessities. When he emerged from serfdom into wagedom he began to obtain, though slowly, more wealth. His wages gradually rose from twopence a day in the thirteenth century to five shillings a day in the nineteenth. With this increase in wages has come increased mobility, larger social opportunities, and consequently a more highly developed and more sensitive character.

Again, as a necessary part of this industrial differentiation and social progress he ceased to be a ward of his master's household, and became simply a seller of service. By this change he gradually became a fractional part of a highly complex system of industry, in which he is an inseparable and almost automatic portion of a vast machine, apart from which he is practically useless as a producer. Consequently, when the factory stops or he is discharged, from whatever cause, he is utterly helpless to procure means for a living, because as an isolated laborer he has lost the power to employ himself. When that point is reached, which the prevalence of enforced idleness shows is painfully frequent, the laborer of to-day is not only more helpless but he is more dangerous to society than were the laborers of the thirteenth century.

When adversity overtook the mediæval laborer, which was very frequently the case, he had the product of a patch of ground or the "offal from his master's table"—all of which he gave up because he could

obtain more wealth and social freedom by working for wages. This has done a thousand times more for him than any form of paternal industry could ever have done. He has been revolutionized in character, passing from a simple life of few wants and necessities to a varied and complex one, where he is more sensitive to social disadvantages and more sensible of his power as a social factor. The product of a little patch of land, which would have satisfied all his wants in the thirteenth century, when he lived in a mud hut without window, chimney, or furniture, would not now be thought of, much less endured, under any circumstances. The social sensibility of the modern laborer is such that it would not only be impossible for him to accept "offal from his master's table," but he cannot, without incurring contempt, accept pauper aid, though it be four times as great in amount as the maximum mediæval wages. And to quietly lie down and die of starvation he will not, as he ought not to do! He has so far outgrown his faith in the divine right of rulers or in the sacredness of the property of the "superior classes" that life is more sacred than all else. To him no interest, no rights, no class, no institutions, and, if the worst comes, even no form of government is as sacred as the social demands of his family. Unlike his mediæval ancestors, rather than sacrifice the latter he will destroy the former, and, Samson-like, pull down the whole structure of society in his own fall. This is clearly shown by the readiness with which he disregards social usages, legal rights, or property interests in inaugurating strikes, industrial riots, and social revolutions in order to obtain redress for his industrial grievances; also by the prevalence of revolutionary organizations seen in Europe and this

country, which openly denounce all claims of vested interests and the social superiority of any class.

For these reasons, together with the fact that there is vastly more accumulated social wealth in the community now than at any previous time, is poverty among the laboring classes more dangerous to the interests of society in general, and to the wealthy classes in particular, than ever before.

Thus it is that while social progress and civilization confers almost unlimited advantages, it at the same time imposes grave responsibilities.

It is a fundamental law in all growth that it should be symmetrical. The top of anything cannot continue to increase in extent and power without the bottom being correspondingly strengthened and enlarged. So it is with society. No portion of it can continuously improve without the progress of the whole. Consequently, the increased wealth, opportunity, and freedom of the "successful classes" can only be permanently secured to them in proportion as the poverty of the masses is diminished and their social opportunities and freedom are enlarged. The dangers that menace society at the top increase exactly in proportion as the development of the bottom, upon which it depends, is neglected. This is demonstrated in the history of every arrested, declining, or fallen nation or civilization the world ever saw.

Therefore, how to eliminate poverty is the problem which concerns alike the wealthy and laboring classes. This can be accomplished in but one way—viz., by *increasing wealth*, and not by taking it from those who have and giving to those who have not. It is impossible to make any important diminution of the poverty of the laboring classes, constituting nearly eighty per

cent of the population, by any redistribution of the present wealth, for the reason that there is not now nor was there ever enough wealth in existence, however divided, to make any appreciable improvement in the general condition of the masses.

Hence the true remedy for poverty is not to be found in any scheme for the arbitrary, artificial manipulation of profits, rents, or taxes, however equitable, because at best such an operation would only be a transfer and not an *increase* of wealth.

Take, for example, Mr. George's plan for abolishing poverty by confiscating the rent, which, he says, "swallows up all the gain" of civilization. When we examine the facts we find that the rent from the land in this country, if equally divided among the people, would, according to the returns for 1880, give about two cents a day per head. What would that do toward abolishing poverty? Simply nothing. It would only be equal to reducing the taxes one half. Any proposition —and this is the most rose-colored one yet heard of— which will only increase the wealth of the masses two cents a day can hardly be worth the effort as a measure for the elimination of poverty.

The same is true of all schemes for the redistribution of present wealth, by whatever means. It is, I repeat, to the increase of the total quantity of wealth produced, so that the laborer can have vastly more without anybody having any less, that we must look for any permanent and general diminution of poverty.

The question, therefore, for the social reformer and statesman to ask is not how can rents be abolished and profits reduced, but how can *the aggregate wealth per capita of the population be increased?* At the very outset of the discussion we are brought face to face

with one of the most important and at the same time the least understood questions connected with economic science—*i.e.*, the true economic relation that consumption, which for the masses means wages, sustains to production. Production and distribution are generally regarded, by both the laboring and employing class, not only as distinct, but quite different questions; as though wealth was produced by one set of economic forces and distributed by another. Hence we find among the workingmen, and especially social reformers, that the great complaint is that "there is too much concentration of wealth and too little distribution;" that existing institutions are "all in the interest of production and against the distribution of wealth;" that it is not a greater production but a more equal or equitable distribution of wealth that is needed," etc.

This view has very naturally given rise to many arbitrary schemes for industrial reform, such as the abolition of interest, profits, rent, etc., many of which would, if undertaken, involve an entire revolution of our industrial and social institutions; while if the true relation that distribution sustains to production were apprehended and clearly set forth, no such mistaken notions would ever obtain.

Distribution as a distinct economic function has no existence apart from production—that is, there is no social factor whose normal function is to distribute wealth. It is true that wealth is produced by and distributed among the various members of the community; but the distinction between production and distribution is purely a metaphysical one, existing only as a mental concept, while as an actual economic fact it has no existence. In a word, economic or industrial

distribution is an inseparable and indispensable
the necessary process of production, and cannot take
place in any other way (except by charity or theft,
which is uneconomic).

For example, the payment of wages is distribution, but it takes place only as an investment in production. The employer pays wages not to dispense wealth, but always to procure more wealth ; therefore, as an employer his economic function is not a distributor, but a producer, the distribution taking place as an inevitable result of his efforts to produce. And for the same reason that there can be no production apart from distribution, the latter cannot take place without the former.* Therefore, to talk of increasing production without enhancing distribution, or of increasing distribution without at the same time enlarging production is the simplest economic nonsense ; and the notion so commonly held by socialistic reformers that all concentration of wealth is injurious to the social well-being of the masses is equally erroneous.

It should be remembered that there are two kinds of wealth—productive wealth and consumable wealth. The former consists of that which is devoted to production as capital, while the latter consists of that proportion of wealth which is capable of directly ministering to our wants and desires. The former—productive wealth or capital—exists mainly in tools and implements of production, such as machinery, buildings, railroads, ships, etc., and these cannot directly minister to our wants ; that is to say, they cannot serve us as food, clothes, shelter, etc., but can only minister to our needs indirectly by producing those

---

* For a full discussion of the relation of consumption to production, the reader must be referred to the second volume.

things which will do so; therefore, the only possible interest the laborer or the community can have in the disposition of this class of wealth is that it shall be so employed as to give the largest amount of products at the least expense to the consumer. If by having $100,000,000 capital concentrated in the hands of a hundred men devoted to the production of shoes in large factories, where as high or higher wages can be paid for labor and the shoes given to the consumer for ten cents a pair less than would be possible by having the same $100,000,000 among a million men with small factories, clearly it is to the interest of both the laborer and the general community to have this wealth concentrated in the hands of the smaller number of persons. And this is what is taking place more and more in every industry in the civilized world. All statistics show that where productive wealth is the most concentrated the products are cheapest and most abundant. Witness England and America as against India and China.

With consumable wealth, however, the case is just the reverse, as this kind of wealth directly ministers to man's wants and desires; the more general its distribution, the more uniform will be the social well-being of all classes of the community. And fortunately for civilization all the influences of economic and social differentiation conspire against the concentration of this kind of wealth. Nobody has any interest in concentrating consumable wealth; and what nobody has any interest in doing will most assuredly never be done.

The only wealth that any class has any interest in concentrating is productive wealth (capital). And it is one of the divine phases of natural law in eco-

nomics that the concentration of productive wealth —which everybody has an interest in promoting—can only take place in proportion as the diffusion of consumable wealth is increased. It is to the interest of the most selfish and sordid capitalist, manufacturer, merchant, or trader to sell his products. Indeed, it is only in proportion as they can thus *dispose* of their consumable wealth that they or the community derive any benefit from the use of their productive wealth (capital).

Accordingly we find the world over that the production of consumable wealth per capita of the population is the greatest and its distribution among the masses the most general where productive wealth is the most concentrated.

In this country and in England, where the concentration of capital is the greatest in the world, the productive capacity per capita is nearly two and a half times that of the average in continental countries, five times as large as that of Italy, Spain, and Portugal,[*] and twelve times that of China and India; and the income per capita[†] is about thirteen times as great as that of India and China, six times that of Italy, Spain, and Portugal, and more than twice that of the average on the European Continent; and the general rate of wages [‡] in England is about ten times that of Asia and nearly double that of Continental Europe; while in this country it is about fifteen times that of Asia, and within a fraction of three times that of the average on the Continent.

In fact, it may be laid down as a fundamental law in

---

[*] Mulhall, "History of Prices," pp. 53–55.
[†] *Ibid.*, "Progress of the World," p. 42.
[‡] *Ibid.*, "History of Prices," p. 126.

economics that consumable wealth is most abundantly produced and most generally and equitably distributed among the masses in proportion as the use of productive wealth (capital) is concentrated.*

When this fact is fully recognized by both capitalists and laborers, one of the chief causes of confusion and misunderstanding in the industrial controversy will have been removed. The employing classes will then abandon the pernicious notion that low wages are conducive to large production and high profits, and the laborers will forever discard the absurd idea that limiting production can in any social or permanent sense tend to increase distribution.

It is because production and distribution are inseparable phases of the same economic movement that large production and extensive consumption per capita are the universal accompaniments of each other. Witness the small production and meagre consumption in India and China, and the large production and relatively varied and extensive consumption per capita in England and this country.

As the diminution of poverty is only possible by a greater diffusion of wealth among the masses, and as any permanent appreciable increase in the distribution of wealth is equally impossible without a larger aggregate production, the problem is, how to increase the wealth per capita, and to enable that increase to find its way to the laboring classes.

The production of wealth, with the exception of the little variation in the muscular power of different individuals, which is too slight to be considered, is wholly a question of tools and implements. The productive

---

* For the full statement of this principle, the reader is referred to the next volume.

capacity of man by hand labor is almost uniform, while that with the aid of tools, machinery, etc., varies many hundred per cent, according to their extent and efficiency : witness the hand-loom and the factory. The distribution of wealth, at least so far as regards the income of the laboring classes, which is what we are concerned with in dealing with poverty, is a question only of wages.* Therefore, to the question, how can the aggregate wealth per capita be increased? the answer is, *by increasing the use of machinery in the process of production.* And to the question, how can that increase of wealth find its way to the laboring classes, the answer is, by *increasing real wages.*

For all practical purposes, then, the labor problem, the problem of diminishing poverty, may be reduced to two simple propositions :

(1) *How can the use of improved methods of production be increased?*

(2) *How can the general rate of real wages be permanently advanced?*

To answer these two questions and thereby show how real wages can be permanently increased and poverty diminished without lessening the income of the profit and rent-receiving classes is the purpose of the following pages.

In order to simplify the treatment of the subject, we have divided it into three parts, as follows :

Part I. Increasing Production : Its Law and Cause.

Part II. The Law of Wages Theoretically Stated and Historically Established.

---

* For a full statement of what constitutes wages, see Chapter II., Part II. The question of rent and profit will be discussed in the next volume.

Part III. Principles and Methods of True Social Reform.

Although these parts each sustain a logical relation to the whole, they are sufficiently monographic in character to admit of being considered independent of each other. Hence, while I should prefer that they were read in the order in which they are presented, the sense would not be seriously affected were any other course adopted.

But while this is true of the parts, it is far from being true of the chapters in each part. Part I. is devoted to production. It consists of two chapters, the first of which treats of the relation human labor, *per se*, sustains to production. The socialistic postulate that " labor is the creator of all wealth"* is shown to be incorrect in fact and inimical to true labor reform. In the second chapter the economic importance of high wages in promoting the use of improved machinery is considered. The capitalistic postulate that the wages and even employment of the laborer primarily depend upon the prosperity of the employer is shown to be an inversion of economic relations. It is demonstrated that the extensive use of machinery and the success of the profit-receiving class finally depend upon the prosperity of the wage-receiving masses. Neither of these chapters can be properly understood without reading the other.

Part II. is exclusively devoted to the subject of wages, and it comprises nine ,chapters. The first is devoted to a critical examination of the popular theories of wages. The second is devoted to a presentation of our own theory of the law of wages. So far as

---

* Platform of Socialistic Labor Party, 1885.

the theoretic treatment of the subject is concerned, this chapter may be regarded as approximately complete. The succeeding five chapters are devoted to an historical review of the movement of wages in different countries and industries from the thirteenth century to the present time. The dawn of wages in the thirteenth century, their marked rise in the fourteenth, their arrest in the fifteenth, their stationary condition during the sixteenth, seventeenth, and eighteenth, and their phenomenal rise in the nineteenth century, in the light of this theory, all become easily explainable. It also affords an adequate explanation of why the rate of wages in the same industries vary in different countries, and vary in the different industries in the same countries ; why they are higher in large cities than in smaller towns ; why, the world over, they are lower in agricultural than in manufacturing and commercial industries, and why the wages of women are universally lower than those of men.

The ninth chapter treats of wages under piece-work, and the last one is devoted to an ultimate analysis of the law of wages.

It is true that we have devoted considerable space to the question of wages. We have been induced to do so for two reasons : (1) Because it constitutes the very kernel of the social problem, which can never be solved until the wages question is philosophically settled, and (2) because it has never received the comprehensive scientific treatment it is entitled to.

Part III., which comprises eight chapters, is devoted to the consideration of practical propositions for industrial reform. As to the means for inaugurating the industrial reform which shall, through the natural operation of social and economic forces, tend to increase

wages without reducing profits or abolishing rents, it is not necessary to say anything here. In closing, however, I may say that every step in that direction has been taken upon a strictly scientific basis. No proposition is suggested which is not based upon sound economic principles and the absolute feasibility of which has not been fully demonstrated by experience.

WEALTH AND PROGRESS.

PART I.

INCREASING PRODUCTION: ITS LAW AND CAUSE.

CHAPTER I.

THE RELATION OF LABOR TO PRODUCTION.

THE idea most prevalent, indeed, well-nigh universal, among workingmen regarding the production of wealth, to use the official language of the largest labor organization in the world,* is: "(1) That labor creates all wealth. (2) That all wealth belongs to those who create it." From this it manifestly follows, "*that all wealth rightfully belongs to the laborer.*" Hence, all who obtain wealth without his consent do so by cheating him out of the product of his labor, and are "thieves and robbers."

This is not merely the official dogma of a single society, but it constitutes the basis of nearly every proposition and the essence of nearly all economic literature put forth in the name of industrial and social reform. With financial reformers the robbery is labelled "interest and usury;" with land reformers it is "rent," and with the socialists, in the language of their own economist, Karl Marx, it is "surplus value," which is

---

* "Polity of the Labor Movement," Vol. I., p. 4, published by the Knights of Labor, 1885.

more sweeping than any of the others, and includes all rents, profits, and interest.

If this formula is correct, and all profits, interest, rents, etc., are "exploitation"—mere plunder of the laborer—clearly the workingmen would be justified in using any means within their power to take possession of all the wealth in the community, as many of their leaders are expecting them some day to do.

But is it correct? If the first proposition is true, the balance of the formula is indisputable; but if it is not true, then the whole fabric falls, and all efforts at social reformation based upon it must surely fail to produce the desired and expected result.

A very little reflection will suffice to show that this proposition, while seemingly true, is essentially false. There unquestionably was a time in the history of man when all wealth was produced by human labor. When man lived on wild berries or such fish and game as he could procure with his own hands, then wealth was all produced by labor; and it may be added that he then got not only all the wealth he produced, but all that was produced. There was then no landlord, capitalist, employer, or politician to take it from him in rent, profits, interest, or taxes. He then both produced all and received all, and it should be remembered that he then got the *least*, and was literally the *poorest* he ever was in the world. From that time to this, just in proportion as he has learned to substitute other forces for human labor in production has the amount of wealth he received increased. Indeed, that is the only condition upon which he would ever consent to change his methods of doing.

Now, suppose the primitive hunter was able by his unaided efforts to procure, on an average, 300 pounds

of game a year, and by devoting two months in the year to making bows and arrows he could with their aid, during the remaining ten months, obtain 400 pounds of game, would the whole 400 pounds be the product of the man's labor? Certainly not. The productive capacity of the man had already been fully tested, and he could only procure 300 pounds a year. The other 100 pounds was, therefore, clearly due to the bow and arrow, which in this case was capital. It may be said that the bow and arrow could not have caught the extra 100 pounds of game without the laborer; true, nor could the laborer have caught it without the bow and arrow, as experience had shown. In fact, that was the only reason he was willing to devote two months a year to making bows and arrows. If he could have procured no more game in the same time with than without the capital, he would have refused to use it. In a word, it is simply because the bow and arrow, in addition to reimbursing him for the two months' labor he has bestowed upon it, makes him a clean present of 100 pounds of game a year, that he is willing to employ it.

Oh, no, says some one, the bow and arrow (capital) gives him nothing; it is simply his own labor in another form. In short, "*capital is stored-up labor.*" Ah! there is where the error begins. That is a metaphysical expression which is a great deal used, and it is very misleading.

What is labor? It is simply human force or energy. Now, human energy cannot be "stored up" in anything but a human being, and only to a very limited extent there. A healthy person would not be enabled to put forth twice as much energy and skill per day during the last half of the year because he had been

idle the first half. It is because of the laborer's inability to "store up" his labor—and if he fails to sell to-day's energy to-day it is lost forever—that enforced idleness has such terrors for him.

But to "store up" human force in anything else than a human being is absolutely impossible. When human energy is devoted to any object it is *expended*, and as human force it is gone forever. If it is wisely directed it will produce wealth; if not it will be wasted. If it produces wealth in the form of a bow and arrow, the bow and arrow is not labor; it is the product of labor. It is a new thing that has come into existence as the result of human energy having been expended upon material objects. The bow and arrow are as distinct and as different from human labor as cotton cloth is from a weaver, or as a rose is from a dunghill.

But assuming for the moment that human labor or force can be "stored up" in material objects, no one will hardly pretend that it can be engendered by them. Therefore, the most that can be claimed by the "storing-up" theory is that the amount of human energy expended in producing an object is transferred to and preserved in that object.

Now, if two months' human force was deposited in bows and arrows, then only two months' human energy could be put forth by the bows and arrows; and if two months were expended on bows and arrows, only ten could be devoted to hunting. We have seen that, unaided, the laborer could only obtain 25 pounds of game a month; hence, in ten months he could only procure 250 pounds; but with the combined force of labor and the bows and arrows he could get 400 pounds. The whole of the additional 150 pounds, however, was not due to the bows and arrows. There

THE LABORER'S SHARE OF THE PRODUCT.   19

were two months' labor deposited in them, and that represented fifty pounds of game, making 300 pounds as the result of the human force and 100 pounds produced by the natural forces combined in the bows and arrows. Thus, whichever way we consider it, the additional 100 pounds of game was produced by capital and not by labor.

But let us carry our illustration a little further, and suppose another person who has an aptitude for making bows and arrows can make a better kind of weapon, one that will kill at a greater distance, and thus enable the hunter to obtain fifty pounds of game a month. He comes to our hunter and says, See here, I can make better bows and arrows than you can, and you can hunt better than I can. Now if you will give me one fourth of the game you catch, I will supply you with these superior bows and arrows, by which you can get 600 pounds of game a year. He accepts the offer, and the result is that, after giving to the man who supplies the capital (bows and arrows) one-fourth of the product, he has 450 pounds.

Now, who has been robbed? Nobody. True, the laborer once got all the wealth, and he now only gets three-fourths; but when he got it all he received fifty per cent less than when he only gets three-fourths of it. And this for the simple reason that the total product had been doubled. Nor is this increased product due to any increased expenditure of labor. There was no more human effort put forth to produce the 600 than was devoted to that of the 300 pounds of game. The increase was wholly due to the use of tools (capital).

When the wealth was all produced by human effort the laborer received it all, and got 300 pounds of game

a year. When he produced a little less than two-thirds of it he received five-sixths, and then got 400 pounds. And when he produced only one-half he got three-fourths of it, and then received 450 pounds a year. Thus it will be seen that instead of the laborer being robbed by capital he from the first received a clear contribution from capital, which constantly increases as its use in the production is extended.

Now, this is just what takes place in all productive enterprises, no matter how subtle and complex the operation may be. There are thus clearly two sets of forces or two kinds of motor power that can be employed in producing wealth. One is labor power engendered and put forth by human beings; the other is natural power engendered and put forth by material objects, as capital (machinery, etc.). The former is slow, clumsy, and ineffectual, and capable of very little increase, while the latter is rapid, exact, and powerful, and is capable of indefinite increase.

Accordingly, in proportion as wealth is produced by human labor is it scant and dear, and the masses are poor and barbarous; and according as it is produced by natural forces (steam, etc.) it is abundant and cheap, and the masses are materially prosperous and socially civilized. Thus, *e.g.*, in India, where wealth is produced mainly by human labor, the annual earnings are about £2 ($10)[*] per capita of the population as against £33 ($165) per capita in this country, where human labor supplies the smallest per cent of the productive power of any country in the world.[†] The same is true of other countries.

---

[*] See Mulhall's "Progress of the World," p. 42.
[†] *Ibid.*, "History of Prices," p. 53.

Hence we find that in England over seventy-eight per cent of the productive power is furnished by steam, as against ten per cent in Russia. In Spain, twenty-four; Italy, thirty-four, and Portugal, forty-two per cent of the productive power is furnished by human labor, as against four per cent in England and America.

In consequence of this difference in the use of natural and human forces in production, Mulhall tells us * " that the united industrial power of six Englishmen and six Americans is equal to that of twenty-four Frenchmen or Germans, thirty-two Austrians, fifty Spaniards, seventy-five Italians, or eighty-four Portuguese." Accordingly we find the general rate of wages in England is nearly twice and in this country three times that of the average in continental countries.

It is thus clear that the laborer is not robbed by capital, but that he always gains by the use of capital, not because of any generosity on the part of the capitalist, but by the inexorable operation of economic law, which prohibits the use of capital except upon the condition that it will yield increasing returns—in other words, that it will give more wealth to the community than it takes from it.

Were this otherwise, social progress would be impossible, as the productive power of the human hand cannot, to any great extent, be increased. Hence, unless some other forces can be harnessed to the production of wealth, man would be doomed to eternal poverty and barbarism, as he has been for ages in those countries where natural forces (machinery) have not—except to the most limited extent—been employed. In short, it is only as capital produces more than it consumes that the laborer is enabled to con-

---

* " History of Prices," p. 54.

sume more than he produces, and social progress becomes possible.

It is therefore clear that human labor does not, except under the most primitive state of savagery, " create all wealth," and that the social condition of the laborer is not necessarily the best when he gets the whole product ; but, on the contrary, wealth is produced by the combined effort of labor and capital, and that, according as the proportion of the total wealth produced by human labor diminishes, the actual amount the laborer receives increases. In other words, the social well-being improves in proportion as nature, instead of man, is made to do the work of producing the world's wealth.

This brings us to the question, How is the use of natural or labor-saving forces in production determined ? which will be the subject of the next chapter.

CHAPTER II.

INCREASED CONSUMPTION BY THE MASSES THE REAL CAUSE OF IMPROVED MACHINERY.

WHAT we have said in the last chapter about the mistaken notions entertained by the laborers regarding their economic relation to production, the employing class will be quick to appreciate. They have no difficulty in seeing that the extensive use of capital is indispensable to a large production of wealth. Nor are they at all slow to observe the fact that rising wages and falling prices accompany the extensive use of labor-saving methods of production. But when we come to question of how the use of improved machinery is determined, we find that the capitalists as a class are very little better informed as to their economic relation to production than are the unlettered laborers. They almost invariably assume and very often offensively insist that the use of machinery is due to their self-denial and sagacity. They hold it is because they have been willing to forego the luxuries others enjoy, and had the wisdom to invest their capital in improved machinery, that laborers are enabled to have higher wages, consumers lower prices, and social progress has been made possible.

With such an inflated estimate of his own importance, backed by economic lore, it is not surprising that the average employer should regard the laborer as an ungrateful wretch when he asks for higher wages, and,

as is often the case, remind him that it is only by the employer's sacrifice and forethought that he has hitherto been enabled to receive any wages at all.

A little closer consideration of the subject, however, will show that this view is as erroneous as is that of the laborer, who assumes that he is the sole producer of wealth. We shall find that instead of the laborer's higher wages and improved social condition being the result of the employer's investment in machinery, the case is just the reverse—viz., that the successful investment of capital in machinery is made possible only by the increased consumption (higher wages) of the masses.* Nor is the reason for this difficult to understand. The fact that man endeavors to satisfy his wants with the minimum effort is as universal as the human race. Hence, as there are two sets of forces, human and natural (labor and capital), by which wealth can be produced, he will naturally use that force which will, under the circumstances, enable him to obtain wealth the easiest. If the primitive hunter could procure as much game and defend himself against attack as well without as with the bow and arrow or other implement, he would not devote any time to making such implements, for the obvious reason that nothing would be gained by so doing.

Upon the same principle, in a highly complex society, where wealth is mostly obtained by exchange, man will use those things which, other things being the same, he can obtain the cheapest. Hence, the use of that which undersells will always supplant that which is undersold. Consequently, just as fast as any commodity can be undersold will the methods by

---

* Brassey's "Work and Wages," ch. v.

which it is produced be driven into disuse. Therefore, whether at any given time or place, labor (human force) or capital (natural forces, machinery, etc.) is most extensively used in the production of wealth will depend upon which of them can produce wealth the cheapest.

It will thus be seen that capital becomes a factor in production only in proportion as it is able to produce wealth *cheaper* than it can be produced by human labor. For the same reason that a man will not devote his labor to production except he can obtain wealth by so doing, will he refuse to devote the products of his labor (capital) to production except he can thereby gain something. Then, as neither the community will use nor the capitalist furnish improved methods of production unless both can obtain more wealth for the same exertion by the undertaking, capital can be permanently employed in production only when it yields more than it costs. In other words, the permanent use of improved machinery is possible only under conditions of increasing returns.

By increasing returns we mean the conditions under which the application of additional capital to production will yield more than a proportional increase of product, which is illustrated in the history of every successful enterprise. Thus, *e.g.*, in the cotton industry in this country, in 1831, there was $651 of capital invested to each operative employed in the manufacture of cotton cloth. The annual product in finished cloth was 956.70 pounds per operative, or 1.46 pounds per dollar invested. In 1880 the capital invested in the business was $1207 per operative, and the annual product was 3519.47 pounds of cloth per operative, or 2.91 pounds per dollar invested ; thus showing that

with an investment in improved machinery of $1207 per operative in 1880, each dollar produced ninety-nine per cent more cloth than it did in 1831, when only $651 per operative were so invested. By this increasing return the laborer could have higher wages, the consumer have the goods at lower prices, and the employer could have a larger aggregate income at even a smaller rate of profit. This is what the history of the present century shows* has taken place wherever increasing returns were possible.

To make natural forces cheaper than human labor as a productive power is to make wealth and civilization cheaper for everybody than poverty and barbarism. Therefore, how to make increasing returns to capital, and hence the general use of machinery possible, is primarily to solve the social or poverty problem. What, then, are the social conditions necessary to make increasing returns and the use of natural force in production *economically* possible?

To begin with, natural forces can only be harnessed to production by the use of capital. For the same reason that the laborer will not devote his labor to production without some reward, the owner of wealth will not devote it to production as capital unless he can gain something thereby. In order to accomplish this he must do one of three things—viz., either give the laborer less, charge the consumer more for his products, or produce a larger amount in the same time. The first is impossible, because the laborer will refuse to work for less than he could get

---

* Carroll D. Wright estimates (1880) that wages in the cotton industry in this country have about doubled since 1828. Since 1826 the price of heavy sheetings has been reduced from 13 to 7½ cents a yard, and that of printed calicoes from 22 to 7 cents a yard.

by hand labor ; the second is equally so, because the consumers will refuse to buy at a higher price than the hand laborer will sell at ; therefore, the third condition—viz., to produce more in the same time—is the only one upon which the owner of capital can gain anything by the transaction, and consequently the only one upon which he will consent to invest his capital in machinery.

Whatever will do this will actually yield increasing returns, and lessen the cost of producing wealth. But there is one other condition that is necessary to make it economically and socially a success. That is that the increased product must *all be sold*. If it cannot be sold it is socially wasted. Wealth that is not consumed in the gratification of human wants is economically as if it had not been produced.

In order to illustrate the operation of this principle, let us suppose that in a given community the consumption of fish is 100 pounds a day. To obtain this amount of fish required the labor of ten men, at $1 a day each. At that rate the fish would cost ten cents per pound. Let us further suppose that by the use of boats, nets, etc., instead of fish-hooks, the same men could catch 300 pounds of fish per day. We will also suppose that the boats, etc., would last two years, and would require the labor of four men one year to make them. That would be equal to constantly employing two men in producing boats, nets, etc. By thus devoting the product of two men's labor to making tools they would be able to increase their production of fish 200 per cent. By this means, provided the product could all be sold, the cost of the fish would be reduced from ten to four cents per pound. But suppose only 200 pounds of the fish were consumed. As the cost

of producing the whole 300 pounds would have to be defrayed out of the income from that portion which was sold—the balance being as if it had not been produced—obviously the 200 pounds consumed would have to be sold at six cents a pound. And for the same reason if only the original 100 pounds were consumed they would cost twelve cents a pound.

It will thus be seen that if the consumption of fish had remained stationary, the small demand of 100 pounds per day could have been supplied at two cents a pound cheaper by the old method than by the new; while if the consumption had grown to 200 pounds a day, by investing as much capital in boats, nets, etc., as would pay for the labor of two men, the product of fish would be doubled, and the cost to the consumer reduced forty per cent. And if the consumption had risen to 300 pounds a day, the same investment of capital would have trebled the product, and reduced the price of the fish sixty per cent. It will thus be seen that with the small consumption (low wages) the products of hand labor were cheaper than those of natural forces (tools); and in proportion as consumption enlarged (wages rose) increasing returns for the use of capital became possible, and consequently the products of natural forces (boats, nets, etc.) became cheaper than those of hand labor. Manifestly, therefore, the social utility and hence the economic possibility of adopting improved methods of production finally depends upon the increased consumption of wealth by the community—by the masses—which, in modern society, means *increasing wages.*

Therefore, instead of the increased wages and improved social condition of the laboring classes being in any true sense due to the "sacrifice" and wisdom

of the employing class, by investing their capital in machinery, the successful use of capital to any considerable extent, and hence the income of the entrepreneur class, ultimately depends upon increasing the economic capacity of the masses to consume wealth—*i.e.*, *the rise of real wages.*

Accordingly, we find that among the American Indians, Esquimaux, Patagonians, and other barbarian tribes there is practically no use for the employing and capitalist class. They cannot get a living among those people, and why? Simply because the consumption of wealth per capita is so small that they can supply their wants with hand labor or by means of the rudest tools cheaper than with modern machinery. And in India and China, where the consumption per capita is a little larger, the chance for the entrepreneur class to obtain a living is a little better. It is a little better still in Russia, Austria, Italy, and Spain, where wages are higher; still better in France and Germany, and best of all in England and the United States, where the wages and consumption per capita are the largest in the world.*

---

* According to Mulhall, in India, with wages at 60 to 70 cents a week, the capital invested in production is only about $35 per head of the population. In Russia, with wages at $3.60 per week, it is $190 per capita. In Austria, Italy, Spain, and Portugal, with wages at $3.76, it is about $350 per capita. In Germany, with wages at $3.84, it is $540 per capita. In France, with wages at about $5, the capital invested is about $1010 per capita, and in England, with wages at $7.74 per week, it is $1300 per capita. Accordingly, in England 78.16 per cent of the products are made by steam as against 10 per cent in Russia, 29 per cent in Austria, 34 per cent in Italy, Portugal, and Scandinavia, and 36 per cent in all Continental countries. And in England and America $4\frac{1}{2}$ per cent of the product is made by hand labor as against 23.19 per cent in Spain, 33.67 per cent in Italy, and 42.37 per cent in Portugal.

An increase in the general rate of wages tends to influence the use of improved methods of production in two ways simultaneously. It not only makes improved machinery possible through a larger consumption, but at the same time, through its tendency to increase the cost of labor, it makes the use of machinery necessary in order to reduce the price as well as increase the quantity of wealth produced.

The first half of this fact is generally recognized and pretty well understood, but the latter half of it is almost uniformly overlooked or ignored. Economists have fully recognized the economic advantage of improved machinery and extensive markets, but they have utterly failed to recognize the necessity of high wages as a means to that end. Adam Smith clearly saw that the division of labor and the use of machinery are " limited by the extent of the market ;" but neither he nor any of the able writers who followed him appear to have perceived the more important double fact—viz.: (1) that the extent of the market is mainly determined by the consumption of the laboring class, whom it is estimated consume about eighty per cent of the *machine-made* products of the world, and (2) that it is only in proportion as real wages rise and labor becomes *dear* that it is worth saving, and the use of cheaper methods (machinery) become an economic necessity.

This partial view is largely due to the mistake of constantly regarding the laborer as only a factor in production and ignoring him as an element in consumption, and consequently viewing wages as an expenditure, as a cost that should be reduced, instead of regarding them as an element of demand and a purchasing force in the market, which should be steadily increased. This fact once thoroughly understood by

the employing class they would soon radically change their attitude toward the labor movement. They would then see that their economic interest and prosperity is finally identified with rising and not with falling or even stationary wages.

Although it is not possible for employers, as such, to arbitrarily raise wages, they would then see that it is alike to their interest and their duty to use all their social and political influence in promoting instead of retarding the free operation of the economic and social forces, which tend to naturally, and therefore gradually and permanently, increase the general rate of wages.

It should always be remembered that a general rise of real wages can never be brought about by any arbitrary and artificial means ; but, as we shall hereafter see, it is always due to the unconscious operation of social influences. Hence the movement, when natural, is always subtle, complex, and very gradual. Consequently, it never injuriously disturbs the economic relations of any class in the community.

Although the upward movement of wages is always subtle and composite, taking place in almost insensible gradations, it is none the less positive and aggressive. The first economic effect arising from the laborer demanding more wages is to increase the pressure upon the employer's profits or the capitalist's interest. The manufacturer, endeavoring to move in the direction of the least resistance, at once tries to avoid this pressure by passing it on to the consumer in the form of higher prices, and the consumer, acting upon the same principle, endeavors to resist the higher prices by refusing to purchase or by buying a smaller quantity of the products. Thus, what the manufacturer gains by increased prices he loses by de-

creased sales. On the other hand, if the employer attempts to resist the upward tendency of wages he is met by the stoppage of his works, which involves an economic loss and a social disturbance, which is always very disagreeable and often ruinous, and will only be encountered as a last resort. Ultimately, therefore, the employer is compelled to choose between the use of an improved process of production, by which his commodities can be made cheaper, or the lowering and perhaps the loss of his profits.

The latter, involving as it does his own impoverishment, is naturally the last thing he will consent to do ; consequently, in obedience to the same law of self-interest which impelled the laborer to demand higher wages and the community to refuse to pay higher prices, he turns for relief to the use of improved machinery* as a means of production.

This result having been reached by the constant, gradual, and almost insensible action and reaction of social influence, he does it not with any conscious reluctance, as a desperate last resort to escape ruin, but rather as an agreeable act of economic strategy, in the laudable endeavor to improve his condition by moving in the direction of the least resistance.

By doing this he unconsciously avoids all the dangers that would beset him in other directions. As in the case of the fisherman in our illustration, by investing as much capital in improved tools and implements as he previously paid in wages to one-fourth of his

---

* Or to a more extensive use of the present machinery, such as a larger factory, etc., by which means he can produce the same amount with less waste, less cost in superintendence, less cost in motive power, etc., which has the same influence on the cost of production as improved machinery.

laborers, he is enabled to produce the same amount at a much less cost. By this means he is not only able to comply with the demand of the laborers for higher wages without any diminution of his profits, but he is also enabled to greatly reduce instead of increase the price of the commodities.

This enables him to sell the products at a lower price and puts them within reach of another large class who were unable to consume them before, thereby greatly extending the market, thus enlarging his income without raising the rate of profits, and at the same time increasing the demand for labor.

This is the way all improved methods of production have come into existence. It was upon this principle that, as an instrument of production, the plough became cheaper than the spade, the mowing-machine cheaper than the scythe, the factory cheaper than the hand-loom and spinning-wheel, the sewing-machine cheaper than the needle, the ocean steamer cheaper than the sailing vessel, and the railroad cheaper than the stage-coach. And it was upon the same principle and in the same manner that woven garments of flax, wool, cotton, and silk became cheaper than skins of animals; that parlor matches were made more economical than the tinder-box, gas undersold tallow candles, and electricity will ultimately be cheaper than either. This explains why machinery, which produces wealth so cheaply in England and America, cannot be employed in Asia. In short, it is a universal law in the world of economics that the use of machinery ultimately depends upon the consumption of wealth by the masses,*

---

* For a more extended treatment of the economic relation of consumption to the production of wealth, the reader is referred to the chapter of the "Law of Production" in the next volume.

and consequently can only be *successfully extended as the general rate of real wages is permanently advanced.* Hence, to promote this is really the first step toward the abolition of enforced idleness and the elimination of poverty.

Therefore, as poverty can only be permanently diminished as the production of wealth per capita is increased, and that can only take place as the use of improved methods of production are extended, which in turn depends upon wages, it is very clear that the first step toward the elimination of poverty is to promote the general permanent increase of real wages.

PART II.

THE LAW OF WAGES STATED AND HISTORICALLY ESTABLISHED.

CHAPTER I.

POPULAR THEORIES OF WAGES CONSIDERED.

SECTION I.—*The Wages-Fund Theory.*

THE "wages-fund" theory is, briefly stated, the doctrine of "supply and demand" applied to wages. This theory, which was suggested by Adam Smith, and subsequently developed by Ricardo, McCulloch, and Mill, constitutes one of the cardinal dogmas upon which the industrial policy of the present century has been based.

According to this doctrine, a certain portion of the capital of every country is set apart exclusively for the payment of wages, which is called the "wages fund." More than that amount, it is held, the laborers cannot receive, and less than that amount the employers cannot pay.* That is to say, the aggregate amount paid in wages in any country, at any given time, is neither more nor less than that contained in this fund, and that, therefore, the rate of wages is regulated solely

---

* Mill, in the *Fortnightly Review* for May, 1869.

by the proportion between the number of the laboring population and the amount of this "wages fund." This being granted, it is held that wages can only be increased by one of two ways: either by increasing that portion of capital devoted to the payment of wages (the wages fund) or by reducing the number of laborers among whom that fund is to be divided. "The well-being and comfort of the laboring classes are, therefore, especially dependent on the relation which their increase bears to the increase of the capital that is to feed and employ them. If they increase faster than capital, their wages will be reduced; and if they increase slower, they will be augmented. . . . *And every scheme for improving the condition of the laborer which is not bottomed on this principle, or which has not an increase of the ratio of capital to population for its object, must be completely nugatory and ineffectual.*"*

"If wages are higher at one time or place than at another, if the subsistence and comfort of the class of hired laborers are more ample, it is for no other reason than because capital bears a greater proportion to population. . . . The condition of the class can be bettered in no other way than by altering that proportion to their advantage; *and every scheme for their benefit which does not proceed on this as its foundation is, for all permanent purposes, a delusion.*" †

American writers have mainly followed in the same strain.‡ Professor Perry, who may be taken as more

---

* McCulloch's "Principles of Political Economy," Part III., sec. 7, p. 174.

† Mill's "Principles of Political Economy," Book II., ch. 11, § 3.

‡ F. A. Walker is an exception, and although not the first to reject the wages-fund theory, was the first to present a counter-theory, which will be considered in the next section.

than an average representative of American economists, accepts this theory of wages as taught by the English writers without qualification.* This theory furnishes the employer with an ever-available defence against raising wages. If a single workman asks for an increase of wages, the employer may sympathizingly assure him that his condition ought to be improved; but on the authority of political economy he can philosophically say: "I would gladly raise your wages if there was anything in the wages fund with which to do it; but you know the wages fund is all divided among you laborers, and, therefore, I could only increase your wages by reducing those of some other laborer, and that would be a great injustice to him." And should the laborers generally ask for an increase of wages, this theory furnishes the employer with an equally conclusive reply. He can say to them: "If you want an increase of ten per cent in your wages, you must first do one of two things: either increase my wages fund ten per cent, or reduce your own numbers one tenth." Unless they will accept one of these alternatives, he can, with the full authority of economic science, declare that no increase in wages is possible.

This doctrine, together with the theory taught by these writers, "that the rate of profits can never be increased but by a *fall in wages*," † goes far to excuse if not sustain the charge "that the current political economy, instead of being a social science, is little else but a specious argument for low wages."

It may be said that this doctrine has been exploded.

---

* "Political Economy," 1st ed., pp. 122, 123.
† Ricardo, "Political Economy and Taxation," ch. 7, p. 75. See also Mill, "Principles of Political Economy," Book II., ch. 15, § 7.

This is a great mistake. No doctrine can properly be regarded as exploded so long as it is the recognized basis of the industrial policy of the civilized world. The theory that wages are determined by the supply and demand of labor is not only acted upon by the capitalists, but it is accepted by the workingmen and reasoned upon by standard economists down to this hour.

In fact, the idea that the price of commodities and of labor rise according as the demand is greater and falls as it is less than the supply, is all but universally accepted. Every argument by economists for limiting the population, every effort by capitalists to corner commodities or regulate the output of products, is based entirely upon this idea. And every strike for higher wages is only the practical application of the same doctrine by the workingmen. It is simply an effort to increase the price of labor by limiting the supply.

When the laborers combine to strike and prevent others from taking their places, they are doing exactly what the capitalists do when they attempt to corner commodities, or arbitrarily regulate the output of products, or impose high tariffs upon competing producers. The employers, economists, and editors, when pouring out their unlimited censure upon the heads of the workingmen for inflicting injury upon themselves and the community by the mistaken notion that strikes can ever permanently increase wages, should remember that in doing this the workingmen are only logically applying the vicious doctrine that for a whole century has been, by both practice and precept, ground into them by the employing classes.

It is true that several writers have taken more or

less pronounced exception to certain phases of this theory, the most vigorous and successful of which was made by Mr. Thornton in his work "On Labor,"* which was sufficiently strong to convert John Stuart Mill, who was its most zealous and able exponent. Even Mr. Thornton, however, only rejected one half of the theory. While he objected to that part of the doctrine which affirms that "no less than the full amount of the wages fund can be paid in wages," both he and Mr. Mill continued to cling to the other half, which says, "More than that amount cannot possibly be paid in wages."

But as neither of them offered any substitute for that portion of the doctrine they had rejected except the vague idea of competition, for which Thornton declares "there is no law," the original theory substantially retains its place in current political economy as the law of wages.

So pronounced is this that Professor Perry, one of the leading economists in this country, in a revised edition of his works (1883) reaffirms the whole doctrine, and Professor Cairnes, one of England's most learned economists, in his recent work † makes an elaborate attempt to defend the wages-fund theory in its original entirety.

In his argument Professor Cairnes squarely admits that there is no economic law or force to prevent any employer from appropriating all or any portion of the wages fund in his possession to any other purpose than that of paying wages if he chooses so to do, and says : ‡

---

* London, 1869.
† "Some Leading Principles in Political Economy," ch. 1, Part II.
‡ *Ibid.*, p. 182.

" Undoubtedly 'there is no specific portion of any individual's capital which the owner must necessarily expend upon wages.' 'There is no law fixing the amount' of any man's 'domestic expenditure, and thereby fixing likewise the balance available for industrial operations.' Nor is any man 'bound to spend' in the payment of labor 'the utmost he can afford to spend.'"

Then, after expressing his surprise that any one should ever have so understood the wages-fund theory, he endeavors to show that the error of the assailants of this doctrine all arises from a misunderstanding of the words "determination" and "predetermination." Speaking of Mr. Thornton in particular, he says :*
" His reasoning from beginning to end proceeds upon a radically erroneous conception of the nature of an economic law, of what is meant by 'predetermination' and 'limitation' in the sphere of economic action. A 'law' in political economy does not mean either legal coercion or physical compulsion, or yet moral obligation, nor does the 'determination' expressed in economic law mean the necessary realization of certain results independently of the human will. What an economic law asserts is, not that men must do so and so, whether they like it or not, but that in given circumstances they will like to do so and so ; that their self-interest or other feelings will lead them to this result. The 'predetermination' in question is of that sort which leads a hungry man to eat his dinner or an honest man to pay his debts, and depends for its fulfilment not upon external compulsion of any sort, but upon the influence of certain inducements on the will,

---

* " Some Leading Principles in Political Economy," pp. 84, 85.

our knowledge of which enables us to say how in given circumstances a man will act. It is in this sense," he adds, "that, speaking for myself, I understand the 'predetermination' of a certain portion of the wealth of a country to the payment of wages." "It is in this sense," he says, "that I understand '*predetermination*.'" Exactly; but what is "*this sense*"? The explanation still needs explaining. In fact, this statement is more ingenious than logical, and tends to elude rather than elucidate the point; or, to use Mr. Cairnes's own expression, it is "simply beside the mark."

The question at issue is not what are the causes which "predetermine" the amount paid in wages; but is the amount so paid "predetermined" at all by any cause? Of what economic importance is it that "a man does so and so whether he likes it or not," or "that he likes to do so and so"? How can it affect the question under consideration whether wages are paid through "external compulsion" or through "the influence of certain inducements on the will," if they are paid? The question is not as to whether or not men "like to do so and so," but whether they always *do* "so and so." What difference does it make to the laborer or the community whether an employer pays wages against his will or not?

In truth, men seldom pay wages because "they like to do so," but because they *must* do so or forego something they like still better. Economic law, Mr. Cairnes's opinion to the contrary notwithstanding, does not recognize motives, or likes and dislikes; it is concerned only with causes and their effects.

But what would Mr. Cairnes have us understand the term "predetermination" to mean? When he talks of "the *predetermination* of a certain portion of the

wealth of a country to the payment of wages," does he not mean that from the operation of some cause, of whatever nature, it is decided, in advance, that the whole of this fund must or will surely be paid out as wages? If so, in what does his position differ from that of Mr. Mill and other wages-fund advocates? If by this statement Mr. Cairnes means that, through "the influence of certain inducements on the will," that amount is *sure* to be spent in wages, it is logically the same as that of Mr. Mill when he said "that amount and no less they (the wage-receivers) cannot but obtain." And his statement that "there is no specific portion of any individual's capital which the owner must necessarily expend upon wages, . . . nor is any man bound to spend in the payment of labor the utmost he can afford to spend," is as complete, though less candid, a surrender of at least that half of the wages-fund doctrine as that of Mr. Mill. If, however, on the other hand, by "the '*predetermination*' of a certain portion of the wealth of a country to the payment of wages," it is not intended to mean that it is previously "determined" or decided that that amount will surely be spent in wages, but only that it may and possibly or even probably will be so spent, what construction are we to put upon the following statement : " The *predetermination* in question is of the sort which leads a hungry man to eat his dinner or an honest man to pay his debts."

If every employer is as sure "to spend in the payment of labor the utmost he can afford to spend" as a hungry man is to eat his dinner, there can be little doubt but that the whole amount of the wages fund will always be spent in wages, which is all the most orthodox advocate of the wages-fund theory ever

claimed. For it is hardly more certain that an apple will fall to the ground than that a hungry man will eat his dinner, or that an honest man will pay his debts. But in order to interpret this statement according to the higgling and hauling of Mr. Cairnes's special effort to show that predetermination does not mean predetermination, we must not say a hungry man will eat his dinner, but only that he *may* and probably will do so, and that an honest man may and probably will pay his debts.

A doctrine which can only be sustained by a use of language, according to which it is doubtful whether a hungry man will eat his dinner or an honest man pay his debts, should only need stating to insure its rejection.

But, again, if the word "predetermination" is not to be understood to mean previously decided, and the wages fund is not a fixed amount to be "unconditionally" devoted to the payment of wages, how can the general rate of wages be regulated by the proportion between the number of the laboring population and the amount of that fund, as claimed by all advocates of this doctrine, Mr. Cairnes included? It would be just as rational to say the price of shoes depends upon the proportion between the number of shoes and the amount spent upon jewelry, as to say the general rate of wages is decided by the proportion between the number of laborers and the amount of a fund that is not necessarily spent in the payment of wages. For how can the average or general price of a thing be determined by the proportion between a definite number and an indefinite quantity?

Yet this is the unenviable position of Professor Cairnes; for while he refuses to admit with Mill, Faw-

cett, Perry, and other wages-fund advocates that " the sum to be divided is a fixed amount," he insists upon their conclusion, which wholly depends upon the truth of that statement—viz., that the " wages of each depend solely on the divisor—the number of participants ;" for he says : " The aggregate capital being less, the wages fund, *cæteris paribus*, would be less ; and unless laborers consent to reduce their numbers, the general rate of wages would fall." * In a word, when Mr. Cairnes admitted that " there is no specific portion of any individual's capital which the owner must necessarily expend upon wages," and that no man is " bound to spend in the payment of labor the utmost he can afford to spend," he allowed the whole wages regulating power to be taken out of his wages-fund theory. And in his painfully inconsistent argument, in which, through the straining of language and twisting of terms, he endeavors to hold on to the conclusions of the theory after its basis is destroyed, he has, if possible, more fully demonstrated the utter indefenceableness of the wages-fund doctrine as the law of wages.

But suppose the wages-fund doctrine, as stated by Mill, were true, and a certain amount of wealth, which could neither be increased nor diminished, is divided among the laborers as wages, would that constitute in any economic sense a law of wages? Certainly not. A law of wages must do more than show how the aggregate amount of wealth paid in wages is determined ; it must explain all the phenomena connected with wages. To say that a given amount divided equally among a given number will yield to each a larger

---

* " Some Leading Principles in Political Economy," p. 223.

amount, according as the number of participants is diminished, and *vice versa*, is merely to state a truism. But it affords no explanation of why some laborers get a much larger portion of this fund than others, and why the same laborers, under different conditions and in different places, obtain quite different amounts for their labor. In short, it explains none of the perturbations connected with wages. Hence, if wholly correct as to fact, it would in no sense furnish a law of wages.

Nor is it in any important respect strengthened by the Thornton-Mill amendment. In the revised form this theory affirms (1) that while less than the full amount of the wages fund ("*actually accumulated capital*") * may be paid in wages, "*no more* than that amount *can possibly* be expended on labor;" † and (2) that wages are governed by the relative demand and supply of laborers, rising as the demand ("actually accumulated capital") exceeds the supply, and conversely falling as the supply of laborers exceeds the demand.

How stand the facts? *First:* Is it true that laborers are never employed until the necessary capital to pay their wages has been "actually accumulated"? Is it true that "no more can possibly be expended on labor" than is then and there in the wages fund? *Most certainly not!* On the contrary, in many employments the reverse is the rule. In new countries, for instance, the wages fund—*i.e.*, the amount of capital actually then and there available for the payment of wages—is seldom sufficient to pay the wages of all

---

* Perry's "Political Economy," p. 122, first edition.
† Thornton "On Labor," p. 85.

the laborers employed at the prevailing rate for a month, a week, or even a day in advance, nor the day, nor week, nor even the month after the labor has been performed, without drawing a part, or all of it, from the products of the laborer during that time. It is simply because the previously accumulated capital (the wages fund) is wholly inadequate to the previous or prompt payment of wages that the laborers have to wait from three to six months for their wages, and sometimes even a longer time. Nor is it necessary to go to Australia, South America, or any other foreign country for the evidence of this fact. It can be seen every day in the United States. It is the common custom among our Western farmers to hire laborers by the season or by the year at a certain stipulated rate of wages, a fraction only of which is or can be paid weekly or monthly, and the balance at the end of the term. Nor is the reason for this mode of fractional payment difficult to understand. It is simply because the amount of his previously accumulated capital (wages fund), which is available for the payment of wages, is too small to enable him to pay the wages in full every week. His capital is mostly invested in stock, tools, machinery, buildings, etc., and the balance is only sufficient to enable him to give each laborer a portion of his wages each week or month, and even that is frequently paid in board and lodgings, or orders on the store, which is only another form of credit to the farmer. It is not until the crop is harvested and taken to market that the farmer is able to pay the laborers their full wages, the amount of which, it will be remembered, was definitely fixed before the laborers' work began. If the amount the farmer paid in wages was limited to his actual "wages fund" on hand at

the time he hired his laborers, it is clear that he would generally be forced to pay from twenty-five to fifty per cent lower wages, or else employ a proportionately smaller number of laborers. But why does he pay a higher rate of wages than his available funds will warrant? some "wages-fund" disciple may inquire. Why, simply because he is compelled to do so or go without the laborers. The reason the farmer cannot get the work done for less is quite another question, which will be fully considered in the next chapter ; it is sufficient for the present purpose to say that he is unable to do so. He pays the least he can, and if he pays a higher rate of wages than his " wages fund " will afford, it is for no other reason than that he cannot get it for less.

Then why, it may be asked, does he not employ fewer laborers ? The answer to this is equally clear : it is for the simple reason that if he employed only the small number of laborers his present " wages fund " would enable him to pay, a much smaller amount of wealth would be produced, and his profits at the end of the year would be proportionately less. It is clear to the unsophisticated farmer, though it may not be to Prof. Cairnes, that by paying the wages of the laborer out of the products of his labor, he is enabled to pay a higher rate of wages, employ a larger number of laborers, produce more wealth, and have a much larger amount as profit, than he would have if his wages-paying possibilities were limited to the amount of capital contained in his previously accumulated " wages fund."

It is, of course, necessary that sufficient capital be accumulated to furnish in advance the tools, stock, etc., with which to work, but this is not true of wages. Labor is almost invariably supplied on credit, wholly

or in part, and that, too, without either bonds, mortgages, or other securities being given, and its wages are paid out of its own future productions, and not from its employer's previous accumulations.

Nor is the operation of this principle limited to new countries or to agriculture, but it obtains with equal force in old countries, and in the most modern manufacturing, mercantile, and commercial industries.

It is true that wages are paid more promptly and with greater frequency in older and more advanced manufacturing countries than in new, thinly settled agricultural countries. In England, for instance, the prevailing custom is to pay wages every week, or at most once a fortnight, and in America the custom in large cities and manufacturing centres is to pay wages at least once a month, and in many cases they are paid fortnightly or weekly. But this greater promptness and frequency in the payment of wages in old and manufacturing than in new and agricultural countries is not due to the existence of a greater proportion of accumulated capital available for the payment of wages (wages fund) in the one case than in the other, but because superior facilities for prompt and easy exchange of the products of labor exist in the former than in the latter communities. The manufacturer in New York and New England can put his goods upon the market and generally sell them a week from the time they leave the factory. He can, therefore, pay his laborers their wages out of the proceeds of their current labor every month, or even fortnightly, with far less inconvenience and difficulty than the Australian or Western farmer can do so every three or six months.

Clearly, therefore, it is not only true that more *can* be and is paid in wages than exists in the previously

accumulated wages fund, but that wages are not drawn from previously accumulated capital, they being paid out of current products of labor and that portion of capital which is invested in tools and raw material. Consequently, neither the aggregate amount nor the general rate of wages can possibly be determined by the existence or condition of any such wages fund.

Second: We now come to the second or regulative phase of the wages-fund doctrine. If this theory were correct as a general statement of fact—*i.e.*, if it were true that "no more can possibly be expended on labor" than is previously accumulated in the wages fund, which we have seen it is not, the question is, Does it afford an explanation of the various phenomena connected with wages? We answer *no!*

After affirming that no more can be divided among the laborers as wages than is contained in the wages fund, it declares that that division is determined by the proportion between the number of laborers and the amount in that fund, as already shown in the former part of this chapter ;* in other words, by the so-called law of supply and demand,† according to which wages will

---

* See J. S. Mill's "Principles of Political Economy," Book II., ch. 11, § 3 ; McCulloch's "Principles of Political Economy," Part III., sec. 7 ; Perry's "Political Economy," pp. 122, 123, first edition ; Fawcett's "Economic Condition of the British Laborer," pp. 120, 137, 183.

† "Finally," says Mill, "there are commodities of which, though capable of being increased or diminished to a great and even an unlimited extent, the value never depends upon *anything but demand and supply.* This is the case in *particular with the commodity Labor.*"— "*Principles of Political Economy,*" Book III., ch. 2, § 5.

'Demand and supply, in their action and reaction on each other, furnish the universal law of wages, as of everything else bought and sold."—*Perry's* "*Political Economy,*" p. 233, 18th edition.

never rise or fall except as the demand for labor is in excess of the supply, or *vice versa*. And, to use the language of Mill, "this rise or fall continues until the demand and supply are again equal to one another"*—that is to say, the rise will continue until the wages fund is *all* divided among the laborers, and the fall will continue until the fund is divided among *all* the laborers. Thus, other things being the same, if the number of laborers is reduced the rate of wages will rise, and the rise will continue until the whole of the fund is divided among the reduced number of laborers. And, on the other hand, if the number of laborers is increased the rate of wages will fall, and the fall will continue until all the laborers can obtain a portion of the fund—*i.e.*, until the rate of wages is sufficiently low to enable the amount in the fund to give employment to the whole of the increased number of laborers at some price.†

How does this accord with the facts of experience? Is it true as a matter of history (1) That wages never rise except when the demand for labor is in excess of the supply? and (2) That "the rise or fall continues until the demand and supply are equal to one another"? Since the close of the fourteenth century there has never been a time (in England) when the supply of labor has not been in excess of the demand. This fact is abundantly established by the almost continuous efforts, legislative and otherwise, to deal with enforced idleness, pauperism, vagrancy, etc., during the last four hundred years, as the history of the poor laws, the act of settlement, the Malthusian

---

* " Principles of Political Economy," Book III., ch. 2, § 4.
† See Perry's " Political Economy," pp. 122, 123, first edition.

crusade, trades-unionism, and modern socialism conclusively show. And still, during this period when the supply of labor has been continuously and sometimes frightfully in excess of the demand, wages, instead of falling, have risen from fivepence to five shillings a day, or about twelve hundred per cent, being in direct opposition to the wages-fund theory. Nor is the claim that "the rise or fall continues until the supply and the demand are equal to one another" any nearer the truth. There has never been a time but once in the industrial history of England,* since the first dawn of the wages system, in the twelfth century, when the demand for labor was distinctly in excess of the supply. That was in the middle of the fourteenth century (1348–50), when over one third of the people were stricken down by the pestilence known as the "Black Death." Did wages continue to rise until the demand and supply were equal? Nothing of the kind. Wages only rose a penny, and, in some rare cases, perhaps twopence a day, although labor was so scarce that "crops rotted in the fields" because there was no one to gather them. And even this small rise was not due to the scarcity, as is shown by the fact that when the supply of labor again became in excess of the demand, wages did not fall again to their previous level.† Not even in the worst days of the Tudors and Stuarts, or at any time since, even in periods of industrial depressions, when enforced idleness has been most prevalent, have wages ever been as low as they were during that time, when the demand for labor was

---

* We take England because its industrial history is more extended, continuous, and complete than that of any other country.
† See Chapter IV., Part II.

more in excess of the supply than at any other time in the world's history.

Again, if it were true that wages always fall when the supply of labor is in excess of the demand, enforced idleness or able-bodied pauperism in any general or permanent sense would be impossible, because wages would not stop falling until the wages fund was divided among all the laborers—*i.e.*, until all the laborers were employed at some wages or the wages system merge back into slavery. So far from this being the case, there is not a country in the world in which it has ever occurred. We do not say that there never was a time in any country when the laborers were all employed, but what we do say is that they were never all so employed by lowering the general rate of wages. History does not afford a single instance of absorbing enforced idleness by reducing wages. In fact, such a thing is economically impossible. On the contrary, however, although enforced idleness (which is the excessive supply of labor) has been more or less general and permanent, as is shown by able-bodied pauperism, wages have increased several fold; clearly showing, not only that wages do not necessarily fall when the supply of labor is in excess of the demand, but that they may and do sometimes even rise under such circumstances.

Manifestly, therefore, as it is not true that the aggregate amount paid in wages is limited to the amount of " previously accumulated " capital (the wages fund), and as the general rate of wages is not determined by the proportion between the number of laborers and that fund, the wages fund or supply and demand theory, either as originally stated or subsequently amended, is wholly inadequate to even approximately explain the law of wages.

Section II.—*Francis A. Walker's Theory.*

Francis A. Walker, who is one of the most liberal and popular economists in this country, is a pronounced opponent to the wages-fund doctrine. Unlike Mr. Thornton, however, he was not content to merely attack the English theory, but he boldly assumed the task of furnishing a new one to supersede it.

This theory, which we shall now briefly consider, will be found stated in Chapter VIII. of his " Wages Question" (1876), also restated in Chapter V., Part IV., of his " Political Economy" (1883). In presenting the new doctrine Mr. Walker says :* The " popular theory of wages . . . is based upon the assumption that wages are paid out of capital, the saved results of the industry of the past. Hence, it is argued, capital must furnish the measure of wages. On the contrary, I hold that wages are, in a philosophical view of the subject, paid out of the product of present industry ; and *hence* that production *furnishes the true measure of wages.*" Again :† " The employer purchases labor with a view to the product of the labor ; and the *kind and amount of that product* determine *what wages he can afford to pay.* . . . If that product is to be greater, he can afford to pay more ; if it is to be smaller, he must, for his own interest, pay less. . . . Thus," he adds, " it is production, not capital, which furnishes the motive for employment and the *measure of wages.*" ‡ In his later work he says :§ " Wages equal the whole product *minus* rent, interest, and profits." " In this

---

* " Wages Question," p. 128. ‡ The italics are ours.
† *Ibid.*, pp. 129, 130. § " Political Economy," p. 284.

view the laboring class receive all they help to produce, subject to deduction on the three several accounts mentioned,"* and in showing how the amount the laborer receives is determined, he says : † " In determining how much in the shape of rent, interest, and profits shall be taken out of the product before it is turned over to the laboring class to have and to enjoy, I hold that the only security which the laboring class can have that no more will be taken than is required by the economical principles governing those shares respectively, is to be found in full and free competition, each man seeking and finding his own best market unhindered by any cause, whether objective or subjective in its origin."

From the above it will be seen that Mr. Walker's doctrine may be briefly stated as follows : (1) That wages " are paid out of the product of present industry," and, therefore, "*production furnishes the measure of wages;*" (2) " That wages equal the whole product *minus* rent, interest and profits," and (3) That the proportion of the whole that will be left for the laborers depends upon " free competition."

Now, assuming that these propositions are all correct, how do they enable us to explain the law of wages ? How does this view enable us to understand why wages are lower in some countries than in others ; lower in rural districts than in large cities ; lower in some industries than in others in the same localities ; lower in agricultural than in manufacturing employments ; and why women's wages are lower than men's ?

Let us see. The first half of the first proposition, viz., " that wages are paid out of the product of pres-

---

* " Political Economy," p. 263. † *Ibid.*, p 285.

ent industry," is unquestionably correct; but how does it necessarily follow from this that " production is the measure of wages"? Because, says Mr. Walker, wages take the " whole product, *minus* rent, interest, and profits," and these three remaining the same the amount paid to labor would increase directly with the increase in the aggregate amount produced.

But this assumes that rent, interest, and profits are taken out of the product before wages are paid. For this assumption Mr. Walker has not given the slightest warrant in either fact or reason. Nay, more, he has not only failed to show that rent, interest, and profits are taken before wages, which he is in logic bound to do before he has the right to thus conclude, but he has conclusively shown that the reverse is true. In discussing the question of rent in the same work * he is ultra-Ricardian, and takes great pains to show that rent does *not* come out of wages, but that it is what is left after wages and other items in the cost of production are paid. That it is because what he calls " no-rent-land " will only yield enough to pay wages and profits that rent cannot be obtained from it, " and that the amount received by the landlord as rent is not paid either by the agricultural laborer or by the consumer of the produce, whether food, fuel, or fibre."† Thus Mr. Walker, like a " Ricardian of Ricardians," as he styles himself, shows that wages are paid *before* rent.

If we turn to his discussion of profits we shall find that Mr. Walker, with the full measure of his usual vigor and force, insists that profits are *not* taken out of wages,

---

* " Political Economy," p. 213, par. 244; see also " Land and Its Rent," pp. 29, 30.
† " Political Economy," p. 248, par. 278.

but, like rent, are what is left after *wages* are paid. He says : * "Do profits, then, come out of wages? Not at all. The entrepreneurs of the lowest industrial grade — the no-profits employers, as we have called them — *must pay wages* sufficient to hire laborers to work under their direction. These wages constitute an essential part of the cost to the employer of the production of the goods. *The fact that these wages are so high is the reason why the employers are unable* (their skill and power in organizing and energizing labor and capital being no greater than they are) *to realize any profits for themselves.*" (The italics are ours.)

Can anything be plainer than this? Here Mr. Walker declares that the reason why unsuccessful employers have no profits is because the product is all taken in *wages* and other costs. In other words, it is because with their skill, capital, methods, etc., they were unable to produce more than would cover *wages*, etc., that they have to go without profit.†

It will be observed, therefore, that, according to Mr. Walker's own showing, rents and profits are not taken out of the product before wages, but, on the contrary, they consist of what remains after wages are paid.

Now, what, under these circumstances, becomes of Mr. Walker's theory that production is the measure of wages? Why, it is entirely demolished. So far as affording any true explanation of the *law of wages*, there is literally nothing left of it. If wages are paid

---

* "Political Economy," p. 254, par. 284.

† In this he is unquestionably correct. Every business failure is a proof of it. It is because the manufacturer or merchant, after paying wages (which legally as well as economically has the first claim) has no profits, or not enough to pay other costs, that he goes into bankruptcy or leaves the business.

before rent and profits, as Mr. Walker shows, then, manifestly, they can exercise no influence in determining wages. It would be just as reasonable to say that a person who will draw water from my well to-morrow by so doing will limit the quantity I can draw from it to-day. Under these circumstances to say " that wages equal the whole product *minus* rent, interest and profits" is merely to utter a truism, which conveys no more information than would the announcement of a boy who hooked a single fish, that his catch equalled all the fish in the sea *minus* those he didn't get.

In what sense, then, is production the measure of wages? The mere fact that wages are drawn from production does not make production the measure of wages. True, wages cannot be more, but they can be and are less than production. The amount produced may determine the former, but it clearly does not regulate the latter. The fact that there is but a hundred cannot possibly be the cause of my not having more or less than fifty. Since wages are the first to draw upon production, and since they do not take all the product, the question is, What determines the amount or the proportion that they do take? It cannot be production, because there is already more produced than they take. It cannot be rent or profits, because, as Mr. Walker has shown us, they only take what is left after wages are determined. Then, how the amount that goes to wages is regulated is still the question. And it is the question to which Mr. Walker's theory, stripped of the errors he himself explodes, affords no answer.

Again, in order to sustain his position that wages are determined by production, he points to the fact that wages are highest where production is largest. Well,

if wages are high because production is large, why is production large? The answer to this is important, because if wages depend upon production, in order to raise wages we must know how to increase production. Now, suppose a given community produce a million dollars' worth of commodities a week and pay half a million dollars in wages, and, after a few years, the product rises to two millions and wages increase to a million dollars a week, if we ask Mr. Walker why the wages increased from half a million to one million a week, he will reply, "Because the product was doubled." But if we follow with the second question, the answer to which is necessary in order to understand the answer to the first, and ask "Why the product was doubled?" his theory has no reply. But if we leave him a moment and seek the true answer to the second question, we shall find that it proves his reply to the first one to be entirely fallacious.

Why was the product doubled? Why were two millions produced instead of one? The answer is very simple. The second million was produced for the same reason that the first was, viz., because it was demanded, the only reason why anything is ever continuously produced. Then, the product was doubled because the demand was doubled. Why was the demand doubled? Because the normal consumption of the masses (wage-receivers) in the community, which is commensurate with and indicated by wages, was doubled. Thus we find that instead of the wages or consumption by the masses being governed by production, as Mr. Walker's theory affirms, the reverse is everywhere true, and production is determined by consumption, or wages.*

---
* See Chapter II.

Again, if it were true, as Mr. Walker would have us believe, that wages rise *because* production is increased, such a thing as a business depression would be impossible. For, as soon as the warehouses began to get overstocked, wages would begin to rise, and the stock would soon be carried off. But we know from bitter experience that the reverse of this is the case; that when the warehouses begin to fill up factories begin to stop, wages fall, and "*hard times*," with all their social evils, overtake us.

It will thus be seen that whichever way we consider Mr. Walker's theory of wages, it is wholly inadequate to explain even the ordinary facts connected with the subject. He, however, affirms an important truth not recognized by the old school, viz., that wages are drawn from the product of present industry instead of from a wages fund. But, in attempting to prove that because wages are paid out of present industry, therefore "production is the measure of wages," he fell into one of the cardinal errors of the old doctrine, which, having assumed that wages are drawn from capital, affirmed that, therefore, capital is the measure of wages.[*]

In order to sustain this assumption Mr. Walker found it necessary to forget the conclusions he had elsewhere established, and adopted the most obvious errors of Henry George by inverting the natural order of economic distribution. Consequently, so far from affording any explanation of the true law of wages, Mr. Walker's theory is really less complete, more inconsistent, and quite as unsound as the English theory.

---

[*] "Wages Question," p. 128.

Section III.—*Henry George's Theory.*

Mr. George's theory of wages, briefly stated in his own words, is as follows :* "In their degree wages rise and fall in obedience to a common law. What is this law? The fundamental principle of human action —the law that is to political economy what the law of gravitation is to physics—is that men seek to gratify their desires with the least exertion. . . . Now, under this principle, what, in conditions of freedom, will be the terms at which one man can hire others to work for him? Evidently they will be fixed by what the men could make if laboring for themselves. . . . Thus the wages which an employer must pay will be measured by the lowest point of natural productiveness to which production extends, and wages will rise or fall as this point rises or falls. . . . Here, then, we have the law of wages as a deduction from a principle most obvious and universal; that wages depend upon the margin of cultivation; that they will be greater or less as the produce which labor can obtain from the highest natural opportunities open to it is greater or less, flows from the principle that men will seek to satisfy their wants with the least exertion."

After devoting seven pages to emphasizing the above idea, he restates his whole conclusions thus :† "The demonstration is complete. The law of wages we have thus obtained as the corollary of the law of rent, and it completely harmonizes with the law of interest. It is that *wages depend upon the margin of production, or*

---

* "Progress and Poverty," pp. 150, 151, 152, popular edition.
† *Ibid.*, pp. 156, 157, popular edition.

HIS THEORY STATED IN HIS OWN WORDS. 61

upon the produce which labor can obtain at the highest point of natural productiveness open to it without the payment of rent."*

To still further emphasize and enforce this theory, he resolves it into three formal propositions as follows :†

"Where land is free and labor is unassisted by capital the whole produce will go to labor as wages.

"Where land is free and labor is assisted by capital, wages will consist of the whole produce, less that part necessary to induce the storing up of labor as capital.

"Where land is subject to ownership and rent arises, wages will be fixed by what labor could secure from the highest natural opportunities open to it without the payment of rent."

Now, it will be seen from the above, all of which is in Mr. George's own words, that his doctrine of wages affirms three propositions :

First. That wages—the laborer's income, when working for an employer—where land is free, is determined by what he could obtain by working for himself on the best land obtainable.

Second. That wages, where land is subject to private ownership and rent is paid, are determined by what the laborer could procure from the best land obtainable without paying rent.

Third. That as private ownership in land extends and rent rises, the margin of cultivation is lowered ; hence, the amount obtainable from *free* or "no-rent" land diminishes and wages fall.

From these propositions it follows, as a logical necessity :

---

* The italics are his own.
† "Progress and Poverty," pp. 156, 157, popular edition.

(1) That wages will always be the highest where land is not subject to private ownership, or where the best land can be had free of rent.

(2) That where private ownership of land obtains, and rent is paid, wages will diminish, or at least be arrested as rent increases; consequently, where rent is the highest wages will be the lowest; or

(3) That where all land is subject to ownership and pays rent, wages will be equal to what the laborer could obtain from the poorest land, *minus* the rent. Consequently, the difference in wages in different communities depends entirely upon the difference in the productivity of the "no-rent" land.

(4) Therefore, the only way real wages can be increased is by reducing or abolishing rent, or, as Mr. George puts it, abolishing "the private ownership in land."

This doctrine, whatever else may be said of it, has the merit of novelty, and, unlike Mr. Walker's, is at least consistent with the general teachings of its author. Indeed, it is a necessary part of Mr. George's scheme to make all economic movement and social progress depend upon rent or the private ownership of land.

But the question that is more important than its consistency with itself or with the general economic doctrines of its author (which we have elsewhere shown[*] to be mainly fallacious) is its consistency with ascertained facts and well-established principles.

Is the doctrine true, and does it afford an explanation of industrial phenomena? is the question. Does it, for instance, explain why wages have risen

---

[*] See article in the *Forum* (N. Y.), for March, 1887, entitled "Henry George's Economic Heresies."

WILL THE THEORY EXPLAIN THE FACTS? 63

in some countries and not in others during the last two hundred years; why wages are higher in some industries than in others in the same localities, and different in the same industries in different localities; why they are higher in large than in small cities; and higher in manufacturing than in agricultural countries and districts; and why men's wages in the same industries and under the same conditions are uniformly higher than those of women? No doctrine which cannot answer these questions can furnish a scientific or philosophic explanation of the economic *law of wages*. Can Mr. George's theory stand this test? Let us see. We will take the propositions in the order named above.

(1) Is it true, then, that wages (*i.e.*, the income of the laboring classes) are the highest where land is not subject to private ownership and where no rent is paid for its use?

The most elementary acquaintance with industrial history is sufficient to prove that the very opposite is everywhere the case.

There never was a time nor place in the world when land was not subject to private ownership, and hence no rent paid for its use, that the laborer's wages were half or even one tenth as much as they are to-day in England and the United States, where rents are the highest of anywhere in the world. "Where land is free and labor is unassisted by capital," says Mr. George, "the whole produce will go to labor as wages." This is true; and whenever or wherever those conditions do or did exist the laborer received the least he ever got in the world. Witness the tribal communities of Australia, India, and Africa, the Esquimaux, the Patagonians, and our American Indians. The

facts on this point are too obvious to need recounting, even to the most uninitiated observer. It is a notorious fact in universal history that the nearer we find man to communal ownership of property, the nearer is he to savagery and starvation. I do not say that communal ownership of property is the cause of his barbarism, but manifestly it does not save him from it, as Mr. George would have us suppose. On this point Mr. George, like many others in whom sentiment dominates over reason, and feeling over facts, appears to assume that if the laborer receives *all* he produces he necessarily has one third more than when he only obtains two thirds of it.* Nothing could be farther from the facts in the case. In any state of society where the laborer receives all the product it is where he produces it all. And wherever all the wealth is produced by human labor and none of it by capital, *i.e.*, by machinery, the whole product per capita is sure to be very small, as in India, China, Africa, Patagonia, Fiji Islands, etc. And wherever a large proportion of the wealth is produced by machinery or capital, the product per capita is sure to be very large, as in America, England, and other machine-using countries.†

If the laborer in the former countries got the whole product he would receive less than one tenth as much as the laborer in the latter countries would get if he only obtained half the product.

As a matter of fact, it is universally true in all industrial communities that where the laborer obtains the whole product he gets far less—often seven tenths less—than where he only obtains one half of it. It should always be remembered that wages are high

---

* See Chapter I., Part I.　　† See Chapter II., Part I.

or low, the laborer is rich or poor, not according as he receives a large or small proportion of the total product, but according as the amount *he actually receives* is great or small. The wages of the laborer who, with the aid of machinery, produces four dollars' worth of wealth a day and receives two dollars, are twenty times (two thousand per cent) higher than those of the laborer who by hand labor produces ten cents' worth of wealth a day and gets it all. Therefore, while it is true that before land was "subject to private ownership" and rent began to be paid or capital was employed in production, "the whole product went to the laborer as wages," it is *not true* that wages were higher, but, on the contrary, that they were very much lower then than they ever have been since rent began to be paid.

(2) Is it true that where private ownership of land obtains and rent is paid, that wages diminish or even stop rising as rent increases?

Not at all, but industrial data show it to be just the reverse. Rents are everywhere the highest in large cities, and it is precisely there where wages reach their maximum the world over without a solitary recorded exception. The same is true of agricultural rents. They are the highest in the vicinity of cities and manufacturing centres, and it is precisely there where the wages of agricultural laborers, as all industrial statistics show, are the highest in every country, even in India.* In fact, on this point Mr. George's theory is directly

---

* See Buchanan's "Travels Through the Countries of Mysore, Canara and Malabar," Vol. I., pp. 124, 125; Leone Levi's "Earnings and Wages," and Rogers's "Six Centuries of Work and Wages," p. 172, show the same to be true in England, and it is proverbially true in this country.

opposed to all the known facts in the case in all countries under normal economic conditions.

(3) Is it true that wages "are fixed," as Mr. George avers, "by what the men could make if laboring for themselves"?

The answer to this question seems too obvious to need stating, and yet there is a large number of workingmen who have not the time or opportunity for study, or mental training necessary to enable them to master the subtleties of economics, who have been misled by the ingenuity with which it has been presented, into accepting this statement, and to a considerable extent are regarding with favor the propositions for reform based upon it. Indeed, it would almost seem as if Mr. George himself believed the statement. After declaring that "this law of wages carries with it its own proof and becomes self-evident by mere statement," he says :* "The average man will not work for an employer for less, all things considered, than he can earn by working for himself ; nor yet will he work for himself for less than he can earn by working for an employer." With the obvious feeling that this logically seals the case, he adds : "And *hence* the return which labor can secure from such natural opportunities as are free to it *must fix the wages which labor everywhere gets.*"

Clearly Mr. George labors under the belief that he has here stated the proposition from the two opposite points of view, viz., that of both the laborer and the employer. But he has done nothing of the kind. Instead of stating the case for both the laborer and

---

* "Progress and Poverty," p. 157, popular edition. The italics are ours.

employer, as he thinks to do, he has in different phraseology merely stated the same thing twice for the laborer.

True, " the average laborer will not work for an employer for less, all things considered, than he can earn by working for himself. Nor yet will he work for himself for less than he can earn by working for an employer." But these statements only affirm what the laborer *will* or *will not* do. How about the employer? Will he give the laborer *more* than he can earn working for himself? That is the question Mr. George did not ask—the true answer to which changes the whole face of the subject. If Mr. George could have shown that, as the laborer will not work for an employer for less, so the employer will not give him more than he can earn working for himself, the case would have been logically closed, and what the laborer could make working for himself would everywhere fix what he could get working for an employer.

But this is exactly what he does not do, and for the best of all reasons, viz., that it is impossible to do it. Now, if it is true that the employer *can* and *will* pay the laborer *more* than he can get working for himself, then Mr. George's whole structure vanishes; because in that case what the laborer could earn working for himself would have nothing whatever to do with deciding what his wages would be when working for another.

Now, then, what are the facts? Is it true, as Mr. George assumes, that the employer does not pay the laborer *more* than he could make by working for himself? Most certainly it is not true.

Other things being the same, the average laborer will work for himself in preference to being employed by a boss. It is only because he can obtain more by

working for another than by employing himself that he will consent to do so. Did the hand-loom weavers abandon their looms, and their wives and daughters the spinning-wheels, and go to work in the factory because they preferred to work for an employer? Not at all! On the contrary, they did everything in their power to avoid it. Indeed, it was to prevent this that the hand-loom weavers went from town to town in England in mobs breaking "*steam-looms.*" They only consented to go into the factory when they were starved out by their productions being undersold by those of the factory. In other words, because the employers would pay them more than they could earn working for themselves.

If the wages of the spinners and weavers to-day were governed by what they could get by working for themselves they would not receive one fourth of their present wages. The same is true of the wages in every other industry in which large capitals and machinery are employed.

Is it true that the average workman, employed in the manufacture of hardware, pottery, furniture, glass, paper, carpets, silks, and broadcloths, the workers in gold and silverware, jewelry, brass, iron, tin, etc., the carpenters, masons, bricklayers, machinists, engineers, and the thousand-and-one other mechanics who work for employers, only obtain as much in wages as they could get by working for themselves, either in the same or any other occupations open to them? The idea is so obviously opposed to the commonest facts of everyday experience, that to seriously mention it is to at once appear absurdly ridiculous.

Is there any truth in Mr. George's last proposition, which he so confidently affirms, and upon the truth of

which his whole theory depends, viz., that "where land is subject to ownership and rent arises, wages will be fixed by what labor could secure from the highest natural opportunities open to it without the payment of rent"? Now, if there is any truth in this proposition, the wages in all industries will be identical with, or, at least, very similar to, what the average laborer can obtain from the land which can be had for nothing. Clearly, if this were true, the wages of agricultural laborers would at least be as high as those in any other industry, especially as they are the standard by which all others are "fixed." The notorious fact, however, is that they are everywhere the lowest. There is not a country in the world in which the wages of artisans are not higher than those of the laborers employed in agriculture. It is true in every country in continental Europe. In England the fact is simply notorious that the wages of the agricultural laborers there are little over one half those of mechanics and artisans. In this country the wages or incomes of the farm laborers and small farmers who work for themselves, as a class, are not only lower than in any other occupation, but in many cases they are nearly one half less.

Again, if "the wages which labor everywhere gets" are fixed by what the laborer can secure from no-rent land, why are the wages of carpenters, painters, masons, bricklayers, tailors, printers, etc., higher in this country than they are in Europe, higher in New York than in smaller cities, and higher in large towns than in the rural districts, and everywhere higher than those of the farm laborer? If the wages of the factory operative and those of the carpenter, painter, mason, and plumber are all "fixed" by what the average laborer can secure from the best no-rent land, why are those

of the former from seventy-five cents to one dollar a day less than those of the latter, or the wages of women everywhere so much lower than those of men? Indeed, if wages were so determined these striking differences would be impossible. The facts nowhere sustain this absurd theory. Industrial data everywhere show that instead of wages being governed by or are equal to what the laborer could get from land obtainable rent free, they nowhere sustain any recognizable relation to it, and are everywhere much higher and frequently double that amount.

It will thus be seen that in whatever way we consider Mr. George's theory of wages, we find it to be not merely inadequate to explain the facts, but everywhere directly controverted by them.

CHAPTER II.

WAGES AND THE LAW OF WAGES.

SECTION I.—*Wages Defined*.

IN any scientific or philosophic view of the subject, the true theory of wages must, as already observed, not only explain how the aggregate amount of wealth that goes to labor is determined, but it must also account for the variations in the general rate of wages in different countries, industries, localities, etc., which, as we have seen in the last chapter, the popular theories have failed to do. In short, the true theory of wages must fully set forth the general principles upon which, under all normal, social, and economic conditions, the movement of wages takes place, and explain the law or order of that movement, and the social influences which tend to impel or retard it.

Before attempting to discuss the *law* by which wages are governed, it may be well to explain what constitutes wages, or, at least, what we wish the term to be understood to mean when used in this work. This is the more necessary, because there is no general agreement, even among economists, as to the exact meaning which, in economic science, is to be attached to the term wages. It is held by some that everything is wages which a person receives in return for his labor. Because all wages are the return for labor, it is held

that all return for labor is wages.* According to this signification of the term, if a man plants corn or catches fish, the corn raised or the fish caught, being the return for his labor, are his "*wages*," just as much as would be the amount he received when working for an employer for a stipulated sum.

Now, this definition is not only inconvenient for the purposes of economic reasoning, but it is incorrect; because it regards two things as identical which are essentially different, both in fact and in the influences by which they are determined. It is true that the corn or fish and the amount paid by the employer are each the return for service, but the amount the laborer will receive under the two sets of circumstances is governed by different principles, and may be very different in amount. The fisherman or farmer who works for himself receives the whole produce, be it little or much. Hence his income is decided wholly by the product of his own labor. But as the man who works for an employer does not own the products of his labor, he receives as his reward a stipulated amount, which is agreed upon in advance, and which may be either more or less, but it is seldom the same, as the product. Thus, while the income of the former is determined by what his labor produces, that of the latter depends upon what another will consent to give for it. In other words, the man who works for himself sells the *products* of his labor, while he who works for another sells nothing but his *labor*, or service. Hence, the income of the former is the whole value of what his labor produces, while that of the latter is only the value or price of his labor as such, which is commonly and very

---

* This is one of the first mistakes Mr. George makes in connection with wages. See "Progress and Poverty," p. 39, popular edition. Mr. Walker, however, does not make this mistake.

properly called *wages*. To confound these two kinds of income, which are thus essentially different in character, and determined by different influences—one being a contingent and the other a stipulated amount—must necessarily lead to confusion and error. Therefore, in order to avoid all misunderstanding on this point, I define wages as *the value or price of labor, or service as such*. Value* (price), in modern society, or wherever exchanges are made through the medium of money, is essentially the same, whether applied to commodities or labor. In economics value never expresses anything but the ratio in which different quantities will exchange for one another. Wages, the price or value of labor, therefore, is not what the laborer produces, nor the value of that product, but what is actually and consciously given in exchange for the service, *per se*. Robinson Crusoe might reap the full reward or product of his labor, but he could not have wages. For the same reason that there can be no value without exchange, there can be no wages—in the sense the term is here used—unless *labor, as such, is bought and sold*.

Popular phrase, which is always the most direct avenue to the mind of the masses, has for once ascribed the correct meaning to an important economic term, enabling us to use the word wages in the same sense that it is used in common language. This is always important, but it is especially so in relation to the subject under consideration, that, more than all others, is the one in which "unlettered laborers" are most deeply interested; hence they should be enabled

---

* The discussion of the whole question of value and price, both of which relate to the ratio of exchange, will be found in the next volume.

to clearly understand it. We shall, therefore, throughout this work always use the term *wages* in the popular sense—*i.e.*, as expressing the *price of labor*, leaving it to those who desire to give the word a different signification to show that something will be gained in clearness by so doing.

It will be observed that this definition of wages includes the incomes, not only of the laborers who work by the day, by the week, or by the month, but those of all, without regard to sex or social status, who *sell their services* as such. That is to say, wages cover all stipulated, as distinguished from contingent, incomes which are received in exchange for personal services.

SECTION II.—*Real and Nominal Wages.*

Before passing to the consideration of the economic law by which wages are governed, it is important to distinguish clearly between real wages and nominal wages. The failure to recognize clearly the distinction between these two kinds of wages is the cause of not a little of the chaos and confusion in which the question of wages has hitherto been all but interminably involved.

By "*Real Wages*" is meant the actual amount of wealth (social well-being) obtainable for a day's labor. By "*Nominal Wages*" is meant the amount of money obtainable for a day's labor. The social well-being of the wage-receiving portion of the community—which is increasing as the complexity of society advances—is always infallibly indicated by the general rate of *real wages*. But this is not necessarily the case with nominal wages. Whether or not a rise in the rate of

nominal wages indicate an improvement in the social condition of the wage-receivers depends entirely upon whether or not it is accompanied by an equal rise of *real* wages. This may or may not be the case. If, *e.g.*, nominal wages should rise from one dollar to one dollar and a half per day, and the price level of commodities upon which those wages were expended rose in the same proportion, there would be no increase in real wages, because the one dollar and a half would exchange for no more of the various commodities than the one dollar previously did. Consequently, no more wealth could be obtained for a day's labor than before, and hence no improvement in the social well-being of the wage-receiver would ensue. And if, as is frequently the case, the rise in the price level should be relatively greater than that in the nominal wages, the amount of wealth procurable for a day's labor would be even less than before. Thus real wages would actually have fallen, while nominal wages rose fifty per cent. And, on the other hand, a fall of ten per cent in the price level would, other things being the same, constitute a rise of ten per cent in real wages without any change in nominal wages.

It will thus be seen that nominal and real wages are not only not identical, but that they may either of them rise or fall without a similar movement in the other, and that it is only by the change of the latter that the economic and social condition of the masses is really affected. Therefore, the relation of real and nominal wages to each other and to the social condition of the masses may be briefly stated as follows :

(1) That the economic and social well-being of the masses is always indicated by the general rate of real wages, but not necessarily by that of nominal wages.

(2) That the movement of nominal wages may or may not be identical with that of real wages ; and that it indicates a change in the social condition of the masses, only to the extent that it reflects the movement of real wages ; and

(3) That, therefore, nothing can improve the social condition of the masses, whether it raises nominal wages or not, which does not increase the general rate of real wages, the degree of which may be universally taken as the accurate measure of social progress. It is therefore with the economic law governing *real* wages that the economist, the statesman, the social reformer, and, above all, the *laboring classes* are most deeply concerned.

With this understanding of what constitutes wages, *per se*, and the distinction between nominal and real wages, we pass to the consideration of that still more important, nay, most important, question connected with social economics, viz., the *law of wages*.

SECTION III.—*The Economic Law of Wages.*

In order to observe distinctly the movement of wages, and understand the law by which it is governed, we must examine it in its earliest and simplest stages—before it has become involved in the subtleties of complex social phenomena. Social industry in its progress to its present state has assumed three distinctive forms, which may be designated as savagery, slavery, and wages. Each of these industrial systems, so-called, had economic characteristics peculiar to itself, one of which was the relation the laborer sustained to the product of his labor, and the condi-

tions which determined the portion of it he should receive.

Social progress being a growth or an evolution, its movement is necessarily gradual, and hitherto has been very slow. Accordingly, industrial systems come and go by insensible gradations; and, while essentially different in their main characteristics, some of the features of each are naturally found to be common to all. Consequently, we find much in slavery that is common to savagery, of which it was the natural outcome. This is equally true of the wages system. Being the outgrowth of the slavery system, it naturally possesses many of the same characteristics.

Under both systems labor is an indispensable factor in the production of wealth. Under both systems the products belong to the master or employer, and not to the laborer. Under both systems labor is bought and sold, and as the service of labor is inseparable from the laborer, under both the presence of the laborer is essential to the delivery of the labor; and as under slavery the master could not obtain the service of the slave without furnishing him with sufficient means to keep him in working condition, so under the wages system it is impossible for the employer to obtain the service of the laborer for less than will afford him a living.* Thus far the two systems are essentially the same; but at this point a change takes place. New elements enter into the wages system which were unknown to that of slavery. While under both systems the employer, in order to obtain the service of the la-

---

* This much is conceded by all leading economists, both English and Continental, and is what they have termed "natural" or "necessary" wages.

borer, is compelled to give him as much of the product as will afford him a living, under slavery what should constitute the standard of that living could be determined by the arbitrary will of the master. Under the wages system his standard of living is determined by the extent of his habitual wants and desires (*i.e.*, the complexity of his social character), which may be and are constantly increased according to the extent and complexity of his social environment.

Although under both systems labor is bought and sold, under slavery, in order to obtain the service, or labor, the master bought the *laborer* as a commodity. Under the wages system he buys only the *labor* as *service*. The result of this new feature is that the person of the laborer not only ceases to be the object of the sale, but, instead of being the sold, as under slavery, he becomes the *seller*. In other words, the employer, under wages, instead of buying and selling laborers, as under slavery, buys service and sells products, and the laborer sells service and buys products. Thus, service, instead of persons, began to be exchanged, and the value or price was transferred from the *laborer* to his *labor*.* Thenceforth the laborer ceased to be a commodity, and became a distinct social as well as an economic factor, which constitutes the essential difference, as we shall hereafter see, between the two industrial systems.

It will thus be observed that during the social differentiation in which slavery was superseded by wages,

---

* It will be observed that it is at this point that the interest of the purchaser of labor, as such, ceases to reside in the personality of the laborer. Whether he lives or dies is no longer a matter of any importance to the buyer or employer of labor, because he now only pays for the service the laborer actually renders or delivers.

service, as such, for the first time became an economic entity, possessing value, and, consequently, subject to the social laws of exchange. We have seen* that under savagery the amount of wealth the laborer obtained—which was the smallest he ever got—was determined by what he produced, because he owned both the labor and the product, such as it was; that, under slavery, the amount was determined by the master, for the same reason, viz., that he owned both the laborer and the product. How that is determined under the present system, where the ownership of labor or service and that of the product are separated, the laborer having possession of the former and the employer that of the latter, and each being able to obtain what he gets from the other only by means of exchange, is now the question.

Manifestly, labor being now subject to all the conditions of exchange, its price (wages) must necessarily be determined by the same general law governing that of all other things in the domain of exchange. Therefore, in seeking the economic law of wages, we are really seeking the law of prices.

The full discussion of prices (value), exchange, etc., in relation to commodities, will be found in another part of this work, which, for reasons already explained, will be published separately.† For our present purpose, therefore, we shall only briefly state the law there elaborately established, and then apply it to wages. It affirms:

(1) That value in economics refers exclusively to the domain of exchange and includes both commodities and services, and always expresses the ratio

---

* Chapter I., Part I. † See preface.

in which quantities, whether of commodities or services, or both, will exchange for one another.

(2) That the ratio in which quantities of different commodities will exchange for one another is not determined by supply and demand, as popularly taught, but that it is primarily governed by the cost of production.

This doctrine does not mean that the price at which each article is actually sold is determined by the cost of producing that particular article. In that case there would be no profits, as everything would be sold for exactly what it cost to make it ; or, if a specific rate of profit is included in the cost, the actual price of every individual article would vary precisely according to the difference in the cost of making it ; in which case everybody would obtain exactly the same rate of profit. Hence there would be no losses, and, consequently, no failures or bankruptcies ; but we know that there are profits, and that they are not uniform ; that in some cases they are very large and in others very small, and that there are many losses, failures, and bankruptcies.* What we mean by saying that prices are determined by the cost of production, is that the general price of any given class of articles is determined by the cost of producing or replacing that portion of the necessary supply of that commodity which is produced under the greatest disadvantage. In other words, the normal price of any commodity in a given market is determined by the cost of producing the most expensive portion of it. Nor is the reason for this difficult to understand. No one can continuously sell an article for less than it costs to produce it ; consequently, that portion of the general supply of a com-

---

* It is estimated that over ninety per cent who go into business fail.

modity which costs the most to produce it must be sold at a price high enough to at least cover the cost of its production. The price at which the most expensive portion of the general supply *must* be sold is, of course, that at which the balance *can* be sold. And, as no one will voluntarily sell for less than the highest price he can with certainty obtain, it follows that the balance *will* be sold at that price. Consequently, that portion of the necessary supply of a commodity which, from closer proximity to the market, improved machinery, easier access to the raw material, or whatsoever, is produced at less than the maximum cost, yields a proportionately larger profit.

Suppose, for example, that A, B, C, and D supplied a given market with shoes of a certain quality; and suppose, also, that A, with the capital, tools, etc., at his command, can barely make these shoes and get his own back at one dollar a pair, and that B, C, and D, through larger capital, superior machinery, favorable location, or any other cause, can furnish the same grade of shoes at ninety-five, ninety, and eighty-five cents a pair respectively. Now, it is very clear that A must sell his shoes at one dollar a pair or leave the business. If A can sell his shoes at one dollar a pair, there is no economic force to prevent B, C, and D from selling theirs at the same price. True, they could afford to sell theirs at less than A, but as they have nothing to gain, and five, ten, and fifteen cents a pair respectively to lose by so doing, they cannot be expected to do so. In fact, they will not do so as long as they can sell their whole product at one dollar a pair.

Suppose, however, D, seeing that by increasing his sales one fourth he could enlarge his factory or put in improved machinery, and in this way be able to

produce the shoes two and a half cents a pair cheaper, actually increase his aggregate profits, and sell the shoes five cents a pair lower, and, in order to undersell his competitors and accomplish this object, he should reduce the price of his shoes to ninety-five cents a pair? Now, other things being equal, people will not give one dollar a pair for shoes when they can get them for ninety-five cents; therefore, in order to sell their shoes, C, B, and A must compete with D and reduce the price. As C and B had ten and five cents a pair profit respectively, they can afford to do so by lowering their profits; but A, who was getting no profits—his shoes costing him one dollar a pair to make them—could make no reduction in the price; hence, he is undersold and driven from the market. Now that A is gone, B's product becomes the most expensive portion of the necessary supply. The minimum at which B can make shoes being ninety-five cents a pair, so long as his shoes are needed ninety-five cents a pair must be paid for them; and for the same reason that B, C, and D could sell for a dollar a pair so long as A's product constituted a part of the necessary supply, C and D can sell at ninety-five cents, and that will therefore be the normal price of the shoes so long as B's product, which is now the most expensive portion of the supply, continues to be required. This is what is constantly taking place in every open market in the world.

This law, which is fully explained elsewhere,* affords an adequate explanation of the constant tendency of prices of a given commodity toward a common level—the great difference in profits in the same industry—

---

* See chapter on " Price and Profits," Vol. II.

the losses, failures, and bankruptcies—the constant tendency toward the concentration of capital into large enterprises, and the consequent crowding out of small ones, with other familiar phenomena in the world of prices and profits, that are inexplicable upon any other theory.

It will thus be seen that the normal price of any commodity is determined by the cost of production, which includes reproduction, but not the cost of making or replacing each particular article, nor the average cost of making that kind of article, but by the cost of making or replacing that portion of the necessary supply which is produced at the greatest cost.

Having found the law of prices (of commodities), let us apply that law to labor, and see if it will afford an adequate explanation of the multifarious and hitherto inexplicable phenomena in the sphere of wages. It will be remembered that in economics, when using the term "law" we do not use it as applying to exact quantities, but only to general tendencies. Hence, when speaking of the "*law* of prices" or the "*law* of wages," we only mean the law which determines the tendency of prices or wages to move in a given direction. According to the principle we have been considering, the law of prices is, "that under normal conditions" the price of commodities always tends toward the cost of production. Applied to labor, then, this law is, that the price of labor (wages) constantly tends toward the cost of producing *labor* or *service*. By the cost of a thing, it will be remembered, is always meant what its owner gave for it, or would have to give to replace it. Now, what constitutes the cost of labor to its owner, the *laborer?* Obviously *the cost of his living*. Upon the same principle that producers

cannot or will not consent to continuously sell a commodity for less than it cost to produce it, or than it would cost to replace it, the laborer cannot or will not long consent to sell his services for less than it cost him—*i.e.*, for less than will afford him a living. The cost of labor to the laborer, therefore, is the cost of his living ; and, other things being the same, the cost of his living will be determined by the number of his habitual wants.

It is not only true that the laborer cannot or will not continuously sell his labor for less than it costs him, *i.e.*, for less than will supply his socially established wants, but it is equally true that he cannot for any considerable time together sell it for more than that amount.

All economic movement may be expressed, as Bastiat truly observes, in " Wants, Efforts, and Satisfactions." This statement not only composes the course of economic movement, but it also expresses the order in which it takes place. (1) Wants, (2) Efforts, (3) Satisfactions. Want supplies the motive, effort the action, and satisfaction is the result. Thus, the only end and aim of effort is satisfaction of some want or desire ; no effort is ever put forth for any other purpose.

Want is thus not only the sole motive, but it is also the only measure of effort. For the same reason that no effort will be put forth except to satisfy some want, *no more* effort will be put forth than is *necessary to* satisfy that want. It is in obedience to this principle that we refuse to give something for nothing, or object to pay for that which we can have free. It is through the operation of the same principle that man everywhere endeavors to obtain the maximum result for the minimum effort, as is exemplified in every division

of labor and improvement in the methods of production. Wants being thus the motive and measure of effort, and wages the price given for the effort, manifestly the laborer's wages can never be permanently much above his wants, as expressed in the standard of his living. Not only is there no motive for him to push the price of his service above the level of what would satisfy his wants,* but if it was arbitrarily raised above that point without his aid it could not long remain so. If, for instance, the general rate of wages in any community should be arbitrarily increased by law or other means twenty-five per cent above the habitual wants—the established standard of living—in the very nature of things it could only be of temporary duration. It could never become permanent, because the very rise itself would set forces in operation that would neutralize it.

Assuming the standard of living to remain the same, wages would ultimately be adjusted to the wants in one of two ways: either the rate of wages per day or week would fall or the laborer would work fewer days in the week or fewer weeks in the year. Never having an incentive to work except to satisfy his wants, he will refuse to work more days than under existing conditions is necessary to enable him to obtain the wherewithal to satisfy those wants, for the same reason that he will not give two dollars for what he can get for one.

Consequently, if the rate of wages per day was not reduced by the employer, the same result would be reached by the number of days' work being reduced by the laborer.

---

* For a definition of economic wants see Chapter VII., Sec. I., Part II.

An arbitrary increase of wages, such as is here supposed, would never become general in any community, for two reasons : (1) Because there is never, under normal economic conditions, sufficient disposable wealth in the hands of the employer to enable him to make any very considerable rise in the general rate of wages without an increase in production. (2) Because if such disposable wealth were at hand, there is no conceivable motive to induce him to give it to the laborer unless he (the laborer) desires, nay, demands it, which nothing but an increase in his wants (his cost of living) can induce him to do.

But, while neither the means nor motives ever exist for making such a thing general, they may and have existed for making it occur locally ; and wherever it has been tried the results have been as we have indicated.

Thus, the experience of Mr. Brassey with the coolies in India, as related by his son, Sir Thomas,* was that " On the railways of India it has been found that the great increase of pay which has taken place has neither augmented the rapidity of execution nor added to the comfort of the laborer. The Hindoo workman knows no other want than his daily portion of rice, and the torrid climate renders water-tight habitations and ample clothing alike unnecessary. The laborer, therefore, desists from work as soon as he has provided for the necessities of the day. Higher pay adds nothing to his comforts ; it serves but to diminish his ordinary industry."

---

* " Work and Wages," pp. 88, 89. See also Smith's " Wealth of Nations," p. 55 ; Hearn's "Theory of Efforts to Satisfy Human Wants," pp. 19, 20.

In fact, it is because it has been observed that a sudden rise of wages, which is always arbitrary, is generally followed by idleness, dissipation, etc., among the laborers, it has been commonly held that "high wages leads to drunkenness and vice." This view is not only held by employers, who eagerly embrace it as a defence for their refusal to increase or their efforts to reduce wages, but it is quite commonly held by philanthropists, moralists, editors, and even some economists. This error arises from the failure to distinguish between arbitrary and economic wages. In a word, when the dollar comes before the want it is very *liable* to be wasted ; when it comes as the result of the want it is *sure* to be utilized.

Thus, from whatever point of view we consider the question, there is no escaping the result that real wages always move toward the level of the wants; or, in other words, the price of labor is finally governed by the standard of living—the cost of its production. The evidence of the truth of this is so universal that no modern writer of note has failed to notice it in some form or other,* although it appears to have been almost wholly ignored in the generalizations of even the most careful economists. Why so important a phenomenon, that is observed by all, should fail to find a place in the theory of any economist, is, indeed, difficult to understand.

---

* "From whatever point of the political compass we may set out at first, we shall find that the cost of production is the grand principle to which we must always come at last. It is this cost that determines the natural or necessary rate of wages, just as it determines the average price of commodities."—*McCulloch's* "*Principles of Political Economy*," p. 178. See also Ricardo's "Principles of Political Economy and Taxation," pp. 52, 75, 93. Also "Wealth of Nations," Book V., ch. 2, pp. 690–93.

Section IV.—*The Standard of Living.*

Having seen that the price of service (wages), like that of everything else in the sphere of exchange, is ultimately determined by the cost of production, and that the cost of producing *labor* is determined by the socially accepted standard of living, it may be well to define a little more clearly what is meant by *the " socially accepted standard of living."* By this expression is meant that state of material comfort and social refinement which is customary, and therefore demanded by the social status of the class to which one belongs, and below which he cannot go without being put to social disadvantage.

Again, the standard of living as here stated must never be understood to mean that of the single individual, but *always* that of the *family*. Nor does this mean that the wages of the worker in each family are determined by the cost of living in that particular family. In that case there could be neither bank accounts nor bad debts incurred among the wage-receivers, the income of each family being always exactly the same as its expenditures. Nor could there be any general rate of wages in any industry, class, or country, if this rule obtained, because in every variety of expenditure in the individual family, whether caused by a higher or a lower standard of living, a larger or a smaller family, extravagance or economy, waste or penuriousness, would then cause a corresponding variation in the income of each family. Thus the expenditure in each family would be a law of wages unto itself. Again, other things being the same, where there were two workers in a family the wages of each would only

be half what they would be were there only one, all of which we know is contrary to experience.

Then in what sense does the cost of living determine wages? In exactly the same sense that the cost of production determines the prices of commodities, which, it will be remembered, is by the cost of producing the most expensive portion of the necessary supply. Therefore, we say *the chief determining influence in the general rate of wages in any country, class, or industry, is the standard of living of the most expensive families furnishing a necessary part of the supply of labor in that country, class, or industry.*

The reason for this is very clear. The laborer cannot and will not work for less than that which will furnish him a living. He will, as experience shows, often work for less than what will supply him with exceptional comforts and luxuries, but he will not continuously work for less than will furnish him with that which, by constant repetition and the force of habit, have become necessities. Before he will forego these he will refuse to work, and inaugurate strikes, riots, and other means of endangering the peace and prosperity of the community.

If two dollars per day is the minimum amount upon which a certain portion of a given class of laborers can or will consent peacefully to live, then that amount must be paid them in order to obtain *their* labor. What the most expensive portion of a given class must receive, the balance may and therefore will receive. In other words, the minimum amount upon which the most expensive laborers will consent to live determines the general rate of wages in that class; and what they will consent to live upon is equally determined by the number of their habitual

wants, or the complexity of their social life. To recapitulate then : (1) Wages are the *price* of labor. (2) The price of labor is governed by (moves toward) the cost of its production—*i.e.*, the cost of producing the most expensive portion of the necessary supply. (3) The cost of producing labor is determined by the standard of living of the *family*. (4) The standard of living is determined by the habitual wants and customs or the social character of the people.

Only this theory will explain why wages are higher in one country than in another ; why the wages of skilled laborers in some places are lower than those of unskilled in others ; why agricultural wages, the world over, are lower than those of the mechanics and artisans ; why some laborers, even of the lowest grade, can save money, while at the same time the best portion of their class can hardly make a living ; why the best portion, and often those who earn the most, as a general thing, are the most discontented and frequently the leaders in strikes ; all of which has hitherto been an economic enigma.

From this view the objectionable features to what has been termed the "iron law of wages" entirely disappear. The idea that under this iron law wages cannot rise, that they constantly tend, as Henry George and Continental Socialists affirm, " to a minimum which will give but a bare living," *i.e.*, barely sustain physical existence and reproduction, will be seen to be wholly erroneous. In truth, there is nothing "*iron*" about it ; on the contrary, it is as elastic as human wants and desires, and capable of as much expansion as the social character of man. There is nothing in this law to prevent the general rate of wages

from rising to $5000 as well as to $500 a year. If it were true, as is generally assumed, that wages, when tending toward the cost of living, tend toward the minimum upon which that portion of the laborers could live who live the cheapest, then all the horrors depicted by Lassalle might be realized. In that case it would be only those whose social habits were the simplest, who would receive sufficient means to gratify their wants. All those whose habitual wants are most varied and expensive would be unable to obtain sufficient to satisfy their normal needs, and hence would be in a constant state of want and misery verging on desperation. Were this "iron law of wages" view correct, it would indeed merit all the damnation which Lassalle, Proudhon, Bakunin, Marx, and others have heaped upon it. To abolish an industrial system of which such a law is a necessary part, would justify revolution—even to overthrowing all existing social and political institutions!

Were this pessimistic doctrine correct it would, of course, also obtain in the sphere of commodities, and consequently prices would be determined by the cost of producing that portion of the supply which cost the least. In this case those who produced the cheapest would sell at cost, and all others who could not produce as cheaply as the lowest would have to sell at a loss, and there would be nowhere any profits. In the sphere of wages this law would fix the price of labor at what would furnish but the bare necessities of those (in that class) who could live on the least; and all whose cost of living was above that point would be in debt, want, and degradation. It is hardly necessary to say that such a state of things never existed in any community. It is an inversion arising from a

misconception of one half of the relation that the cost of living sustains to wages.*

While it is true that the price of labor (wages), like that of everything else, tends toward the minimum cost of production, it is the minimum cost not of the cheapest, but of the dearest, portion of the necessary supply. This makes all the difference between what really is, and what would be, the case if the "iron law" view were correct. In this, the true view of the case, in the sphere of commodities, the normal prices being determined by the cost of producing the most expensive portion of the supply, clearly all who by their superior skill, or by the aid of machinery and tools, produce commodities at less cost than the most expensive, can have the difference as profit; consequently, instead of all producing at a loss except those who can produce the cheapest, and nobody having any profits, everybody has a profit except those who produce the most expensive portion of the necessary supply, and this is what is universally taking place.

So it is with wages. Instead of the rate of wages in any class being determined by the cost of living of those who live the cheapest, the reverse is true; it being governed by that of those whose cost of living (for the family) is the highest; they constituting the most expensive portion of the supply. Consequently, instead of all laborers in a given class whose standard of living is higher than the lowest in that class, necessarily (when in steady employment) being constantly in want, debt, and difficulty, the case is exactly the

---

* It is especially strange that F. A. Walker, who more clearly than any economist has recognized the operation of this law in the sphere of commodities, should have failed to observe its equally obvious application in the domain of wages.

reverse. It is only that portion of the class whose cost of living is the greatest that are in that condition, and all whose cost of living, from whatever cause, is lower than the highest can indulge in extras or save money.

And the reason for this is not difficult to understand. We know that the general rate of wages in the same industry and locality is nearly uniform. We know, for instance, that weavers, spinners, shoemakers, carpenters, bricklayers, etc., working in the same shop or factory, or on the same job, get the same rate of pay for work at their respective trades, whether they are single or married, have large or small families, or live more or less expensively than their fellow-laborers. We also know, for reasons already given, that the most expensive among them must obtain for his service that which will supply his family with what to them (as a class) are the necessities. What will be sufficient to supply the urgent necessities of the most expensive portion of any class of laborers, to induce them to continue to work, will furnish all those whose cost of living is less with a margin proportionate to the difference, which may be spent in what to them are luxuries—dress, amusements, pictures, etc.

This explains why we always find those whose families are largest, or those who have more cultivated tastes and wants, and, therefore, their cost of living is higher than the great mass of their class, are constantly chafing under the pressure of their unsatisfied demands. This pressure increases in severity in proportion as the standard of living rises above that of the average. Consequently, we find in every class of laborers a portion who are in almost perpetual rebellion against the smallness of their wages, and what to them is almost

unendurable poverty ; while the single men, and those whose families are smaller, or who maintain a lower standard of living, while receiving the same wages, can either save money or use it in dissipation.

This is the reason why the Asiatic and European laborer can come here and accumulate wealth (or dissipate *) upon wages which will supply the American laborer's family with only the bare necessities ; as can be seen in the fact that a large majority of the wage-receivers who own their homes or have bank deposits (so commonly regarded as evidence of thrift and superior character) are foreigners and the children of foreigners. It is only because of the laborer's habits of life—his standard of living being lower than those of the highest of his class—that he is able to save at all. Accordingly, we almost always find, other things being the same, that the home appointments, sanitation, and the social relations of the wage-receivers who own their homes—mere shanties most of them—are quite inferior to those of their class who hire their homes and have no bank deposits. If the possession of a bank account, or the ownership of what is so patronizingly styled "a little home," is the evidence of superior character in those who acquire them, why did they not give the same kind of evidence in their own country ? It may be replied that it is because the general rate of wages there was so low that it left no margin above what would give them a bare living. True, but why is there no margin in their own country ? Why is there no margin for the best class of Chinamen in China, of Germans in Germany, English-

---

* In 1880 thirteen per cent of our population were foreigners, and they furnished thirty per cent of our criminals.

men in England, and Americans in America, while there is a margin in almost any country in Continental Europe for the Asiatic, a margin in England for both the Asiatic and Continental laborer, and a margin in the United States for the laborers of every other country, but no margin for the American laborer in any country in the world? The answer is very clear. There is no margin upon which the best class of laborers can save in their own country simply because there the general rate of wages is determined by their own standard of living. They can get wages which will leave them a margin over the cost of living, only by going where the price of labor is determined by a social character and standard of living *higher than their own;* or, if in their own country, by adopting a standard of living lower than the highest of the class to which they socially belong. Why the foreign laborer, who can hardly procure a living at home, can accumulate here, while the American laborer can only obtain sufficient to satisfy his normal social needs, is for the first time explained by the operation of this economic law. And should the standard of living of the American laborer ever be reduced to the level of that of the European or Asiatic, then it would be as impossible for the foreign laborer to save money here as at home, and for the same reason.

It will thus be seen that the rate of wages, and, consequently, the social prosperity of the masses, is not kept up and promoted by the influence of those whose standard of living is below the maximum or the average, but by the constant pressure of the unsatisfied desires of those whose standard of living is the highest in their class. In other words, social progress and civilization are promoted, not so much by saving as by

consuming wealth. Those who save, especially among the wage-receivers, are enabled to do so, other things being the same, solely because others consume. If everybody saved, who would consume ? and if nobody consumed, who could save ?

Thus it is that, in accordance with the same principle that production is finally determined by consumption, the laborer's income, under wage-conditions, is governed by his expenditures. In other words, the standard of living is the economic law of wages.

SECTION V.—*The Cost of Living.*

The cost of living is a resultant of two factors : (1) The price of the commodities that the laborer habitually consumes ; and, (2) The quantity of commodities which enter into his habitual daily consumption. The former depends upon the price of the commodities, and the latter upon the number of established wants ; in other words, the social character of the laborer.

Therefore, the cost of living (price of labor) may be affected by two sets of influences : (1) by affecting the price of the commodities consumed ; and (2) by affecting the number of habitual wants, and, consequently, the number of commodities consumed by the laborer.

An increase in prices would be a rise in the *cost* of living, but not a rise in the *standard* of living. It would increase the wages but not the wealth the laborer receives for a day's services. It would be a rise of what we defined as "nominal wages," but not a rise of real wages. An increase in the habitual wants involving an increase in the number of commod-

ities habitually consumed would constitute a rise in the *standard of living;* it would increase the amount of wealth the laborers would receive for a day's work, and would therefore constitute a rise of what we defined as *real wages.* It will be seen that while nominal wages will always rise with a rise in the cost of living, it will only represent more wealth for the laborer when it is accompanied by a rise in the *standard of living*, which is real wages. It may therefore be laid down that the general rate of real wages always tends toward the *standard of living*, and that nominal wages always tend toward the cost of living.

From this it follows that, prices being the same, wages will vary according to the standard of living— *i.e.*, according to the quantity and variety of commodities which enter into the laborer's normal daily consumption ; and the standard of living being the same, wages will vary according to the price of commodities.

It should be observed, however, in this connection, that although any permanent change in the cost of living will surely be followed by a corresponding change in wages, it does not follow that if the cost of living should change, from a sudden rise or fall of prices, that the change in nominal wages would be equally sudden. If, for instance, the cost of living should be increased by a sudden rise in prices, wages would not immediately rise in the same ratio, but they would be sure to begin to move in that direction ; and if the rise in prices became permanent, the wages would finally be adjusted to them. In the same way, if prices should suddenly fall, wages would not immediately fall in the same proportion, but they would soon begin to gravitate in that direction ; and if the low prices became

permanent, wages would ultimately fall to the same extent. Consequently, the variation between wages and the cost of living produced by such causes can never become permanent; they are merely accidental perturbations which can only exist during the time necessary for the wages to become adjusted to the new prices.*

Whether the laborer will lose or gain by such a change will depend upon whether prices rise or fall. If they rise he is the loser until his wages have also risen, and if they fall, he is the gainer until his wages are reduced in the same ratio. This is an important distinction which should never be lost sight of, and to which we shall have occasion to refer more at length hereafter. Therefore, if the doctrine we have laid down is sound, and our generalizations are correct, the proposition that wages are determined by the cost of living will be in full accord with all experience under wage-paying conditions. Wherever wages constitute the sole or main income of the laborer, the general rate of wages will always be found to sustain a general uniform relation to the cost of supplying the laborer's wants according to the socially accepted standard of living.

---

* This is the case when any sudden change in prices and wages occurs as the result of a variation in the value of money. Witness the inflation period in this country during our Civil War, and the subsequent contraction of the currency.

CHAPTER III.

THE SIMILARITY OF WAGES IN ASIA AND EUROPE IN THE THIRTEENTH CENTURY.

THE theory of wages presented in the previous chapter, if sound, should afford an adequate explanation of wage-phenomena under all conditions. According to this doctrine, wherever it is possible to trace the general rate of wages and the cost of living from century to century, or from generation to generation, we ought to find that they sustain a general uniform relation to each other. Do the facts sustain the theory? Let us see.

If we can accept the universal testimony of travellers and historians, the cost of living among the laboring classes in the leading countries in Asia, Africa, and South America, has always been exceedingly low, and their wages, so far as wages have been paid at all, have ever been correspondingly small. In India the working class, or "lower ranks," called the "*sudras*," which compose the great mass of the people, live mainly upon rice, ragi or millet, with salt and occasionally a little oil or chili for seasoning.

This diet can be supplied for about three or four cents a day. "A quantity sufficient for two meals," says Gibson, "can be purchased for a half penny" (one cent).* Turner, who made an extensive tour through

---

* "Indian Agriculture," in Journal of Asiatic Society, Vol. III., p. 100.

Bengal in the last quarter of the eighteenth century, speaking of the cost of living among the common people, says: "The value of this can seldom amount to more than one penny a day, even allowing him to make his meal of two pounds of boiled rice, a due proportion of salt, oil, vegetables, fish and chili." *
"From the earliest period to which our knowledge of India extends," says Buckle,† "an immense majority of the people, pinched by the most galling poverty, and just living from hand to mouth, always have remained in a state of stupid debasement."

The truth of this is also shown by the fact that in most parts of India it is established, both by law and custom, that if a laborer is unable to pay his debts, which is a common thing, he or his wife and children, if he has any, become the property of the creditor, and by this means, in many places, a large portion of the laborers have become slaves.‡

Nor is this exceptional. Turner declares§ that "the lower ranks without scruple dispose of their children for slaves to any purchaser, and that, too, for a very trifling consideration; nor yet, though in a traffic so unnatural, is the agency of a third person ever employed. Nothing is more common than to see a mother dress up her child and bring it to the market with no other hope, no other view, than to enhance the price she may procure for it."

If we had no other evidence of the simple life, low wages, and consequent social degradation of the masses

---

* "Embassy to the Court of Thibet," p. 11.

† "History of Civilization," pp. 52, 53.

‡ Buchanan's "Journey Through the Countries of Mysore, Canara and Malabar," Vol. II., pp. 320-562.

§ "Embassy to the Court of Thibet," pp. 10, 11.

in India, it is fully shown in their civil and religious code, the "Institute of Menu,"* which, we are told, "is still the basis of Hindu jurisprudence, and the principal features remain to the present day." † According to this remarkable code a *sudra* (laborer) has no rights that any superior is bound to respect. For the slightest offence to a Brahmin he can be cruelly tortured or put to death. For him to read, or even listen to the reading of the sacred books, is a most heinous crime, visited by terrible penalty, and he is expressly forbidden to attempt to accumulate wealth.‡

But we are not confined to these general statements for evidence that wages and the cost of living in India go hand in hand. Buchanan, unlike most travellers in that country, did not content himself with a mere general survey of the social and industrial condition of the laboring classes, but in each place he visited he took special pains to ascertain how the people lived and what their living cost. Also how much they were paid, and what they were paid in—whether in goods or in money; also the kind of money, and its value in gold.§

---

* The "Institute of Menu," Buckle thinks, was drawn up about 900 B.C., but some writers have put it at a much more ancient date. See also the works of Sir W. Jones.

† Elphinstone's "History of India," p. 83.

‡ Buckle's "History of Civilization," Vol. I., pp. 56, 57.

§ According to Buchanan, wages in India range from six to nine cents a day in gold; fifty to fifty-five cents a month when the laborer gets one meal a day from the master, etc.

For an extensive statement of wages and the cost of living in India, which we regret we cannot spare the space to quote, the reader is referred to his "Journey Through the Countries of Mysore, Canara and Malabar," Vol. I., pp. 124, 125, 133, 171, 216, 217, 298, 390, 415; Vol. II., pp. 12, 19, 22, 90, 108, 132, 217, 218, 481, 523, 525, 562; Vol. III., 181, 363, 364, 428, etc.

His investigations were not confined to a single locality, but they cover the greater part of Southern India. They were taken from places so distinct that different modes of payment prevailed, and even different kinds of money were used. Notwithstanding all this social isolation and industrial difference, real wages are everywhere clearly governed by the same law; for whether we find the laborer receiving his wages in food, cloth, house rent and money, or in grain, without house rent, cloth, or money, or all in money, makes little or no real difference. In all cases the laborer's income, of whatever it consists, is, generally speaking, in close conformity to the cost or standard of living, and that is the only thing to which wages appear to sustain any uniform consistency.

What Buchanan found in the last quarter of the eighteenth century, the elder Mr. Brassey found in the middle of the nineteenth.

Speaking of the laborers of India employed by his father in building railroads in that country, Sir Thomas Brassey says : * " Their food consists of two pounds of rice a day, mixed with a little curry, and the cost of living on this, their usual diet, is only a shilling (twenty-four cents) a week." " In India, wages," says the same writer, " ranged from fourpence to fourpence-half-penny (nine to ten cents) a day," which are substantially the same as those given by Buchanan.

If we turn from India to China we find a similar state of things. While it is difficult to get reliable data as to the industrial system of China, the little we have confirms the view we have taken. The testimony of travellers, inconsistent in many other respects, all goes

---

* " Work and Wages," p. 88, ninth edition.

to show that the wants of the laboring classes in China are very few—that their diet consists mainly of rice and a few vegetables—that their costumes are of the simplest and cheapest kind. They huddle together, large numbers crowding into small apartments,* almost without furniture—if tin cans, chop-sticks, and board bunks and benches admit of such a designation—and, consequently, the cost of their living is but a few cents a day. All this is fully confirmed by what we see of the habits and modes of living of Chinese laborers who have emigrated to other countries, especially to Australia and this country—notably in California—where they have settled in sufficiently large numbers to carry with them their national habits.

While parents do not sell their children in open market for slaves in China, as in India, they frequently destroy them because of their inability to give them a living. "Marriage is encouraged in China," says Adam Smith, "not by the profitableness of children, but by the liberty of destroying them. In all great towns several (children) are every night exposed in the streets, or drowned like puppies in the water. The performance of this horrid office is even said to be the avowed business by which some people earn their subsistence." †

True, the political and social institutions of China are in many respects essentially different, and, perhaps,

---

* "Their wants are few and they are easily satisfied. The poorer classes live almost entirely on rice and vegetables, to which they sometimes add small pieces of fish or meat. Their clothes are of the cheapest kind, and they are so accustomed to crowded apartments that house rent forms an insignificant item in a Chinaman's expenditures."
—"*Encyclopædia Britannica*," Vol. V., p. 671.

† "Wealth of Nations," Book I., ch. 8, pp. 55, 56.

superior, to those of India. In China education is general, if not universal; "it being intended," says Draper,* "that every Chinese shall know how to read and write;" and, public officers being selected by "competitive examination, the way to public advancement is (theoretically, at least) open to all;" while in India the laborer not only receives little or no education, but is forbidden even to associate with those who do. He is also excluded, by the combined force of caste, custom, and law, from the possibility of social distinction or political power.† But, notwithstanding the constitutional difference between the political and social institutions of the two countries, there is one thing in which the *sudra* of India and the laborer in China are very similar—that is, in their mode and their cost of living. In both countries the main diet of the laborers is rice, or some other equally cheap vegetable, with a little seasoning; in both countries house rent is a mere fractional item, and furniture almost out of the question. In both countries clothing is of the simplest and cheapest kind; but in China, if it is not dearer, a rather larger quantity is used.

Thus, with the exception of clothing, the cost of living in the two countries is very much the same. Therefore, if the doctrine that *the cost of* living is the law of wages be true, for the same reason that wages are low in India may we expect to find them nearly as low in China, and, so far as reliable data is obtainable, this is precisely what we do find. Accordingly, while wages vary from five to eight cents a day in India, they are from six to ten cents a day in China.

---

* "Intellectual Development of Europe," p. 618.
† Buckle's "History of Civilization," pp. 56, 57.

If we leave Asia and go to Europe—if we turn our attention from the industrial systems of India and China to that of England*—though the seeming is different, the fact is the same. While in other respects the conditions of society in England are entirely different from those of India and China, we find the same principle obtains in relation to wages. Although at the time the laboring classes in England began to emerge from the system of slavery (or serfdom) to that of wages, the political, social, and religious institutions under which they lived were entirely different from those existing in Asiatic countries, there was still one feature common to them all, viz., *their material condition*.

In England, as in India and China, the laborer's mode of life was simple, his wants were few, and his living was cheap. What rice was to the Hindoo and Chinese laborers, wheat was to the English.† While in the former countries the laborer's diet mainly consisted of rice or ragi, with a little fish and seasoning, in the latter it consisted, for the most part, of bread, herring, and beer.‡ Nor can the habitation of the

---

* We take England because it is there that the wages system has been in existence the longest and has become the most general, and also because reliable industrial data is more abundant in that country than in any other. As Rogers observes, " the archives of English history are more copious and more continuous than those of any other people. . . . The information from which the economical history of England and the facts of its material progress can be derived, become plentiful and remain continuously numerous from about the last ten or twelve years of the reign of Henry III.," or about the middle of the thirteenth century.

† There are, however, certain other facts, which prove the same position, that the Englishman of the Middle Ages subsisted on wheaten bread and barley beer."—*Rogers's* " *Work and Wages,*" p. 60.

‡ " At this period (the thirteenth century) the food of laborers con-

English laborer be said to be any better than that of his Asiatic brother. We find him in the thirteenth century existing—for living it can hardly be called—in a hut that would barely keep out the snow and rain, which had neither windows nor chimneys, with the bare ground for the floor, rushes for a bed, and, some writers say, "a block of wood for a pillow." * And, with the exception of an iron pot for cooking, and earthen vessels, their furniture, which was of the roughest kind, was home-made, all of which, according to the inventories made in the taxing rolls of Edward I., were valued at a few shillings.†

Consequently, we find his wages correspondingly low. According to some writers, wages in England, in the thirteenth century, were only " a penny a day in har-

---

sisted principally of fish, chiefly herrings, and a small quantity of bread and beer."—*Wade's* "*History of the Middle and Working Classes,*" p. 8.

* "In the houses of these villages (in the thirteenth century) the floor was the bare earth. . . . The wood fire was on a hub of clay. Chimneys were unknown, except in castles and manor houses, and the smoke escaped through the door or whatever aperture it could reach. The house of the peasant cottager was ruder still."—*Rogers's* "*Six Centuries of Work and Wages,*" pp. 67, 68.

Wade describes them as even worse. See "History of the Middle and Working Classes," pp. 8, 9, 12.

† The following is a copy of an inventory of household furniture of a peasant taken in 1301, six years before the death of Edwar I. :

A maize cup.............................	£0 0s. 6d.
A bed...................................	0 1 6
A tripod................................	0 0 3
A brass pot	0 1 0
A " cup.............................	0 0 6
An andiron.............................	0 0 3½
A brass dish............................	0 0 6
A gridiron..............................	0 0 6
A rug or coverlet.......................	0 0 8
	£0 5s. 8½d.

—*Eden's* "*State of the Poor,*" Vol. I., p. 22.

vest and a half-penny at other seasons."* This is so very small that one is tempted to regard it as exceptional, although Hallam † finds "a bailiff's account of expenses" more than a century later, in 1387, "where it appears that a ploughman had sixpence (twelve cents) a week, and five shillings (one dollar and twenty cents) a year, with an allowance of diet, which seems to have been only pottage." Thorold Rogers says :‡ "His wants were few, and most of them were satisfied on the spot. . . . The bailiff hired hands by the year, but these were constantly paid in allowances of grain and a small sum of money. Where one does find day work paid for, it is at about the rate of twopence (four cents) a day for men, one penny (two cents) for women, half-penny (one cent) for boys."

But, as "agricultural laborers were rarely paid by the day," this price was only paid occasionally, and was evidently exceptionally high, for, when speaking of the wages of those who had constant employment throughout the year, he says : " When the hinds were hired by the year they received a quarter of corn at, say, four shillings every eight weeks, and six shillings, money wages, *i.e.*, about the value of thirty-two shillings a year. They were always, however, boarded in harvest time and at periods of exceptional employment. This board, as I find from other sources, was reputed to cost from one and a quarter to one and a half-pence (two and a half to three cents) a day, and if we take six weeks as the time thus employed, the real wages which they received would be in the aggregate

---

* Wade's "History of the Middle and Working Classes," p. 8.
† "History of the Middle Ages," Vol. II., ch. 9 ; Part II., p. 310.
‡ "Work and Wages," pp. 169, 170.

about thirty-five shillings and eightpence a year," equal to seventeen cents a week, or about three cents a day. If we allow for the difference in the value of money, a penny then representing about as much silver as threepence does now, wages would be about from six to nine cents a day. Thus we see that the cost of living and also the wages of the English laborer in the thirteenth century were substantially the same as those of the laborer in India and China.

Since the close of the thirteenth century, however, a great difference has arisen between the material as well as the political and social condition of the working classes in England and that of those in Asia. In China, and for the most part in India, the wants (standard of living) of the laboring classes are practically unchanged, while in England they have undergone a most wonderful development. The laborer in China and the *sudra* of India still live mainly upon rice, while the diet of the English laborer to-day includes not only every variety of home production, but also many of the delicate luxuries produced in almost every country on the earth. While the Chinaman still huddles in a hole,* eats with chop-sticks, and sleeps on a board, and the *sudra* inhabits a hut without furniture, the English laborer lives in a house well built and better furnished than were those of the nobility in the thirteenth century.†

Accordingly, if the principle we have laid down is correct, this radical difference in the wants and, consequently, in the cost of living, between the English and Asiatic laborer will be accompanied by a proportion-

---

* An apartment six feet by five can hardly be called anything else.
† Henry II. slept on a bed of rushes.

ate difference in their wages. And so it is. Indeed, this is the only circumstance which fully explains the reason why we find the laborer in Asia to-day working for about the same wages he received six centuries ago, while those of the British workman have risen over a thousand per cent. And if we trace the progress of the English laborer from the thirteenth century to the present time we shall find that every movement in his wages from that day to this has been in accordance with the same law.

CHAPTER IV.

THE RISE OF REAL WAGES IN ENGLAND IN THE FOURTEENTH CENTURY.

SECTION I.—*Why Real Wages Rose After the Famine in* 1315–21.

BECAUSE prices sometimes rise without an immediate proportionate rise in wages taking place, Adam Smith, and most of the able economists who have followed him—including Thorold Rogers—have concluded that wages are not controlled by the cost of living, but by supply and demand. It is no valid objection to our theory to find a marked difference between wages and the cost of living at any given time. On the contrary, such disparities are, for reasons already explained,* in perfect harmony with this theory, and what we may always expect to find wherever prices are subject to sudden changes. One of the earliest illustrations of the operation of this law is shown in the first distinctive rise of wages that took place in England. It was at the time of the great famine in the first quarter of the fourteenth century (1315–21). Through the failure of the crops the cost of raising a bushel of wheat was greatly increased. Now, wages did not rise simultaneously with the rise in the price of provisions—*they never do*—but they immediately began to move in that direction. Had the failure of the

---

* Chapter II., Sec. V., Part II.

crops in 1315 been followed by a good harvest in 1316 wages might have risen but slightly, as in that case the prices would have returned to the wages. But the scarcity continued more or less severe for seven years, during which time wages increased thirty per cent.*

Thorold Rogers, who is forced to recognize the fact that a great rise of wages did follow this increase in the cost of living, is manifestly either very loath to admit, or unable to see, that they rose on that account, and he makes a strenuous endeavor to explain it on the theory of supply and demand. In doing this he affords a striking illustration of the length to which great men may sometimes be led in creating facts to sustain a theory, instead of making their theory wholly depend upon its ability to explain the facts. Upon the hypothesis that wages can rise *only* when laborers are scarce,† and finding that wages did rise, he concludes that there must have been a falling off in the supply of laborers ; hence, in order to explain this increase in wages, he assumes that the people must have died from famine, and says :‡ " That the famines of this unfortunate period led to a considerable loss of life is proved by the unquestionable rise in the rate of agricultural wages after their occurrence." This conclusion is philosophically unsound, and, to say the least,

---

* " The immediate rise in the wages of labor after the famine of Edward II.'s reign is as much as from twenty-three to thirty per cent, and a considerable amount of this becomes a permanent charge on the costs of agriculture."—*Rogers's* " *Work and Wages,*" p. 218.

† " Now it is generally the case that, unless the laborer is paid at a rate which leaves him no margin over his necessary subsistence, an increase in the price of his food is not followed by an increase in the rate of wages, this result being arrived at only when there is a scarcity of hands."—" *Work and Wages,*" p. 217.

‡ *Ibid.*, p. 217.

historically doubtful. If it were true, as assumed by Mr. Rogers and others, that wages never rise except when the demand for labor is in excess of the supply, there could have been no increase of wages in England from the last quarter of the fourteenth century to the present time. There has not been a time in the history of England, from the Black Death to this hour, when the number of laborers in that country has not been in excess of the demand.

Still, wages have continued to rise, and are to-day many hundred per cent higher than they were in the fourteenth century, when labor was the scarcest it was ever known to be. Therefore, the fact that wages rose does not of itself justify the assumption that the population had decreased or that the supply of laborers was inadequate to the demand. Nor is it at all clear that any such increased mortality occurred as to warrant such a conclusion. There can be little doubt but that the famine inflicted terrible hardships upon the poor, and that many died of starvation, but the evidence appears to be entirely wanting of any such terrible death-rate as would cause a sufficiently marked scarcity of labor to account for an increase of thirty per cent in wages. Although the historical data of that period is very meagre, a circumstance which struck down the population by starvation would hardly have escaped the notice of the best writers, such as Hallam, Eden, and others, and especially as it occurred only about thirty years before the Black Death Plague, which struck terror into all Europe. Indeed, Mr. Rogers obviously draws his conclusions as to the increased death-rate more from inference than from fact, and, instead of connecting the rise of wages with the historical fact of the falling off of the population, he infers

the increased mortality from the fact that wages rose, and says :* "Considerable *loss of life* is *proved by* the unquestionable rise in the rate of agricultural wages." The rise of wages does not *prove* any such thing. Again, this inference is greatly weakened by another circumstance which he relates on the same page. "It is said by chroniclers," he adds, "that in the universal scarcity numbers of servants and domestics were discharged ; that, made desperate, these people became banditti ; and that the country folk were constrained to associate themselves in arms in order to check the depredations of those starving outlaws." Now, if this be true—and there can be little doubt about it, both because of the frequency with which it is referred to by other writers, and that it is just what would naturally occur under such circumstances—it greatly impairs the value of the conclusion above, that the rise of wages was the result of the increased mortality among the laboring classes. Indeed, the two circumstances are incompatible with each other. If it were true that, through the increased death-rate, laborers had become so scarce that thirty per cent higher wages had to be offered in order to obtain them, it is impossible that discharged laborers should have become "starving outlaws," and desperate, roving "banditti," for want of employment.

But, when we view the rise of wages as resulting from the increased cost of living instead of from the scarcity of labor, the whole phenomena at once becomes explainable and appears perfectly natural, and the increased idleness and increased wages become quite compatible with each other. The rise in the

---

* "Work and Wages," p. 217.

price of provisions that would naturally accompany such a general failure of crops must have been such as to make an increase of wages for those who work inevitable, although the unemployed should be doubled or trebled. It is obvious that, however many laborers were out of work, it was impossible for those who did work to do so for less than would give them a living; and we may be quite sure that, under such circumstances, even the increased rate of wages would not more than barely do that. Nor is it less certain that the numbers of the unemployed would be increased. With both provisions and wages at famine prices it is very natural that the number of laborers and domestics would be reduced to the minimum, and, in many instances, would be dispensed with altogether. Thus, it is not only possible, but it is perfectly natural that, in a state of protracted scarcity, money wages should rise and the number of tramps increase at the same time, which was the case in the reign of Edward II., and has been many times the case since, a set of circumstances entirely unexplainable upon any other theory of wages.

This seven years of scarcity, however, was followed by a quarter of a century of uninterrupted plenty. We are told—and on this point authorities generally agree—that during the last five years of the reign of Edward II., and the first twenty of that of Edward III., the harvests were very good, crops of all kinds being abundant. This is manifest also from the fact that the price of wheat, the average of which, in 1316, was sixteen shillings a quarter, some being sold as high as twenty-six shillings and eightpence,* fell to "five

---

* Rogers's "Six Centuries of Work and Wages," ch. 8, p. 215.

shillings and fourpence, the average of the first twenty-five years of the reign of Edward III." *

The most remarkable feature of this extraordinary period, however, is the fact that, although wages rose with the rise in the price of provisions during the famine, they did not fall with the fall in prices after the famine. And, it may be added, they never have fallen to the same point since. This, at first sight, may have a paradoxical seeming, and suggest the query that, if the cost of living is the law of wages and a rise of prices causes a rise of wages, how comes it that a fall in prices does not also cause a fall in wages? On a moment's reflection, however, the reason for this becomes apparent.

It will be remembered that there are nominal wages and real wages. The former are governed by the cost of living and move in the direction of the price of commodities. The latter are governed by the standard of living and move in the direction of the wants, or quantity of wealth consumed. Hence, whether or not nominal or money wages will fall as well as rise with the rise of prices, will depend entirely upon whether the causes that affect both nominal and real wages, or only those that affect nominal wages, have been operating. If, for instance, the standard of living is un-

---

* Tooke's "History of Prices," Vol. I., ch. 3, p. 21. Speaking of the same period, Rogers says : " The period which intervened between the last of three bad harvests (1321) and the great event to which I shall next advert (the Black Death, 1349) was one of exceptional prosperity. The harvests were generally abundant, the wages of labor had been permanently improved, and all kinds of produce were cheap."—"*Six Centuries of Work and Wages,*" p. 219.

See also table of prices in "Wealth of Nations," Book I., ch. 11, and Hallam's "History of the Middle Ages," Vol. II., ch. 9, Part II., p. 268.

changed, then for the same reason that money wages will tend to rise with the rise of prices, will they tend to fall with the fall of prices; but if the causes which affect the standard of living have also operated, the result may be very different. If the prices rise and wants increase at the same time, although money wages will rise with the rise in prices, they will not necessarily fall with them. For in that case when the fall in prices occurs, instead of nominal wages falling in the same ratio, the surplus is absorbed in supplying the new wants, thereby constituting a *bonâ fide* rise of real wages.

Now, this is just what took place at the period of which we are writing and explains why wages did not fall with the fall of prices after the famine of 1315-21. The rise of money wages at that time was unquestionably due to the exceedingly high prices, but the increase in real wages which became visible when the price of labor failed to fall with the price of provisions was due to an entirely different cause, as the movement of real wages always is. This was not the result of any circumstance immediately connected with the famine, the effects of which upon wages disappeared with the return of plenty.

The rise of real wages was the result of social causes which had been in operation for fully a century before that time. During the last quarter of the twelfth and the whole of the thirteenth centuries, through causes which I cannot now stop to describe, the free towns and cities made great progress.* These free cities,

---

* The rise and development of the free cities and towns, and their relation to the progress of industrial prosperity and the growth of social and political freedom among the masses, will be found in the opening chapters of the next volume of this work, where it will be

which were the outcome of the baronial towns of the tenth and eleventh centuries, by the thirteenth century had become the centres of trade and industry.* In their struggles to protect themselves against the plundering of the barons on the one hand and the exactions of the king on the other, the towns were compelled to resort to all the means of strengthening themselves within their reach. Consequently, in the struggle between the feudal lords and the monarchy for supremacy, which lasted several centuries, the towns or cities would side with the barons and help them to resist the exactions of the king, if they would increase their town privileges. And, on the other hand, they would fight for the king if he would grant them greater charter privileges, exempting them from the authority of the barons, whose property they originally were. This he was naturally willing to do, because by that means he weakened the power of the barons, who were his standing enemies. By this and kindred means the towns gradually acquired commercial privileges, and finally the right of self-government.†

---

shown that the free cities were really the birthplace and nursery of modern civilization.

* " From the middle of the twelfth century to that of the thirteenth, the traders of England became more and more prosperous. The towns on the southern coast exported tin and other metals in exchange for the wines of France ; those on the eastern sent corn to Norway ; the Cinque-ports bartered wool against the stuffs of Flanders." —*Hallam's " History of the Middle Ages,"* Vol. II., p. 80.

† " Under such a system of arbitrary taxation, however, it was evident to the most selfish tyrant that the wealth of his burgesses was his wealth, and their prosperity his interest ; much more were liberal and sagacious monarchs, like Henry II., inclined to encourage them by privileges. From the time of William Rufus (1087 to 1100), there was no reign in which charters were not granted to different towns, of exemption from tolls on rivers and at markets—those lighter manacles of

118   WEALTH AND PROGRESS.

It was in this way the great *Magna Charta*, which declared all existing charters of the towns, and especially that of the city of London, inviolable, was wrung from the treacherous and cowardly King John on that memorable 15th of June, 1214. By these charters the towns, as just remarked, finally acquired the right of self-government, frequently to the extent of electing their own magistrates, levying taxes, supporting their own military, etc.*

In order to increase their numbers, wealth and strength, both for defensive and offensive purposes, against either the barons or the king, the cities offered an asylum to all who should escape thither, and, after one year's residence within the walls of the city, even serfs were declared free, and were granted all the rights and privileges of citizenship,† which was not only to participate in defending, but also in governing, the city.

The necessary result of this was, not only that serfs began to flee to the towns and cities for freedom, "but," as Guizot says,‡ "frequently men of considerable rank and wealth . . . upon being attacked by more powerful neighbors or by the king himself,"

---

feudal tyranny ; or of commercial franchises ; or of immunity from the ordinary jurisdictions ; or, lastly, of internal self-regulation."—*Hallam's "History of the Middle Ages,"* Vol. II., p. 78.

* See Guizot's " History of Civilization," p. 153.

† " In order to swell their numbers," says Hallam, " it became the practice to admit all who came to reside within their walls to the rights of burghership, even though they were villeins—appurtenants to the soil of a master, from whom they had escaped." And he adds in a note : " One of the most remarkable privileges of chartered towns was that of conferring freedom on runaway serfs."—" *History of the Middle Ages,*" Vol. I., p. 170.

See also Guizot's " History of Civilization," pp. 153-157. Wade's " History of the English Working Classes," p. 9.

‡ " History of Civilization," p. 157.

would "carry away all the property they could rake together and enter the city" for safety and protection. By these means the population, wealth, power, and social character of the towns rapidly increased, so that early in the third quarter of the thirteenth century (1264) they began to be represented in Parliament.*

The natural result of these changed social conditions was that the power of the feudal lords gave way to that of the commoners, the serfs and villeins became hired laborers,† and by the end of the thirteenth century feudalism was virtually overthrown and the period of free labor was inaugurated.

It will thus be seen that during the hundred years immediately preceding the time of which we are writing—from the granting of the *Magna Charta* in 1214 to the famine in 1315—circumstances occurred that radically changed the social and economic condition of the laborers. During this period they had ceased to be mere serfs of the soil, inseparable from the lord's estate, without rights except by his decree. They had become hired laborers, with the legal right, at least, to go whithersoever their labor was in demand, or tenants paying rent for the land either in money or its equivalent in service. All this change in the industrial conditions, the greater social contact consequent upon the increasing variety of social duties and industrial calling, arising from the growing prosperity and social complexity of the free cities,‡ in the government of

---

* Hallam's "History of the Middle Ages," Vol. II., p. 83. See also Guizot's "History of Civilization," p. 172.

† Hallam's "History of the Middle Ages," Vol. II., p. 204.

‡ For evidence of the prosperity of the free towns see Rogers's "Six Centuries of Work and Wages," pp. 115-117; Hallam's "History of the Middle Ages," Vol. II., pp. 76-80, 266-268, 271, 272; Wade's

which they also took part, naturally produced considerable change in the social needs, desires, and aspirations—wants and character—of the people, as the history of that period abundantly shows. Indeed, it was impossible that this should be otherwise. Consequently, when prices fell after the famine (1321), all the conditions were ready for transforming the rise of nominal wages which had occurred during the famine into a permanent rise of real wages. There is nothing surprising, therefore, in the fact that wages did not fall again with the fall of prices, but, on the contrary, that the greater part of the rise in nominal wages should be converted into a rise of real wages was the natural effect of the changed condition of the masses, arising from the general economic movement of the period, and would, from the nature of things, have taken place if the famine had never occurred. It might, and probably would, have been less sudden and noticeable at that particular time, but it would have been no less sure. If we trace the history of labor from that time to this we shall find that wages have always moved in accordance with the same law, and real wages have everywhere risen or remained stationary according to the advancing or stationary condition of the laborer's social character and standard of living. But what appears to me the most remarkable of all is that this fact should be so generally observed by economists,[*] and

---

"History of the English Working Classes," pp. 9-11; Guizot's "History of Civilization," ch. 7.

[*] See Smith's "Wealth of Nations," Book V., ch. 2, p. 691; Torren's "Essay on the External Corn Trade," pp. 57, 58; Ricardo's "Principles of Political Economy and Taxation," pp. 50, 52, 75, 93; M. Say's "Treatise on Political Economy," pp. 336, 337; McCulloch's "Principles of Political Economy," Part III., sec. 7, pp. 177, 178,

yet its economic relation to wages be almost entirely overlooked.

Section II.—*The Black Death not the Real Cause of the Rise of Wages in* 1350-51.

The next important epoch in the history of wages occurred about the middle of the fourteenth century. About that time (1349) a fearful pestilence, known as the Black Death, which is said to have arisen in China several years before, after working havoc in most of the countries of Europe, reached England,* when about one third of the population died in a few months. In 1350 there was a marked rise in the rate of wages, and the rise not only became permanent, but it continued its upward tendency until well into the second quarter of the next century. Here, again, our economic historian, Thorold Rogers, endeavors to put the stamp of English political economy upon industrial history. Upon the erroneous theory that wages only rise when labor is scarce, for the same reason that he assumed exceptional mortality among the laborers to account for the rise of wages in 1322, he attributes the rise of wages in 1350 and 1351, and the prosperous condition of the masses during the last half of the fourteenth

---

181, 182, 184; Brassey's "Work and Wages," pp. 15, 16, 59-61, 70, 88, 89, 93-96, 105, 108.

* "The disease began in the Levant about 1346, from whence Italian travellers brought it to Sicily, Pisa, and Genoa. In 1348 it passed the Alps and spread over France and Spain; in the next year it reached Britain, and in 1350 laid waste Germany and other northern states, lasting generally about five months in each country. At Florence, more than three out of five died."—*Hallam's* "*History of the Middle Ages,*" Vol. I., p. 44.

and the first half of the fifteenth century to the scarcity of labor by the Black Death in 1349. A little examination of the industrial phenomena of the period, however, shows that this circumstance is inadequate to account for the industrial events that followed. The pestilence in 1349, like the famine in 1315, was the circumstance which unquestionably made it possible for the rise in wages to be more sudden than it otherwise would have been, but neither event of itself could ever cause a permanent rise in *real* wages. The only way such events can affect wages is through their influence upon prices, which, as before explained, *cæteris paribus*, affect nominal but never real wages. Indeed, if famine, pestilence, and their sister evil, war, were the promoters of real wages, then the laboring classes in Europe, from the ninth to the nineteenth century, would surely have been in the most opulent circumstances, for they were seldom free from one or other, and often all, of these wealth and life-destroying agents. Such an idea could only be born of the rankest economic heresy.

That the increase in real wages which commenced in 1350–51 was the result of the same general causes as that in 1322, and must have taken place if the plague had never appeared, is shown by all the industrial data of the period. Now, if the rise of wages in 1350 was, as Mr. Rogers says,* "the actual effect of this great and sudden scarcity of labor," they would have fallen again to their former level when the scarcity of labor ceased, which, he admits, was very soon.† But, in-

---

* " Six Centuries of Work and Wages in England," p. 227.

† " I make no doubt that the population speedily righted itself, as it has done on many other occasions, when a sudden or abnormal

stead of that they continued to rise for half a century after the scarcity disappeared, and, despite the subsequent and almost continuous redundance of labor, they have never fallen to the same point since.

Again, if this scarcity of labor was the real cause of the rise of wages, why was not the effect somewhat proportionate to the cause? With such a sudden diminution in the population, taking his own estimate of one third, there could be nothing, at least so far as the supply of laborers was concerned, to prevent them from fixing their own price upon their labor, limited only by the ability of the employer to pay. Indeed, he tells us * that such was the scarcity of labor "that crops were often suffered to rot in the fields for want of hands," and "that cattle and sheep roamed at large over the country for lack of herdsmen."

Now, why, under these circumstances, did not wages rise to a shilling or even to two or three shillings a day? Why did the laborers only aspire to fivepence (ten cents) a day when, according to the supply and demand theory, they could have had many times as much? Why wages could not be kept at threepence a day seems clear to Mr. Rogers, but why they should not rise above fivepence a day his "scarcity of labor" doctrine is wholly unable to explain. Considered in the light of the theory we have presented, however, this whole phenomena at once becomes, not merely explainable, but perfectly natural. Viewed from the doctrine that the *standard of living*, instead of the abundance or scarcity of labor, is the determining in-

---

destruction of human life has occurred in a people and the people has a recuperative power. That they had this power is proved by the events which followed."—"*Work and Wages*," p. 226.

* "Work and Wages," p. 227. American edition.

fluence in wages, the reason why wages did not rise above fivepence a day at once becomes as clear as that of the inability of the authorities to keep them at threepence. It was simply because fivepence a day was sufficient to defray their cost of living. A permanent rise in the rate of real wages never occurs except from a rise in the laborer's social character and standard of living; and hence is always proportionate thereto. And this the pestilence, like the famine, in the very nature of things, could not produce.

A brief glance at the events of that period will suffice to show that the increase of from two to four cents a day in wages after 1350 was the natural result of the same general influences which led to the rise of from two to three cents a day in real wages after 1320–22. It was simply a part of the same social and industrial movement already referred to, which had its rise in the free towns in the twelfth, and continued to gain momentum till the last quarter of the fourteenth century. The circumstances which contributed so largely to the growth and prosperity of the free towns during the thirteenth century began to operate with greater force after the first quarter of the fourteenth.

Rogers tells us that the period between the famine and the plague (1322–50) "was one of exceptional prosperity. The harvests were generally abundant, the wages of labor had been permanently improved, and all kinds of produce was cheap. The early days of the war did not impair the general well-being of the English people." * It was during this period (1331) that Edward III., whom Hallam calls "the father of English commerce," invited the Flemish manu-

---

* "Work and Wages," p. 219.

facturers to settle in England,* in order to promote the manufacture of fine woollen, for which England has ever since been so famous.

The Hanseatic Confederacy had now become well established, and the English towns were fast acquiring a prosperous foreign trade. "This opening of the northern market," says the same author, "powerfully accelerated the growth of our own commercial opulence, especially after the woollen manufacture had begun to thrive. From about the middle of the fourteenth century, we find continual evidence of a rapid increase of wealth." † In brief, this was really the dawn of a new industrial system, which created new wants among the laboring classes, and consequently increased the cost by raising the standard of living. Not that things were dearer, but a greater quantity of them was needed. The demand for more home comforts was becoming general. The hovels contentedly occupied by the laborer of the thirteenth century now failed to give satisfaction. This is shown by the fact that houses with chimneys,‡ which were

---

* The following remarkable inducements offered by Edward III. to the Flemish manufacturers to settle in England are quoted by Blomefield in the history of Norfolk, from Fuller's "Church History": "Here they should feed on fat beef and mutton till nothing but their fulness should stint their stomachs. Their beds should be good, and their bedfellows better, seeing the richest yeomen in England would not disdain to marry their daughters unto them, and such the English beauties that the most envious foreigners could not but commend them."—See *Hallam's* "*History of the Middle Ages*," Vol. II., p. 268.

† Hallam's "History of the Middle Ages," Vol. II., pp. 271, 272.

‡ "The two most essential improvements in architecture during this period, which had been missed by the sagacity of Greece and Rome, were chimneys and glass windows. Nothing apparently can be more simple than the former, yet the wisdom of ancient times was

previously only known to the rich, now began to be demanded by the laborer, which was soon followed by the additional comfort of windows, first of lattice, then of horn, and by the end of the century we are told glass was used.* This would very naturally stimulate the desire for something in the way of furniture—not upholstery, indeed, but something better than mere blocks of wood hewn into shape with a broad-axe and spokeshave, as was the case prior to the fourteenth century.†

This increase in the daily wants, and, therefore, the cost of living, of the masses, being the result of natural causes which had been in operation for more than a century previous,‡ not only prepared the way for a

---

content to let the smoke escape by an aperture in the centre of the roof. . . . About the middle of the fourteenth century, the use of chimneys is distinctly mentioned in England and Italy, but they were found in several of our castles which bear a much earlier date."—*Hallam's " History of the Middle Ages,"* Vol. II., p. 293.

* Hallam's "History of the Middle Ages," Vol. II., pp. 293, 294.

† Some idea of the quality of the household furniture of the laborer before this time may be gathered from the fact that a full set of carpenters' tools, according to the inventories made in the reign of Edward I. (1301), consisted of

A broad-axe..............value..................		5*d*.
Another axe...............	"	3
An adze...................	"	2
A square..................	"	1
A marger, or spokeshave...	"	1
Total value.............................		1*s*.

For a full statement of this period the reader is referred to Eden's "State of the Poor," Vol. III.

‡ " A silent alteration had been wrought in the condition and character of the lower classes during the reign of Edward III. This was the effect of increased knowledge and refinement, which had been making a considerable progress for full half a century, though they did not readily permeate the cold region of poverty and ignorance."
—*Hallam's "History of the Middle Ages,"* Vol. II., p. 204.

rise of wages, but had made that event inevitable. Consequently, when the pestilence came and struck down "one third of the population," the rise of wages, which we have seen had already commenced, and would otherwise have been gradual, now took place suddenly.

But, although the rise in wages was somewhat sudden, it was not abnormal. Being governed by the cost of living, wages very naturally rose only as that had been increased. Unlike the rise of 1321, there was now no increase in prices, the harvests having for many years previous been very good. Therefore, the increase in the cost of living in this instance was mainly due to the higher standard of living, caused by the new wants which had been developed by the influences to which we have referred. To meet the demands of these new wants a rise of from one and a half pence to twopence (three to four cents) a day was demanded, which increased wages to about fivepence (ten cents) a day. Nor is it surprising that they did not rise to tenpence (twenty cents) a day; indeed, it was just as natural that they should not rise to tenpence as it was that they should rise to fivepence, because fivepence being sufficient to satisfy their normal wants, tenpence would be more than they could consume, and, therefore, would have tended to induce idleness rather than to stimulate industry.* Hence, they had no motive for demanding it.

But, another, and the most conclusive proof that the rise of wages was the natural effect of the improved

---

* See Brassey's experience in raising wages in India above the wants of the Hindu, as stated in his book "Work and Wages," pp. 88, 89.

standard of living, is shown by the fact that the united power of wealth, law, and royal authority was not able to force them down again. The plague struck England in August, 1348, and continued till January or February of the next year. Consequently, during the spring and summer of 1349 wages suddenly rose. The lords, tenants, farmers, and employers generally, became alarmed at the prospect. Parliament being broken up through the plague, they appealed to the king, who, being himself an extensive landowner and employer, shared their consternation. There having been no rise in the price of provisions, the cost of living, so far as they could see, was unchanged. They could hardly be expected to recognize the claims of new wants at that early time, when the political economy and the statesmanship of the nineteenth century still regard all indulgence of new wants as extravagance needing to be suppressed; and, as the most modern employers often do, they insisted that the demands of the laborers were unnecessary and unjust and should therefore be resisted by the iron hand of authority. Accordingly, in 1349 the king issued a proclamation decreeing that no higher than customary wages should be paid. It was soon seen, however, that the king's mandate was unavailing. His majesty then announced that not only would laborers be punished for asking higher than the customary rate of wages, but severe penalties would also be inflicted upon all tenant occupiers, crown tenants, or even upon inferior barons, priors or abbots who should be known to do so. Many laborers, we are told, were put into prison for disobeying the royal edict.

But all to no effect. The next year (1350) Parliament was again called together, for the first time after

the pestilence, when by its vote the substance of the royal mandate became a law, under that famous title "*The Statute of Laborers*," which was the first legislative attempt to deal with wages. And it remained upon the statute-book over two hundred years. The preamble of this statute complains of the "insolence of the servants," who asked for higher wages than had been previously paid, "to the great detriment of the lords and commons," and ordains

(1) That no person under sixty years of age, serf or free, except those who possessed property, lived by merchandise, or occupied land, should refuse to labor for the same wages they were accustomed to receive in the twentieth year of the king's reign (1347), which it fixes for weeders and haymakers at one penny a day, reapers for the first week in August at twopence, and the remainder of harvest threepence a day, and mowers fivepence an acre. They were to be hired by the year, month, or day, and receive these wages in wheat or money, as the master might decide.

(2) That the lord shall have the first claim to the labor of the serf, and those who refuse to work for him or others at the fixed price are to be sent to the common jail.

(3) That all persons who leave their employments before the expiration of their contracts shall be punished by imprisonment.

(4) That even the lords of the manor who shall pay more than this amount shall be fined in treble damages.

(5) That artificers, under which title are enumerated "saddlers, tanners, farriers, shoemakers, tailors, smiths, carpenters, masons, tilers, pargetters, carters, and others," are liable to the same damages.

(6) That food must be sold at reasonable prices.

(7) That alms shall not be given to able-bodied laborers.

(8) That any excess of wages, either given or taken, shall be seized for the king's use, etc.*

Notwithstanding the fulness and severity of this act, the enforcement of which, we may be sure, lacked

---

* See Hallam's "History of the Middle Ages," Vol. II., p. 310; Rogers's "Work and Wages," p. 228; Wade's "History of the English Working Classes," p. 9; "Wealth of Nations," Book I., ch. 11, Part III., p. 141.

nothing the king and the lords could do, wages rose. But while imprisonment of laborers served to increase the amount of ungathered crops, it did not prevent the ultimate and permanent rise of wages. In spite of the royal mandate, statute law, and the personal power of the barons, wages rose, as is shown by the bailiffs' rolls for the same year, from fifty to seventy-five per cent, and, in some instances, even more, although at first, in order to harvest their crops and avoid the penalties of the statute, which were, doubtless, for some time at least, mercilessly inflicted, the bailiffs in their entries frequently drew a line through the new price, "*fivepence a day*," and substituted the legal price, "*threepence.*" * The new prices were soon openly and regularly paid, however, as is seen alike by the bailiffs' rolls and the frequent complaints of employers that the statute was not enforced.

When the terrors of the pestilence, the royal edict, and the new statute had spent themselves, and "the prices paid for labor had been steadied by custom," it was found that, regardless of all authority, wages had obeyed the natural law, and adjusted themselves to the new standard of living, and, accordingly, rose from fifty to seventy-five per cent.† Indeed, "the result," to use the language of Rogers, "is marked, universal, permanent, and conclusive, even if we had not on record the complaints of the landowners in Parliament, that the 'Statute of Laborers' was entirely inoperative." ‡

The inability of the combined power of baronial in-

---

* "Work and Wages," p. 229.
† *Ibid.*, p. 233.
‡ *Ibid.*, p. 237. See also Eden's "State of the Poor."

fluence, royal authority, and statute law to prevent wages from gravitating toward the cost of living was shown by the utter failure of this statute; and the principle that wants govern wages is unconsciously inscribed upon all subsequent legislation on wages, which was almost incessant during the next four centuries.

CHAPTER V.

THE RISE OF REAL WAGES ARRESTED BEFORE 1450. HOW IT WAS BROUGHT ABOUT.

FINDING that all the pains and penalties the governing classes were able to inflict could not prevent wages from rising to the level of the *wants* of the people, they began to legislate upon what those wants should be—*i.e.*, to fix the standard of living by statute law. In 1363, in response to the numerous complaints that the "Statute of Laborers" was not enforced, although it had been re-enacted three years previous (1360) with the penalty of imprisonment and the branding of the forehead with a red-hot iron for its violation,* a law was enacted fixing the quantity, quality and price of both the food and clothes the laborer should have.

This statute ordains that the servants or laborers of lords, artificers or tradesmen shall receive meat, fish, or the offal of other victuals, etc., according to their station, and that laborers shall wear but one kind of cloth, of which the whole piece did not cost more than a shilling a yard.†

---

* "In 1360 the 'Statute of Laborers' was confirmed by Parliament, and the observance of it was enforced, under the penalty of imprisonment for fifteen days and burning in the forehead with a red-hot iron in the form of the letter 'F.' If they fled into a town the magistrate was to deliver them up under a penalty of £10 to the king, and £5 to the master who should reclaim them."—*Eden's "State of the Poor,"* Vol. I., p. 36.

† Eden's "State of the Poor," pp. 38, 39. See also Wade's "History of the English Working Classes," p. 9.

It was soon discovered, however, that the statute of 1363, fixing the diet and apparel, like its predecessor in 1350, fixing the wages, had come too late to be effectual. The new wants, which had been gradually developing for more than a century previous, had become too firmly established by custom to be wiped out by any mere statutory enactment; nothing short of physical force could now produce that effect.

The causes which had produced this irrepressible change in the wants, and hence in the wages, were still active. The trade and commerce of the towns was still prosperous, and the social intercourse and the needs of the laboring classes were steadily progressing, not merely in regard to their food, which is so often erroneously taken, even by economists, as the only measure of the cost of living, but also in regard to dress, furniture, and amusements, which are more civilizing than diet. No better evidence of this is needed than the general outcry of the rulers and writers of the times against the extravagance of the poor.* Knyghton declares that "in 1388 the vanity of the common people in dress was so great that it was impossible to distinguish the rich from the poor, the high from the low, or the clergy from the laity by their appearance. Fashions were changing constantly, and every one was trying to outdo his neighbor." This is unquestionably a greatly overdrawn picture of the situation, but the very exaggeration proves the fact. If the wants of the laborers for dress, etc., had not been materially increased, and caused them to become troublesome

---

* "The extravagance of dress was the common topic of complaint among the historians of that period (last quarter of the fourteenth century)."—*Eden's* "*State of the Poor*," Vol. I., p. 37.

in their demands for higher wages, there could have been no ground for this alarm, and no motive for exaggeration ; in fact, nothing to exaggerate.*

The rolls of Parliament for that period contain evidence of the same fact. They inform us that " in the year 1376 the Commons made great complaint that the masters are obliged to give their servants and laborers great wages to prevent them from running away." † Again, in 1378, we are told that " the Commons complained in Parliament that the ' Statute of Laborers ' was not attended to, but that persons employed in husbandry *fled* into the cities and became artificers, mariners, and clerks, to the great detriment of agriculture." ‡

It is thus evident that the employing classes now began to recognize the fact that this rise of wages, which all the powers of government had so far failed to suppress, originated in what was very naturally regarded as the " *evil influences of the cities and towns.* " Having treacherously slain Wat Tyler, put to death most of his associates, and at least formally suppressed his insurrection, Parliament, in 1388, again resumed its onerous task of fixing the wants and wages of the laboring classes. They now commenced to direct their efforts against the real cause of " all their woes," viz., the opportunities for social intercourse which had for

---

* In referring to Knyghton's clamor against the irrepressible demands of these increasing wants of the people, Sir Frederick Eden wisely observes : " A poor man's vanity would in vain have coveted finer clothes than he was used to had not his industry and the improvement in manufactures afforded him the means of gratifying it."
—"*State of the Poor,*" Vol. I., p. 37.

† Eden's " State of the Poor," Vol. I., pp. 42, 43.

‡ *Ibid.*, Vol. I., p. 43.

a century and a half been gradually revolutionizing the habits and customs of the people.

This statute,* after prescribing a schedule of prices to be paid in the different occupations, which were somewhat higher than those of the previous statutes, " directs that no servant or laborer should depart from one part of the country to another to serve or to reside elsewhere, or under pretence of going on a pilgrimage, without a *letter patent* under the king's seal, specifying the cause of his departure and the time of his return, which might be granted by a justice of the peace. Every vagrant who could not produce a letter patent was to be taken up, put into the stocks and imprisoned until he found surety to return to his former master." †

Previous legislation had all been directed against the results of the new wants, and, consequently, produced no real effect upon wages, but this statute directly related to the causes which determined the standard of living; and hence, as we shall presently see, was attended with most disastrous consequences to wages. From the date of this statute the causes began to operate which finally arrested the rise of wages, and, consequently, the prosperity of the English laborers, which afterward became practically stationary for more than three centuries. Although wages did not immediately stop rising, it was this and similar statutes which followed it that laid the foundation for the fearful arrest of material prosperity which was consummated before the middle of the fifteenth century, and

---

* 12th Richard II., ch. 3.

† Eden's "State of the Poor," Vol. I., p. 44. "By a very harsh statute in the 12th of Richard II. no servant or laborer could depart, even at the expiration of his service, from the hundred in which he lived without permission under the king's seal."—"*History of the Middle Ages,*" Vol. II., p. 207.

became so marked in the sixteenth. In fact, this enactment really sustained the same relation to the low wages and poverty of the masses during the sixteenth, seventeenth, and eighteenth centuries that the chartered towns of the thirteenth century did to the increased wages, prosperity, and progress of the fourteenth and fifteenth centuries. What the charters gave this statute took away. The free towns afforded opportunity for industrial contact and social intercourse and association, which naturally tended to increase the wants and develop the social and intellectual character of the laborer, and to prepare him for the freedom he thereby acquired. While the purpose and effect of this legislation, so far as it was operative, was to destroy all opportunity for travel and social intercourse, it prohibited all association, prevented the development of new tastes and wants, and prepared the laborer for the despotism and degradation which followed for nearly three centuries after the death of Henry VII.*

That the law of 1388 was rigidly enforced is manifest from what immediately followed. The "uplandish folk," as the country people were called, properly envying the prosperity and freedom enjoyed in the towns,† and being now prohibited from leaving the place of their birth or changing their occupation after twelve years of age, began to send their children under that age into the towns, and bind them as ap-

---

* Rogers's "Work and Wages," p. 508.

† "It was natural," says Hallam, "that the country people or 'uplandish folk,' as they were called, should repine at the exclusion from that enjoyment of competence and security for the fruits of their labor which the inhabitants of towns so fully possessed."—"*History of the Middle Ages*," Vol. II., pp. 204, 205.

prentices to learn some trade or craft—become "artificers." In order, therefore, to complete the statute of 1388, and make it operate as effectually upon children under twelve as it had done upon all over that age, it was further enacted in 1406 * " that no person whosoever, unless possessed of land or rental of twenty shillings a year, shall put a child of any age apprentice to any trade or mystery in any city or borough, but that children should be brought up in the occupations of their parents, or other business suitable to their station ;" and this was further strengthened by another statute of similar import in 1483.

It was thus during what Rogers calls " the golden age of the English laborer" that the foundation of his degradation was laid. The machinery for arresting the growth of new tastes and wants among the masses was now put into full operation, and we shall soon see with what result. Although the tendency of wages continued upward for a time, long before the middle of the fifteenth century the rise was completely and permanently arrested. This is clearly shown by the rates of wages as fixed by subsequent statutes, that of 23d Henry VI., in 1444, being from seventy to ninety per cent above that fixed by the statutes of Edward III., Richard II., and Henry IV. in 1350, 1388, and 1406,† and was the highest point they ever reached until the depreciation of the currency by Henry VIII. in 1545–46 and Edward VI. in 1549–51, which, though it increased nominal wages, had no tendency to advance real wages. In fact, while through the variation

---

* 7th Henry IV., ch. 17. See Eden's " State of the Poor," Vol. I., p. 63 ; also Hallam's " History of the Middle Ages," Vol. II., p. 207.

† See Eden's " State of the Poor," Vol. I., pp 65, 66.

of prices produced by changes in the value of money and bad harvests, nominal wages frequently rose during the sixteenth, seventeenth, and eighteenth centuries, historians agree in assuring us that the general rate of *real* wages never again rose till the present century.

The effect of this legislation soon began to show itself, and finally proved to be as disastrous to the prosperity and progress of the laboring class as its most sanguine projectors could have hoped or desired. Indeed, were all other evidence wanting of the fact that the rise of wages was permanently arrested before the middle of the fifteenth century, it is fully demonstrated by the statute of Henry VII., Chapter XI., in 1496, and that of Henry VIII. in 1514; for, although nearly three-quarters of a century had elapsed between the statutes of the Sixth and Eighth Henrys, during which time several laws regulating the price of labor had been passed,* the rate of wages as fixed by them all was substantially the same, as is clearly shown by the following schedule of wages fixed by the statutes of Henrys VI., VII., and VIII., in 1444, 1496, and 1514:

---

* See Rogers's "History of Prices," Vol. IV., pp. 17–23; also Eden's "State of the Poor," Vol. I., pp. 30–75.

† The wages of the bailiff in the statute of 1496 are stated by some early writers at sixteen shillings and eightpence, which is clearly an error. Eden thinks it should be one pound, sixteen shillings and eightpence. But this appears to be equally improbable, as that is as much out of proportion to the rate fixed by other statutes as sixteen shillings and eightpence. What seems to be more probable, however, is that in the earlier copying the figures 1 and 6 have got placed together as 16s. instead of £1 6s. The probable correctness of this view is sustained by the fact, that in the statute of 1514 where all the other wages are exactly the same as in that of 1496, the bailiff's wages are one pound six shillings and eightpence. Rogers appears to have taken this view also, as he has put it at one pound six shillings and eightpence in his "History of Prices."

RATE OF WAGES IN 1444, 1496, AND 1514.

	1444		1496		1514	
YEARLY WAGES IN HUSBANDRY.	Yearly Wages with Food.	Yearly Allowance for Clothing.	Yearly Wages with Food.	Yearly Allowance for Clothing.	Yearly Wages with Food.	Yearly Allowance for Clothing.
	£ s. d.	£ s. d.	£ s. d.	£ s. d.	£ s. d.	£ s. d.
Bailiff...........................	1 3 4	0 5 0	1 6 8	0 5 0	1 6 8	0 5 0
Chief hind and shepherd.........	1 0 0	0 4 0	1 0 0	0 4 0	1 0 0	0 4 0
Common laborer.................	0 15 0	0 3 4	0 16 0	0 4 0	0 16 0	0 4 0
Women...........................	0 10 0	0 4 0	0 10 0	0 4 0	0 10 0	0 4 0
Children under 14 years........	0 6 0	0 3 0	0 6 8	0 4 0	0 6 8	0 4 0

	1444		1496		1514	
DAY WAGES OF ARTISANS AS FIXED BY SAME STATUTES.	Daily Wages.		Daily Wages.		Daily Wages.	
	With Diet.	Without Diet.	With Diet.	Without Diet.	With Diet.	Without Diet.
	£ s. d.	£ s. d.	£ s. d.	£ s. d.	£ s. d.	£ s. d.
Free mason.....................	0 0 4	0 0 5½	0 0 4	0 0 6	0 0 4	0 0 6
Carpenters.....................	0 0 4	0 0 5½	0 0 4	0 0 6	0 0 4	0 0 6
Rough mason....................	0 0 3	0 0 4½	0 0 4	0 0 6	0 0 4	0 0 6
Common carpenter...............	0 0 3	0 0 4½	0 0 4	0 0 6	0 0 4	0 0 6
Master tiler...................	0 0 3	0 0 4½	0 0 4	0 0 6	0 0 4	0 0 6
Common laborers................	0 0 2	0 0 3½	0 0 2	0 0 4	0 0 2	0 0 4
Glazier........................			0 0 4	0 0 6	0 0 4	0 0 6
Joiner.........................			0 0 4	0 0 6	0 0 4	0 0 6
Carver.........................			0 0 4	0 0 6	0 0 4	0 0 6
Plumbers.......................			0 0 4	0 0 6	0 0 4	0 0 6

† See note on p. 138.

It is difficult to ascertain the exact cost of provisions for each year in the foregoing table, but all authorities agree that the price of wheat was lower in the first than in either of the other years.* If we take Thorold Rogers, who, being the most recent writer on prices, has had the best opportunities for forming a correct estimate, we find that the price of wheat in 1444 † was three shillings and elevenpence three farthings a quarter. In 1496,‡ according to the same writer, it was five shillings and fivepence halfpenny, and in 1514 § it was five shillings and fourpence. If we take the average for the decades in which each of these years occur, which is still better, we find the result to be the same. The average price of wheat from 1441 to 1450 ‖ was five shillings and threepence three farthings; from 1491 to 1500 it was five shillings and three farthings, and from 1511 to 1520 it was six shillings and eightpence three farthings.

It is therefore very clear that while nominal wages in a few cases were a fraction lower, real wages were, if anything, higher in 1444 than at either of the other periods, which conclusively shows that the rise of real wages was unmistakably arrested before the middle of the fifteenth century.

Nor were the evil effects of those enactments confined to the "uplandish folk," but it affected the towns also. The statutes of Richard II. and Henry IV. virtually cut off the industrial and social intercourse be-

---

* See Tooke's "History of Prices," Vol. VI., pp. 423, 424, 425; "Wealth of Nations," conclusion of Book I., p. 206; Arthur Young's "Progressive Value of Money;" Eden's "State of the Poor," and Rogers's "History of Prices," Vol. IV.
† "History of Prices," Vol. IV., p. 284.
‡ *Ibid.*, p. 286.   § *Ibid.*, p. 288.   ‖ *Ibid.*, p. 292.

tween the laboring classes in the country and those in the towns, which was necessarily very inimical to the growth of the population and prosperity of the latter. Several circumstances contributed to this result. Under these conditions the population of the country, or "open towns," as they were called, naturally increased. While the police system was as yet by no means perfect, the necessity of walled towns to protect the industry and commerce of the burgesses against the depredations of the lords had largely disappeared. With the fall of feudalism and the abolition of serfdom and villeinage there had naturally begun to grow up a middle class, who were neither barons nor laborers; and as the exclusive privilege of the Guilds in the chartered towns prohibited all except members from entering trade or manufacture, this class naturally settled down in the open towns, where they were free from the exactions of the Guilds, which had now become very despotic.

Thus manufacture, trade, and commerce began to develop in the open towns,* and in the chartered towns they began to decline.†

So marked was this that by the end of the fifteenth, or early in the sixteenth, century the chartered towns

---

* Birmingham and Manchester were very prosperous towns early in the sixteenth century. In the 33d Henry VIII., Manchester is referred to as having a large industrious population " well set to work in making of cloths as well of linen as of woollen, whereby the inhabitants of said towns have gotten and come unto riches and wealthy living," etc.

† "It is highly probable," says Rogers, "that some of this decay is due to the spread of woollen manufacture into country places where the charges of the Guilds did not apply."—" *Six Centuries of Work and Wages.*"

Hume and Wade say substantially the same thing.

and cities had lost all their power and prestige. The preamble of 3d Henry VIII. complained that "most cities, boroughs, and towns corporate had fallen into decay and were no longer inhabited by merchants and men of substance," and the 6th Henry VIII. (in 1515) also complained of the decay of the towns, setting forth that the number of men, women, and children occupied in industry was lessened; that husbandry had decayed, and that churches were destroyed, divine offices neglected or suspended,* and* before the middle of the century they had not only lost their political power, but the property of the Guilds was confiscated by the king.

Thus, although the statutes of 1388 and 1406 did not produce any immediate effect upon wages, by cutting off the opportunities for the development of new wants among the laborers, they set in operation the causes by which, before the middle of the fifteenth century, the rise of wages was permanently arrested, the free towns finally overthrown, and the people prepared for the degradation and despotism that awaited them at the hands of their Tudor and Stuart rulers. So long as the statutes were enacted against the wages based upon the wants already developed, they were economically harmless, but when they were directed against the *opportunities* which create the wants, they at once became disastrously effective. Thus the terrible industrial events that followed the accession of Henry VIII., if not the inevitable result of, were certainly made possible by those which preceded it. The Act of Settlement of Charles II., in 1662, though

---

* See Wade's "History of the English Working Classes," p. 17; also Rogers's "Work and Wages," p. 339.

enacted for opposite reasons, was the natural result of that of Richard II., in 1388.

I have dwelt more at length upon these facts than would have been necessary in a treatise of this nature, had not their connection to wages hitherto been entirely overlooked by both historians and economists. Even Mr. Rogers, in his excellent work, in which he takes both characters, has omitted to notice their economic importance. He appears to have fallen into that common mistake of attributing the rise or fall of wages to the circumstance most prominent at the time or immediately preceding the change, which is almost certain to be erroneous. Cause and effect in economic movements are seldom prominently in view at the same time. The operation of natural law in economics is so slow and gradual that the cause of any real and permanent change in wages and industrial conditions is invariably to be sought for in circumstances that have ceased to be prominent long before the effects are generally observable.

Thus, instead of ascribing the rise of real wages and consequent prosperity and progress that took place in the fourteenth and fifteenth centuries to the natural causes which began to operate in the early part of the thirteenth century, he attributes it to accidental circumstances (the famine and the plague), which occurred the same year the rise took place. And, again, instead of attributing the stagnant, if not declining economic status of the English laborer during the sixteenth, seventeenth, and eighteenth centuries to the causes which began to operate in the last quarter of the fourteenth, and succeeded in permanently arresting the rise of wages before the middle of the fifteenth century, he ascribes it all to the vicious blunders of

Henry VIII.* In truth, however, if the causes which produced the change in the fourteenth century had been allowed to continue, the mere debasement of the currency or plunder of the Guilds by Henry could not have produced any permanent change in real wages. In fact, the natural causes which develop the wants and tend to increase real wages ceased to operate at the close of the fourteenth, and did not commence again on a general scale till the latter part of the eighteenth century; consequently, there was no permanent rise of real wages for nearly four centuries.

---

* "Work and Wages," pp. 324, 325, 345, 378.

CHAPTER VI.

MOVEMENT OF WAGES FROM THE FIFTEENTH TO THE NINETEENTH CENTURY.

SECTION I.—*Why Nominal Wages do not Rise and Fall with the Rise and Fall of Prices.*

WE have seen in the previous chapter that the social influences which tend to develop new wants in the laborer, and consequently raise his standard of living and advance real wages, were effectually arrested by the second quarter of the fifteenth century, and that real wages were practically stationary during the greater part of the four following centuries.

During this period, therefore, the cost of living was affected only by those causes which operate upon the price of commodities, such as changes in the currency, good and bad harvests, and only influenced nominal wages. Consequently, if our theory be correct, wages (nominal wages, of course) will be found not only to rise with the rise of prices, but also to fall with the fall of prices; which is just what the industrial history of the sixteenth, seventeenth, and eighteenth centuries shows us did take place. Although there was, for the reasons before stated, no appreciable rise of real wages, nominal wages rose more than fourfold. This is the more remarkable because during that time wages were not allowed to freely follow the natural course of economic movement, but were fixed by authority, with the persistent effort to keep them at the minimum.

Although the monarchical power was more absolute at this period than it was in the fourteenth century, it proved to be as impossible for royal authority and statute law to prevent wages from gravitating toward the cost of living under the Tudors and Stuarts as it did under the Plantagenets.

It should always be remembered, however, that in thus laying it down that real wages are governed by the standard of living, and that, *cæteris paribus*, nominal wages are ultimately governed by prices, it is not claimed that nominal wages always rise and fall simultaneously with the rise and fall of prices. If prices never varied except from the gradual operation of social and economic causes, this would be true, or so nearly true that no general disparity between prices and wages would ever exist. But this is not, nor is it possible that it can be, the case where the change of prices is sudden and artificial. The price of labor is always less susceptible to the sudden influence of artificial causes than that of commodities. The reason for this, on a moment's reflection, becomes very clear. The sellers of labor are more numerous, and, therefore, each one possesses a much smaller proportion of the whole amount offered for sale than the sellers of commodities. Besides, they are more ignorant, more necessitous, and that which they have to sell is much more perishable. Therefore, if they have the incentive—which they have not—they have neither the ability nor opportunity to study and anticipate the sudden changes in prices produced by artificial causes, as is constantly being done by the sellers of commodities. For example, in the case of a bad harvest, or other cause known to affect the price of commodities, it is a common occurrence for merchants to put

up the price of wheat, coal, or whatever is on hand, long before any portion of the short supply reaches the market. But this is not the case with labor. Upon learning that, through a failure of crops or a change in the value of money, the prices of provisions are likely to advance, the laborer does not at once put up the price of his labor, nor does he do this immediately after the advance of prices. It is not until his wages fail to procure for him what, according to his established habits, have become necessities, that he, with any degree of seriousness, begins to insist upon having a higher price for his labor.

It is because wages thus move much slower than prices—when the latter are suddenly affected—that we often see prices rise and fall again, without any change taking place in wages. But while wages are slow to rise, they are for the same reason slow to fall.* Although the laborer is very tardy in making a demand for higher wages, he is also very reluctant to submit to a reduction, which fact explains why so many strikes are instituted to resist a *fall*, and so few to enforce a *rise* of wages.

---

* According to all experience, whether within modern observation or recorded in history, it may be laid down as an established maxim that labor is the last of the objects of exchange to rise in consequence of dearth or depreciation, and that commonly the price of labor is the last to fall in consequence of increased abundance of commodities or increased value of money."—*Tooke's "History of Prices,"* Vol. I., p. 71.

SECTION II.—*Wages and Prices in the Sixteenth Century—The Effect of Henry VIII.'s Depreciation of the Currency.*

In considering the *law of wages,* however, the question is not what decides wages at any particular time, but what determines the general direction or tendency of wages through all time. Consequently, the question is not what are the facts for this or that year, nor for any particular years in this or that decade, but what are the facts for a considerable number of years or decades taken together. For it is impossible to form any approximately correct conclusion as to the economic tendency of wages unless our observations extend over a sufficiently long period for the causes that have operated upon both wages and prices to have fully spent themselves. This is what Thorold Rogers, in discussing the movement of wages during this period, fails to do. As an historian he may, in the main, be relied upon; but as an economist he is erratic, inconsistent, and often unsound, his conclusions frequently being strangely at variance with his own data. This is strikingly apparent in his discussion of the movement of wages from the fifteenth to the nineteenth century. Because during that period there was at times a disparity between the movement of wages and that of prices, he concludes that they sustain no important economic relation to each other.

Upon the assumption that wages "do not rise with prices," he concludes that every advance in prices is necessarily inimical to the laborer,* as the increase

---

* "As, therefore, wages do not rise with prices, no crime against labor is more injurious than expedients adopted on the part of Government which tend to raise prices."—"*Work and Wages,*" p. 429.

goes to profits at the expense of wages.* The fact that during the period under consideration, through depreciations of the currency, bad harvests, etc., prices of provisions rose, he affirms that the economic condition of the laborer was worse, very much worse, during the seventeenth, eighteenth, and the first half of the nineteenth centuries than it was in the fifteenth. Indeed, he even goes so far as to say that the highest-paid mechanics in London at the close of the third quarter of the nineteenth century had not reached the economic eminence occupied by their ancestors in the middle of the fifteenth century. In other words, that the English laborer was not as well off in " 1877 " with " forty-two shillings and ninepence a week" (ten dollars and seventeen cents), and occupying a four or six-room house with modern appointments, as he was in 1450 with " three shillings and fourpence a week" (eighty cents), occupying a hut without chimney, window, or sanitation, or anything that can be properly dignified by the name furniture. The fact that some of Mr. Rogers's most pessimistic and least warranted statements regarding the relative economic condition of the laborer during these periods are constantly being quoted to sustain palpable economic heresies is my apology for dwelling here upon what otherwise might be properly regarded as unnecessary detail.

In support of his statements that " wages do not rise with prices, and that the condition of the laborer was from fifty to seventy per cent better in the fifteenth than it was in the seventeenth and eighteenth centuries," he compares wages and the price of wheat at

---

* " It is assuredly from the stint of wages that the profits of middlemen have been derived."—"*Work and Wages*," p. 544.

the close of the former with those of exceptionally dear years during the latter centuries.

Of course, if we compare the wages and the price of wheat in 1495 with those of 1725, 1770, and 1795, the dates to which Mr. Rogers most delights to refer, we shall find that the legal wages did enable the laborer to procure more food in the former than in the latter years. But this fact does not necessarily prove either that wages do not tend to rise with the rise of prices or that the laborer's general condition was really worse in the latter period than in the former. While these facts are correct, their comparison for such a purpose is extremely treacherous and misleading. True, they give the actual state at particular dates, but they contribute little toward showing the general condition, and nothing toward establishing general tendencies, simply because they represent only temporary extremes. The price of wheat in 1495 was four shillings and three farthings* a quarter, being, with two or three exceptions, lower than at any time for two hundred years. In 1725, 1770, and 1795 it was at famine prices, in the last-named year being five pounds and four shillings,† the highest ever known down to that date. In each of these years, however, as the facts given elsewhere by Mr. Rogers show, wages began to rise toward the prices, and were frequently supplemented from other sources, as we shall hereafter see. Therefore, to cite the wages and prices at such dates to indicate the general industrial condition of the period, is not only unfair, but fallacious.

---

* Rogers's "Work and Wages," p. 389. Adam Smith puts it at three shillings and fourpence.
† *Ibid.*, p. 486.

No data, we repeat, can be of any real importance for such a purpose that does not enable us to compare the wages and prices of both good and bad years taken together for a considerable period—say several decades, at least.

Fortunately, however, such data is at hand sufficient to clearly indicate the direction of the general movement of both prices and wages. From the middle of the reign of Henry VI. to that of Henry VIII. (1444–1540) both real and nominal wages were practically unchanged, the average wages of the artisans throughout the country being about sixpence, and those of common laborers fourpence a day.* Henry VIII. began to issue what Rogers so bitterly designates "base money" in 1545–46, which example was followed by his son, Edward VI., in 1549–51; and it was restored nine years afterward (1560) by Elizabeth. This change in the currency was, of course, followed by a general rise in prices, to which Mr. Rogers attributes all the ills of the English laborer from the middle of the sixteenth to that of the nineteenth century.†

Now, Mr. Rogers has himself furnished us with a complete schedule of wages and the price of wheat,‡ which is the best indication of the cost of living during that period—for six and a half successive decades of the most important part of the sixteenth century—viz., from 1520 to 1582, inclusive, as here given:

---

* Rogers's "Work and Wages," p. 388.

† "The effect of Henry's and Edward's base money, though it lasted only sixteen years, was potent enough to dominate in the history of labor and wages from the sixteenth century to the present time (1880)."—"*Work and Wages*," p. 345.

‡ "History of Prices," Vol. IV., p. 731.

Years.	Price of Wheat per Quarter.		Weekly Wages.		Years.	Price of Wheat per Quarter.		Weekly Wages.	
						s.	d.	s.	d.
	s.	d.	s.	d.	1551......	20	4	4	1½
1520......	9	4½	2	9	1552......	10	6¾	3	11½
1521......	7	8½	2	7½	1553......	10	0	4	6½
1522......	6	0¼	2	8	1554......	18	8¼	3	11½
1523......	5	6	2	7½	1555......	22	0½	4	0½
1524......	5	1½	2	8	1556......	28	5½	4	3¼
1525......	5	5	2	7½	1557......	8	4¾	3	10¼
1526......	6	2½	2	8¼	1558......	9	3½	3	6
1527	12	11	2	10½	1559......	11	0¾	4	0¾
1528......	8	10¼	2	9½	1560......	14	2¾	5	0
1529......	8	10	2	9	1561......	15	8	4	9¼
1530......	8	5	2	8	1562......	10	11¼	4	9¼
1531......	8	2¼	2	8½	1563......	19	9¼	4	0½
1532......	8	0	2	8¼	1564......	10	10½	4	7
1533......	7	8	2	9¼	1565......	10	7	4	7¾
1534......	7	0	2	10	1566......	16	5¼	4	8¾
1535......	10	3½	2	11¼	1567......	11	1	5	1½
1536......	10	7¼	2	10¼	1568......	11	3½	4	6½
1537	7	1	2	7¾	1569......	11	9¼	4	11
1538......	6	11½	2	11½	1570......	9	10	4	7
1539......	5	7¼	2	8¼	1571......	12	5½	4	7¾
1540......	5	8½	2	9¼	1572......	13	6¾	4	10¼
1541......	9	0¼	2	10½	1573......	26	3¾	4	11½
1542......	7	11¼	2	10½	1574......	14	2¾	4	8
1543......	9	3¼	2	11	1575......	15	11	4	11
1544......	9	0¼	2	10½	1576......	22	2½	4	8¼
1545......	15	6¾	2	10½	1577......	20	2	4	10¾
1546......	8	3½	2	7¾	1578......	17	4¼	4	8
1547......	4	11	2	10¾	1579......	17	6¼	4	9½
1548......	8	1¾	3	2½	1580......	20	0	4	11½
1549......	16	4	3	6	1581......	21	5¼	5	5½
1550......	18	0	3	4	1582......	19	1½	4	10
Average..	8	7½	2	9¾	Average..	15	8	4	6¾

This table includes thirty-one years before and thirty-two years after Henry's and Edward's depreciation of the currency, and therefore affords a good opportunity for observing whether or not nominal wages tend to move in the same direction as prices. It will be observed from the table that many times during those sixty-three years there appears to be a great difference between the movement of prices and

that of wages. For example, in 1526 the average price of wheat was six shillings and twopence halfpenny per quarter, and wages two shillings and eightpence farthing per week. The next year, 1527, wheat rose over one hundred per cent, the average price being twelve shillings and elevenpence ; but there was a good harvest in 1528, and wheat fell again to eight shillings and tenpence farthing. Meantime, wages only rose to two shillings and ninepence halfpenny. Thus, while the price of wheat rose over one hundred per cent, it remained up so short a time that wages only rose twopence, or about sixteen per cent. On the other hand, in 1556 wheat had risen to twenty-eight shillings and fivepence halfpenny per quarter, and wages to four shillings and threepence farthing a week. The next year the price of wheat fell to eight shillings and fourpence three farthings, or about seventy-five per cent, while wages only fell to three shillings and tenpence farthing, or about ten per cent.

If, however, we take the average wages and the price of wheat for the whole three decades before the issue of the "base money"—1520 to 1550, inclusive—we find that wheat for the whole period was eight shillings and sevenpence halfpenny per quarter, and wages were two shillings and ninepence three farthings a week. Thus, as compared with 1520, the price of wheat fell eight per cent, while wages remained about the same. Taking the thirty-two years after the change in the currency, the average price of wheat was fifteen shillings and eightpence per quarter, and wages were four shillings and sevenpence a week. Hence, as compared with 1551 (the first of the thirty-two years), the average price of wheat fell about twenty-three per cent, and the aver-

age wages for the same period rose about ten per cent. If we take the whole period, which is the only true way, we find the average price of wheat for the sixty-three years was twelve shillings and twopence three farthings per quarter, and wages were three shillings and eightpence one farthing. Thus, as compared with 1520, the price of wheat rose twenty-eight per cent and wages twenty-seven per cent.

If we examine the statutes fixing the legal rate of wages during that period, the object of which was to prevent wages from rising, we shall find that they, too, followed the movement of prices. Early under the reign of Elizabeth (1563) an act was passed authorizing the county magistrates to meet twice a year and "fix the rate of wages in accordance with the times." The preamble of this statute dilates upon "the grief and burdens of the poor laborer and hired man," and solemnly declares that on account of the high prices *"the wages of laborers are too small and not answerable to these times."* Even if this was all hypocritical cant, and the whole purpose of the statute was to prevent wages from rising, as Mr. Rogers claims, it only the more clearly proves the impossibility of preventing wages from gravitating toward the cost of living.

In pursuance of this statute, the magistrates throughout the country met at Michaelmas and Easter (spring and fall) to fix the rate of wages according, in the words of the Rutland magistrates in 1564, to "the price of linen, woollen, leather, corn (wheat), and other victuals." In doing this, it is needless to say, they put them up as little and down as much as possible. But the records of the semi-yearly proclamations of these magistrates clearly show that the wages were increased and diminished according to the rise

and fall in prices, mainly of wheat, which was then the staple article of food.*

To such an extent was the cost of living unconsciously recognized as the standard of wages, that a sliding scale was adopted by which wages should rise and fall with the variation in the price of bread. In 1795 the Berkshire magistrates decided that when the "gallon loaf" cost one shilling the laborer should receive from the parish sixpence a day and threepence a day for each of his family,† and for every rise of one penny in the price of the loaf, he should receive an increase of threepence a week for himself and one penny a week for each of his children. This plan was so popular that bills were twice introduced into Parliament to make it a law, and, although it failed to become a statute, it was sustained by the courts,‡ and became a general practice, supplanting the system of fixing wages by statute law. But economic wages being governed by the cost of living, the allowance system could make no permanent difference to the laborer. While it might enable the employer to pay less, it did not give the laborer more. What he lost in wages he received in allowance, and what he received in allowance he lost in wages. This, indeed, is now generally admitted by all economists.

"There is a rate of wages," says Mill,§ "either the lowest on which the people can, or the lowest on which they will consent, to live. . . . Their habits

---

* See Rogers's "Work and Wages;" also Eden's "State of the Poor."
† See Eden's "State of the Poor," Vol. I., p. 577.
‡ "Work and Wages," p. 437.
§ "Principles of Political Economy," Book II., ch. 12, § 4, pp. 450–452.

will not be altered for the better by giving them parish pay. . . . It is well known that the allowance system did practically operate in the mode described, and that under its influence wages sank to a lower rate than had been known in England before. . . All subsidies in aid of wages enable the laborer to do with less remuneration, and therefore ultimately bring down the price of labor by the full amount, unless a change be wrought in the ideas and requirements of the laboring class—an alteration in the relative value which they set upon the gratification of their instincts and upon the increase of their comforts and the comforts of those connected with them."

SECTION III.—*Wages and Prices during the Seventeenth, Eighteenth, and Nineteenth Centuries.*

If we examine the general movement of wages and prices during the seventeenth, eighteenth, and nineteenth centuries we find the same tendency constantly observable. The average price of wheat during the first decade in the seventeenth century was twenty-nine shillings per quarter, and, according to Arthur Young, the average price for the whole century was thirty-eight shillings and twopence, being a rise of a little less than one third for the whole century. The average rate of wages at the commencement of the century was four shillings a week, and, according to the above authority, the average rate of wages for the century was tenpence and three farthings a day, or about five shillings and fivepence a week, being a rise of thirty per cent for the whole period. So, too, with the eighteenth century. The price of wheat at

the commencement of the century (1701) was, according to Tooke, twenty-eight shillings and fivepence per quarter, and the average for the whole century was thirty-eight shillings and sevenpence one farthing, or a rise of about one fourth, although, as will be seen, it is only fivepence a quarter higher than the average for the previous century. The average wages at the beginning of the eighteenth century were about six shillings a week—agricultural laborers five shillings and sixpence, and artisans seven shillings and sixpence a week. The average wages from 1701 to 1730 rose to six shillings for agricultural laborers and nine shillings for artisans. From 1731 to 1800 they were eight shillings a week for the former and sixteen shillings for the latter, the average for the century being about seven shillings a week for agricultural laborers and twelve shillings and sixpence for artisans, or, both taken together, eight shillings and threepence a week, showing an average rise for the whole period of forty per cent.* Thus it will be observed that the average rise in the price of wheat and labor for the whole century over that which prevailed at the commencement of the century is about the same ; but, as compared with the average of the previous century, it will be seen that wages rose over fifty per cent, while wheat rose less than ten per cent. Therefore, although during the greater part of this period wages were nominally fixed by authority, while prices were left free to move in accordance with economic influ-

---

* For more full information upon this point we refer the reader to Arthur Young's "Journey Through England" (1767), Eden's "State of the Poor," Tooke's "History of Prices," Rogers's "History of Prices," Porter's "Progress of the Nation," Wade's "History of the Working Classes," and Levi's "Wages and Earnings."

ences, the united power of wealth and law could not prevent them from moving in the same direction.

It is true that during this period the whole influence of the authorities was used to keep wages at the minimum, and often with considerable success; but it is also true that in proportion as the government succeeded in preventing wages from keeping pace with prices or the cost of living, it was compelled to call for and finally by law enforce public contributions, as under the poor law and the allowance system, to make up the deficiency. By this means, which was the inevitable result of arbitrary interference with the natural movement of wages, the laborer's income, as before stated, was eked out from the public funds, according to the size of his family and the price of provisions.*

Thus, for the same reason that the pains and penalties of Edward III. and Richard II. were unable to prevent real wages from moving in the direction of the improved standard of living in the fourteenth century, those of the Tudors and Stuarts and Brunswicks were unable to prevent nominal wages from moving in the same direction as prices in the sixteenth, seventeenth, and eighteenth centuries. When we reach the nineteenth century, however, we find the other set of causes to which we have so often referred as affecting real wages again beginning to operate. From causes fully set forth in another chapter,† the spinning-jenny and the power-loom came into existence, which

---

* A full table of the scale by which the wages were to be supplemented by parish allowance, according to the price of bread and the number of the family, will be found on page 577 of Vol. I. of Eden's "State of the Poor."

† This chapter is unavoidably deferred to the next volume.

made congregated industry and the factory system of production possible. The towns thus again became manufacturing and commercial centres, through which industrial and, consequently, social contact again became an active force among the masses, at least among those engaged in the manufacturing and mechanical industries.

From these changed conditions new desires and wants soon arose, and new habits began to be formed, the influence of which, though unconsciously exercised, soon became visible in a higher standard of living and, consequently, a general and gradual but persistent and continuous rise in *real* wages. This fact was clearly observed by Tooke, who, speaking of the rise of wages at the commencement of the present century, says : " The wages of agricultural laborers and artisans had been doubled, or nearly so. Salaries from the lowest clerk up to the highest functionaries, as well as professional fees, had been considerably raised on the *plea* of greatly increased expenses of living, *not only* by the increased price of necessaries, but *by a higher scale of general expenditure or style of living incidental to the progress of wealth and civilization.*" *

From this time on, quantity instead of price again became the controlling element in the cost of living ; and, consequently, we find wages in the nineteenth century, as in the fourteenth, constantly moving toward the standard of living rather than the price of commodities, which is the only movement of wages that can ever increase the wealth of the laborer and really promote human progress. This also explains why, during the present century, wages have risen and prices fallen

---

* " History of Prices," Vol. I., pp. 329, 330.

at the same time, instead of the former constantly following the latter, as in the sixteenth, seventeenth, and eighteenth centuries.

This, I repeat, is because during the former period the wants, habits, and standard of living, and, consequently, real wages were practically stationary ; and, therefore, all variation in wages was merely nominal, rising and falling only as the prices of the commodities used by the laborer rose and fell, the quantity of wealth he received remaining essentially the same ; while in the present century the wants and habits of the laboring classes have greatly improved, and when, through the use of machinery, the price of commodities fell, instead of wages falling in the same ratio, as formerly, the new wants, as in the fourteenth century, absorbed the difference, thereby raising the standard of living and increasing real wages.

The operation of this principle is clearly seen in the striking difference between the movement of the wages of the agricultural laborers and that of those of the artisans and others engaged in manufacturing industries generally. It will be remembered that during the three centuries in which the standard of living was stationary, the wages of the artisans and laborers in husbandry always rose and fell together, and that, too, in a similar if not in the same ratio. But during the present century the wages of the agricultural laborers have made very little progress, while those in the manufacturing industries have risen, in most cases, over a hundred per cent.* Nor is the reason for this

---

* See Levi's "Earnings and Wages ;" Porter's "Progress of the Nation ;" Inaugural Address of the President of the London Statistical Society, 1883 ; Report of Bureau of Statistics of Labor, Massachusetts, 1884-85.

very difficult to understand. It is because the social influences which develop the wants and raise the standard of living among the laborers in the manufacturing and commercial centres have not operated upon the agricultural laborers, and, consequently, their wages have done little more than follow the movement of prices.*

---

* It is notorious, however, that agricultural wages are always higher in the immediate vicinity of manufacturing centres. Rogers has observed this fact, and says: "The wages paid to agricultural laborers in the manufacturing districts of England are far in excess of those customary in purely rural parts."—"*Work and Wages*," p. 172.

CHAPTER VII.

UNIVERSALITY OF THE LAW OF WAGES.

SECTION I.—*Wages and Cost of Living in Different Countries and Industries.*

THE doctrine that wages are ultimately governed by the cost of living is susceptible of universal application. It furnishes as complete an explanation of the variation in wages in different countries, localities, and industries as we have seen it does of the different periods in the same country. The cost of living is higher in large cities than in small towns for two reasons: first, because the price of a few things, such as house rent, is higher in the cities than in the country, and, second, because a larger number of expenditures enter into the daily economy of the laborers in the cities than in that of those in the country. To the extent that this is due to the former cause it affects only nominal wages, and to the extent that it arises from the latter influence it affects real wages. But by whatever cause this is produced, the fact is universal; and the fact that wages in similar industries are higher in large cities than in the country is, and ever has been, equally universal. And for the same reason we find wages the world over are invariably lower in agricultural than in manufacturing industries. Even in India, Buchanan found the wages of the Sudras much higher in the cities and immediate vicinity than in the

country.* Accordingly, wages are always higher in London than in Manchester, Birmingham, Leeds, or Edinburgh, and higher in these places than in the rural towns.

In the thirteenth century, when the wages system first began to dawn in England, Rogers tells us † "the wages of agricultural labor were higher in the eastern counties and the *neighborhood of London* than in the rest of England." And he adds : ‡ In London "the wages were from twenty-five to thirty per cent over the rates paid in other places." When considering "the present situation," he says : § "London wages were about twenty-five per cent more than country wages of the same kind." Adam Smith observed the same fact, which was evidently as marked in his day as it is at the present time, for he says : ‖ "The wages of labor in a great town and its neighborhood are frequently a fourth or a fifth part, twenty or five and twenty per cent, higher than at a few miles distance. Eighteenpence a day may be reckoned the common price of labor in London and its neighborhood. At a few miles distant it falls to fourteen and fifteenpence. Tenpence may be reckoned its price in Edinburgh and its neighborhood ; at a few miles distant it falls to eightpence."

The same is true of this and all other countries where wage conditions prevail. The fact that wages in the various trades in New York City are from twenty-five to seventy-five cents a day more than in

---

* Buchanan's " Journey Through the Countries of Mysore, Canara, and Malabar," pp. 124, 125.
† " Work and Wages," p. 171.
‡ *Ibid.*, p. 327. § *Ibid.*, pp. 180, 536.
‖ " Wealth of Nations," Book I., ch. 8, pp. 57, 58.

the small cities and towns in that and other States, is explainable only on the same principle.

In Fall River, Mass., for example, the wages of carpenters, painters, masons, and bricklayers are (1886) from two dollars and fifty cents to three dollars a day; while in New York City they are from three dollars and fifty cents to four dollars and fifty cents. Common laborers in the former city receive from one dollar and twenty-five cents to one dollar and fifty cents a day, while those in New York receive from one dollar and seventy-five cents to two dollars, and those employed by the city two dollars and fifty cents. So universally is this true that it is recognized by both employer and employed. Even trades unions' schedules and masters' prices, both in Europe and this country, are based upon it. Not that they agree upon any theory of wages, but because they are both compelled to observe the fact. This is equally true of the same industries in different countries. Without regard to climate, political institutions, or social conditions, wherever the cost of living is low, whether from the cheapness of things or the fewness of the wants, small wages are invariably paid, and *vice versa.*

The testimony of Sir Thomas Brassey upon this point is ample and conclusive; and his evidence is especially important because of his exceptional opportunities for obtaining the facts in relation to wages and cost of living in so many different countries, with the data of his father's experience, who employed a larger number and greater variety of laborers in more different countries than any other man. He says :* " The minimum is determined by the cost of living, accord-

---

* Brassey's "Work and Wages," pp. 94 95.

ing to the standard adopted by the people. . . . As we recede from the more civilized countries of Europe the standard of comfort is reduced, and the laborer is content to receive lower wages. In Eastern Europe," he continues,* "the standard of living is very low, and the earnings of the laboring people are scanty in proportion. The Galicians live principally upon black bread, schnapps—a spirit distilled from Indian corn—and potatoes. The inhabitants of Bukovina and Moldavia live on Indian corn and schnapps, at a cost of from four to fivepence a day. Ninepence may be considered the ordinary wages."

In Russia the food, which, he says, consists of "black bread and water," "costs from five to six shillings a month," and wages are from four to sixpence a day."† In Germany day wages are from one shilling and twopence to one shilling and ninepence, and board and lodgings tenpence a day.‡ In Hungary wages are one shilling and threepence a day, the cost of living for an average family being about one shilling a day.§

McCulloch, who was a strong wages-fund advocate, admits that the difference in the wages in "England, Ireland, China, and Hindustan is the result of the difference in the standard of living in those countries."

---

* Brassey's "Work and Wages," p. 89.
† *Ibid.*, pp. 61, 103. ‡ *Ibid.*, pp. 15, 16.
§ See pp. 44–105. In a later edition Mr. Brassey has extended his observations on this subject, in which he says (pp. 160, 161) : " The cost of labor rose thirty per cent in the last ten years because of a rise in the cost of living ;" and on pp. 164, 165 he adds : " The wages in France had grown with the augmented cost of living." " The enhanced value of provisions had produced the same influence on the price of labor in Belgium as in France."

He says :* "In England (1824), for example, the laborers principally subsist on wheaten bread and beef, in Ireland on potatoes, and in China and Hindustan on rice. . . . In Ireland the peasantry live in miserable mud-cabins, without either a window or a chimney; while in England the cottages of the peasantry have all glass windows and chimneys, are well furnished, and are as much distinguished for their neatness, cleanliness, and comfort as those of the Irish for their filth and misery. In consequence of these different habits, there is an extreme difference, not in the rate of necessary wages merely, but in their actual or market rate in these countries; so much so, that while the average market price of a day's labor in England may be taken at from twentypence to two shillings, it cannot be taken at more than fivepence in Ireland and threepence in Hindustan."

The wages in the building trades in London † average about seven shillings and three halfpence (one dollar and seventy-one cents) a day, or rather less than the common laborer, and more than a dollar a day less than those employed in similar industries in New York City.

If we examine the rate of wages paid in the different industries in the same localities, we shall find that the rate of wages paid to masons and bricklayers is generally higher than that paid to carpenters and painters, and that of carpenters and painters is considerably above that of the factory operatives. For example, in Fall River, Mass., the "spindle city of

---

* "Principles of Political Economy," p. 181.

† Thorold Rogers's "Work and Wages," p. 539. See also George Howell's "Capital and Labor;" Leone Levi's "Wages and Earnings."

America," in 1885 the wages of bricklayers and masons—I am quoting union prices—were from three dollars to three dollars and fifty cents per day, and those of the painters and carpenters from two dollars to two dollars and fifty cents per day, while those of factory operatives were only about one dollar and forty cents.

Why, it may be asked, if wages are governed by the cost of living, is the rate paid to masons and bricklayers higher than that of carpenters and painters in the same town, since, as a class, their standard, and, consequently, their cost of living, is practically the same. It is true that the general standard of living of the bricklayer and mason in the same locality is virtually the same as that of the carpenter and painter, and so are their aggregate wages. The former get a slightly higher rate of wages per day, but they are more exposed to the weather, and work fewer days in the year. Consequently, while their rate per day is higher, their actual income throughout the year is about the same.

SECTION II.—*The Income of the Family not Increased by the Wages of the Wife and Children.*

Although the regularity or irregularity of employment in various occupations will explain the difference in the ratio of wages in the building trades, this fact, it may be said, is inadequate to explain the extraordinary difference between the rate of wages in the building trades and that paid to the factory operatives. The employment of the latter is more constant than that of those in any branch of the building trade.

It is also true that in the same locality the general standard of living of the operative is lower than that of the former. But it is no less obvious that both of these causes are insufficient to explain the striking difference in their wages. It should be remembered, as we have repeatedly stated, that when comparing the wages and cost of living, we do not mean *merely* the rate of wages, *when they work*, and the price of board for a single person, but the average wages and cost of living of the average family in any given class or industry; because if our doctrine is sound, and the income of the wage-receiving class is governed by their expenditures, the cost of living being given, the rate of wages will fall in proportion as the number of workers increases; or, to be more strictly correct, as the amount earned by other members of the family increases. Consequently, other things being the same, in those industries where the wife and children work the rate of wages for the man will be the lowest.

"The habits of the people," says Mill* "(as has already been so often remarked), everywhere require some particular scale of living, and no more, as the condition without which they will not bring up a family. Whether the income which maintains them in this condition comes from one source or from two makes no difference; if there is a second source of income they require less from the first. . . . For the same reason it is found that, *cæteris paribus*, those trades are generally the worst paid in which the wife and children of the artisan aid in the work. The income which the

---

* "Principles of Political Economy," Book II., ch. xiv., p. 488. See also Report of Massachusetts Bureau of Statistics of Labor, 1876, p. 71.

habits of the class demand, and down to which they are almost sure to multiply, is made up, in those trades, by the earnings of the whole family, while in others the same income must be obtained by the labor of the man alone." It is this fact which explains the striking difference in the rate of wages paid to factory operatives and that of those employed in the building trades. Among factory operatives, all branches taken together, the wives and children who contribute to the support of the family are, on an average, as one and a quarter to each family, while among those employed in the building trades the average of wives and children who work is only one to every four families. Hence, in the building trades the wages of the man supply about ninety-seven and one half per cent of the total cost of the family's living, while among the factory operatives the wages of the man only supply sixty-six per cent, or two thirds, of the cost of the family's living, because the other one third is furnished by the labor of the wife or children. Nor is this because the cost of living in the factory operative's family is greater than that of the laborer in the building trades, for while the average family in the building trade contains four and one half persons, that of the factory operative contains five and seven eighths persons. The total cost of living in the former is about fifty dollars a year more than in the latter, and the wages of the man in the former are nearly two hundred and fifty dollars a year more than those of the latter.

Upon this point also ample data has been collected in Massachusetts for the most conclusive generalizations. The sixth (1875) report of the Labor Bureau of that State furnishes a full individual statement of

the wages, cost of living, etc., of three hundred and ninety-three families employed in the different industries. Of this number fifty-seven represent the building trades, including bricklayers, carpenters, masons, painters, plasterers, ship-carpenters, and stair-builders; thirty-nine are taken from the boot, shoe, and leather trades, which include boot and shoemakers, tanners, shoe-chandlers, cutters, lasters, trimmers, curriers, and morocco-dressers; sixty-one are taken from the metal-workers, and include blacksmiths, boilermakers, cutlers, engine-builders, iron-moulders, iron-roller makers, machinists, nailmakers, jewellers, and watchmakers; seventeen are taken from the laborers in cutlery and iron works, machine and boiler shops, roller-mills, etc.; thirty-five represent factory operatives, and under this head are included pressers, section hands, spinners, and weavers; thirty-eight represent the other operatives employed in the factories, under the head of mill laborers; ninety-eight are taken from the various outdoor employments, such as laborers for builders, street laborers, wharf laborers, fishermen, etc.; ten represent quarrymen and teamsters; twenty-four are taken from shop trades, such as cabinetmakers, carriage-builders, hatters, cigarmakers, mechanics, stone-cutters, and whipmakers, and ten from the laborers in these shop trades.

The statement of each of these families gives the amount the father earns, the whole number of the family, the number who work, the amount earned by each, the total amount earned by all, how they live, and what it costs. The average yearly earnings of the father, the wife and children, and the cost of living in those industries are as follows:

Trades.	Father's Yearly Wages.	No. in Family.	Wife and Children Working.	Total Earnings of Wife and Children.	Total Yearly Earnings of Family.	Total Cost of Living.
Shop trades..........	$752.36	4¾	¼	$69.04	$821.40	$772.21
Metal-workers	739.30	4½	⅓	90.51	829.81	723.00
Building trades.......	721.32	4½	⅓	73.00	794.32	740.03
Teamsters.............	630.02	5½	½	105.00	735.02	729.04
Shoe and Leather trade	540.00	4¾	1	209.00	749.00	693.13
Metal-workers' laborers...............	458.09	5½	1⅛	256.08	714.17	697.92
Mill operatives........	572.10	5	1	250.35	822.45	755.04
Mill laborers.........	386.04	6¾	1½	284.08	670.12	638.99
Shop laborers........	433.06	5 9/10	1 1/10	232.02	665.08	642.08
Out-door laborers....	424.12	6½	1⅓	257.93	682.05	650.81

From these facts, which are ample and reliable, three things are manifest: (1) That the aggregate earnings of the average family in any given class of wage-receivers is always proportioned to the cost of living in the average family in that class. (2) That in proportion as the wife and children contribute to the support of the family the wages of the father are reduced. (3) That the standard of living and, consequently, the total income of the family is the lowest where the wife and children contribute the most toward its support.*

Paradoxical as the last statement may at first appear, it is perfectly natural—indeed, it could not be otherwise; because where the mother and children go to

---

* "Thus it is seen that in neither of the cases where the man is assisted by his wife or children does he earn as much as other laborers. Also, that in the case where he is assisted by both wife and children he earns the least."—*Report on the Statistics of Labor*, 1876 p. 71.

the mill it is impossible for the wants, which result from the refining influences of social life, to be developed to the same extent as where the mother presides at the home and the children attend school. Accordingly, if we take the shoe trades, metal-workers, and the building trades together, where the proportion of children that work is only as one to every three families, the average earnings of the father come within seven dollars and forty-two cents a year of the total cost of the family's living; whereas, if the metal-workers' laborers, mill laborers, shop laborers, and outdoor laborers are taken together, where the number of children that work are as one and one quarter to each family, the average earnings of the father are two hundred and thirty-two dollars and twelve cents a year less than the cost of the family's living. This difference is still greater when we consider the fact that the average total cost of living in the latter class is nearly one hundred dollars a year less than in the former.

The same is true of women, the marked difference between their wages and those of men being explained upon the same principle. It may be urged that the cost of a woman's living, other things being the same, is as great as that of a man's. If the cost of living was measured by the personal expenses of the single individual, instead of by that of the family, as we have explained, this would be to some extent true; but the cost of living of the workers always includes that of the non-workers also. Hence, in proportion as the non-workers are reduced are the demands upon the earnings of the workers lessened and their wages accordingly reduced. It is for this reason that the wages of the father, as shown above, are reduced in

proportion as the wife and children contribute to the support of the family.

As the man is much more generally the head and chief earner of the family, a much larger number are dependent upon the wages of the average man than upon those of the average woman. Again, although the wants of the average woman in the same social environment, for amusements, travel, etc., are equal to those of the average man, they are generally furnished by the man, as father, friend, or lover, and therefore really constitute an item in the normal expenses of the man, instead of those of the woman. It will thus be seen that, other things being the same, the cost of living of the average man is much greater than that of the average woman, and his wages are correspondingly higher, as shown in following tables.*

WAGES AND COST OF LIVING OF MALES.

Counties.	Persons Dependent.	Yearly Wages.	Cost of Living.
Barnstable	2.86	$338.86	$387.89
Berkshire	3.39	431.00	430.38
Bristol	3.13	456.05	479.85
Dukes	3.61	359.28	398.24
Essex	2.96	461.65	486.53
Franklin	2.99	438.19	426.51
Hampden	3.03	563.48	569.59
Hampshire	3.10	408.01	413.77
Middlesex	3.11	496.58	503.69
Nantucket	2.00	327.73	532.50
Norfolk	3.18	447.18	479.27
Plymouth	3.06	403.30	423.85
Suffolk	3.03	576.19	559.87
Worcester	3.04	490.78	485.45
For the State	3.08	482.72	488.96

* Seventh Annual Report of the Massachusetts Bureau of Statistics of Labor for 1876, pp. 66–69. These tables are based upon 71,339 schedules.

WAGES AND COST OF LIVING OF FEMALES.

Counties.	Persons Dependent.	Yearly Wages.	Cost of Living.
Barnstable...	1.71	$133.44	$130.40
Berkshire...	2.27	179.40	180.82
Bristol...	1.93	213.02	185.98
Dukes...	1.50	149.56	136.50
Essex...	1.95	212.22	203.10
Franklin...	1.74	178.74	152.81
Hampden...	1.71	219.59	192.84
Hampshire...	1.56	192.13	169.61
Middlesex...	1.60	205.24	178.82
Nantucket...	1.00	88.67	81.25
Norfolk...	1.81	148.54	190.60
Plymouth...	2.09	182.14	185.39
Suffolk...	1.81	197.87	184.55
Worcester...	1.65	191.07	175.77
For the State...	1.78	198.76	182.86

It will thus be seen that the number of persons sustained by the earnings of the average woman throughout the State is only one and seventy-eight hundredths, while that of those dependent upon the earnings of the average man is three and eight hundredths. Hence the yearly wages of the woman are only one hundred and ninety-eight dollars and seventy-six cents, and the cost of her living is one hundred and eighty-two dollars and eighty-six cents; while the wages of the average man are four hundred and eighty-two dollars and seventy-two cents, and the cost of his living is four hundred and eighty-eight dollars and ninety-six cents.

Although this principle has never been understood by economists and statesmen, it has long been unconsciously acted upon by practical men. It is upon this principle that employers import low-paid laborers from distant countries. The English manufacturers imported agricultural laborers into Lancashire, and

American capitalists import Asiatic and European laborers to this country for no other reason than that they could live upon less and therefore work for lower wages than could the Lancashire and American laborers.

SECTION III.—*The Theory Further Sustained by Dr. Engel's Law of Expenditures.*

Moreover, the doctrine here laid down is not only sustained by all industrial history, but it is also in full accord with the known principles of consumption as established by "Engel's law" of expenditure. Dr. Engel, the famous Prussian statistician, by exhaustive investigations has discovered that the incomes of the wages and salaried classes * are, on an average, divided in the various channels of expenditure as follows : (1) That the greater the income the smaller the relative percentage of outlay for subsistence ; (2) that the percentage of outlay for clothes, rent, fuel, light, etc., is approximately the same, whatever the income ; and (3) that as the income increases in amount the percentage of outlay for sundries—*i.e.*, education, literature, art, travel, amusement, etc.—increases.†

---

* All who receive stipulated incomes for service are properly wage-receivers. See definition of wages, pp. 73, 74.

† These conclusions have been fully tested by extensive investigations in Prussia, England, and America, and especially in Massachusetts, where more complete data has been collected than in any other place in the world. Colonel Wright, after comparing the averages for Prussia, England, Illinois, and Massachusetts, says : " The remarkable harmony in the items of expenditure shown by a percentage of total expenditure must establish the soundness of the economic law propounded by Dr. Engel. The column of averages should, therefore, be taken as the very best results of that law, sustained by a wide range of data from three great countries."—*Report of Massachusetts Labor Bureau*, 1885, p. 153.

It will be seen from the above that that portion of the general consumption which goes to satisfy the physical necessities is susceptible of very little increase ; that the portion which goes for clothes, rent, and home conditions generally, is capable of a much larger increase, while the possibility of enlarging the demand for that portion which goes to satisfy the intellectual, moral, and social wants of man is practically unlimited. This being true, it follows : (1) That in proportion as the laborer's wants are limited to his physical necessities will his wages be low and practically stationary, as in Asia, Africa, and Eastern Europe. (2) That only in proportion as his domestic, social, and æsthetic wants are increased—*i.e.*, the standard of living is elevated—will real wages rise.

The truth of this principle will be more clearly seen by comparing the weekly wages and the number of days' labor devoted to procuring food and those given to the gratification of the higher social wants in the different countries, as shown in the following table :*

Countries.	Weekly Wages.	Food.	Clothes, Rent, and Sundries.	Taxes.	Total Working Days in the Year.
United States.............	$10.80	113	154	33	300
Great Britain.............	7.44	114	154	32	300
France....................	5.04	120	135	45	300
Germany..................	3.84	155	107	38	300
Italy.....................	3.60	162	78	60	300
Belgium...................	4.80	133	134	33	300
Russia....................	3.60	180	83	37	300
Austria...................	3.84	159	107	34	300
Spain	3.84	164	80	56	300
Scandinavia	3.60	147	123	30	300

* This table is all taken from Mulhall's "History of Prices," 1885, except the wages for the United States, which is taken from the Massachusetts Labor Bureau Report for 1884.

From this table it will be seen that in those countries where the largest number of days' labor a year is devoted to obtaining food, and the higher social wants are the fewest, wages are the lowest, and where the largest number of days' labor is given to supply the higher social wants, wages are the highest. Thus, *e.g.*, the laborer in the United States and Great Britain gives one hundred and thirteen and one hundred and fourteen days a year respectively to the procuring of food, as compared with one hundred and sixty-two in Italy, one hundred and sixty-four in Spain, and one hundred and eighty in Russia; and for the gratification of higher social wants the former gives one hundred and fifty-four days' labor a year as against seventy-eight in Italy, eighty in Spain, and eighty-three in Russia. Hence we find the wages in this country are ten dollars and eighty cents, and in England seven dollars and forty-four cents a week, as against three dollars and sixty cents in Italy, three dollars and eighty-four cents in Spain, and three dollars and sixty cents in Russia. Or, to state the case another way, the American and Englishman, after furnishing food, clothing, rent, and taxes—the first three of which are superior to those in any other country—have left to supply luxuries and to gratify æsthetic wants the products of fourteen days a year more than the Frenchman, twenty-three more than the Scandinavian, forty-one more than the Austrian, forty-three more than the German, sixty-eight more than the Spaniard, sixty-nine more than the Russian, and seventy-three more than the Italian. Accordingly, we see the wages of the American are double the European and more than two and a half times those of the continental average;

and those of England are nearly double the average of those on the continent.

Clearly, therefore, from whatever point of view we consider the subject, and whatever class of data we examine, the evidence is ample and conclusive that the standard of living is the economic law of wages.

CHAPTER VIII.

WAGES UNDER PIECE-WORK.

"PIECE-WORK" is one of the most delusive expressions in the whole economic vocabulary. It implies, and the idea is generally accepted among both laborers and employers, that wages are governed by a different principle under "piece-work" than under "day-work"; that under the former the amount the laborer receives is determined by the quantity he produces, while under the latter it is governed by the number of days he works. Although this has the appearance of truth, it contains the very essence of error. "Day-work" and "piece-work" are merely different methods for buying and selling given quantities of labor, and not different principles for regulating the price of labor. The fact that wages are sometimes measured by the number of hours, and sometimes by the amount of labor performed or the result accomplished, in no way affects the principle by which the daily amount received is finally determined. Economic prices are governed by the same law, by whatever method the sale takes place.

For the same reason that potatoes would be neither cheaper nor dearer because they were sold by the peck or by the pound are wages ultimately neither higher nor lower because work is done by the day or by the piece. If it cost three cents a yard to manufacture a certain grade of cotton cloth, three cents a yard is the

lowest at which that cloth can be continuously sold. If it was sold by the pound the manufacturer could not afford to take any less, nor would the consumer consent to give any more for it on that account. If seven yards weigh a pound, for the same reason that three cents is the lowest that can be taken for a yard, twenty-one cents is the lowest that can be taken for a pound. As we have seen, what the cost of production is to the price of commodities, the cost of living is to the price of labor. Hence, for the same reason that under " day-work" the daily wages are governed by the daily wants (cost of living), under " piece-work" the price per " piece" is governed by the amount produced per day.*

The " piece-work" price always moves in an inverse ratio with the quantity produced. Both movements, however, are governed by the same law. Therefore, the fact that under " piece-work" the price per piece rises and falls in an *inverse* ratio with the quantity produced, is as constant and universal as that under " day-work" the price per day rises and falls in a direct ratio with the cost of living. It is by the operation of this principle that the price of commodities is reduced by improved methods of production. If the same price per yard for weaving, spinning, etc., was paid with the power-loom and self-acting mule as with the

---

* So generally is this fact recognized, that it is a common thing to find workmen agreeing among themselves not to do more than a certain quantity of work, because repeated experience has taught them that if they do their wages will soon be proportionately reduced. That is why, in some trades, the unions forbid the men to produce more than a given quantity per day, which is so bitterly denounced as one of the injurious features of trades unions. This practice is adopted the most when new kinds of work or new machinery are introduced, in order to keep the price " per piece" as high as possible.

spinning-wheel and hand-loom, woven fabrics would be as dear to-day as they were a hundred years ago.

Although this law has never been understood, it has always been implicitly obeyed. Consequently, wherever the wages system prevails, whether the price of labor is fixed by royal proclamation, statute law, or competition, we find the rate of wages tends to conform to the cost of living, and the price of "piece-work" to the rate of wages for "day-work." This fact was clearly recognized by Karl Marx, who says :* " Piece wages are only another form of time wages, although it appears as though in this kind of wages the price of labor was determined by the quantity of product yielded. In fixing the piece wages the following questions arise : What is the duration of the customary working day ? What quantity of goods does a laborer of the average industriousness and ability make in this time ? What are the daily wages under these circumstances ? Suppose we find out that, on an average, thirty pieces of one commodity can be produced by a laborer in a working day of twelve hours, for which he receives a day's wages of one dollar and fifty cents, then the piece wages for one piece of this commodity will be five cents, for thirty pieces one dollar and fifty cents. Therefore the laborer will derive no benefit from this form of wages, but the capitalist knows well how to take advantage of it."

Accordingly, in the various statutes regulating wages in England from the fourteenth to the eighteenth centuries, we find the price fixed for "piece-work" always sustained a uniform relation to that of "day-work." For instance, threshing a quarter or

---

* Extracts from "Capital," p. 26, Weydemeyer's translation.

mowing an acre of wheat was always regarded as a day's work. Hence, in the thirteenth century, when harvest wages were threepence a day, the price of mowing an acre or threshing a quarter of wheat was threepence also. During the same period, when artisans' wages were threepence halfpenny a day,* the price for a pair of sawyers to saw a hundred planks—which was always reckoned a day's work †—was sevenpence. And when "day-wages" rose after the pestilence to fivepence a day, the "piece-work" price of threshing and mowing rose to fivepence also,‡ and that of sawing one hundred planks to a shilling.§

So, when wages rose after the rise in prices in the sixteenth, seventeenth, and eighteenth centuries, the price of "piece-work" always rose correspondingly with that of "day-work." Thus, in 1651, when the Essex magistrates fixed the wages of common laborers at one shilling and twopence a day, the price of sawing one hundred planks was fixed at two shillings and sixpence, or one shilling and threepence for each sawyer. And if we compare the price paid for "piece-work" in the same industries in different countries or localities where similar methods of production are employed, we shall find that the rate paid will vary according to the difference in the cost of living. Thus, other things being the same, the price of "piece-work," like that of "day-work," is always higher in large cities than in small towns. The price of labor, whether paid by the piece or by the day, has always been from twenty-five to sixty per cent higher in

---

* "Work and Wages," p. 180.
† "The sawing a hundred of planks was always estimated from early times as a day's work."—Rogers's *Work and Wages,* p. 392.
‡ *Ibid.,* p. 229.   § *Ibid.,* pp. 236, 237.

London than in the country. And for the same reason "piece-work" as well as "day-work" prices are higher in New York City than in London—higher in this country generally than in England, and higher in England than on the continent. Industrial statistics, as we have seen, conclusively show that the yearly earnings and the cost of living of weavers, spinners, shoemakers, tailors, printers, etc., who work by the piece, sustain as close and consistent a relation to each other as do those of bricklayers, carpenters, iron-workers, and outdoor laborers, who work by the day.

Again, in manufacturing industries, where machinery is extensively used and "piece-work" is the general practice, although the average wages keep pace with the average cost of living, the price of "piece-work" always varies inversely with the productive capacity of the machinery. In the cotton industry evidence of this fact is constantly in view. Through the changes in machinery, which are mostly gradual, it sometimes happens that two kinds of machinery (the new and the old) are in use in the same factory, and very often in the same locality, at the same time, and accordingly we frequently find two different prices paid for the same work in the same town, and even in the same establishment—not a different *rate of wages*, but a different *scale of prices*, in order to equalize the rate of wages. And sometimes, in order to avoid two scales of prices for the same work, one will be put on "day-work," the rate of wages being fixed upon the average earnings of the other. In fact, this is the general practice on new machinery, until its productive capacity is correctly ascertained, after which the scale of prices is fixed accordingly.

I have, myself, seen three different prices paid for

weaving the same cloth in the same room, all because it was woven in different kinds of looms. For example, a fifty-inch loom will not run as fast as a thirty-inch loom—*i.e.*, the shuttle will not, *cæteris paribus*, pass as many times a minute across a fifty-inch space as it will across a thirty-inch space. While the former to-day will run at the rate of from one hundred and thirty to one hundred and fifty picks a minute, the latter will average from one hundred and eighty to two hundred picks a minute. It will thus be seen that when thirty-inch cloth is woven in forty or fifty-inch looms, the weavers on the broad looms cannot weave as many yards per day as those on the narrow looms; hence a higher price per cut or per yard is always paid for weaving narrow cloth in broad than in narrow looms. This has been strikingly illustrated by the operations of sheeting manufacturers in Rhode Island and the print-cloth manufacturers of Fall River, Mass.* During the periods of depression in the cotton trade the print-cloth manufacturers in Fall River have several times stopped or run short time, in order to reduce the stock of goods in the market, and the sheeting manufacturers of Rhode Island, in order to produce the same effect upon the sheeting market, suspended the production of sheetings, and went to making print-cloths;† and when they came to weave print-cloth in sheeting looms, notwithstanding the depressed state of trade and the falling state of the labor market, they paid three and four cents a cut more for weaving

---

* The manufacturers of Fall River produce over one fifth of the total output of print cloth in the United States.

† This has frequently been made the excuse for reducing wages instead of stopping or running short time by the Fall River manufacturers.

print-cloth than was paid by the print-cloth manufacturers. In fact, this practice is so general that in England, in the accepted schedules of prices for weaving which are agreed upon by the trades unions and the employers' associations, allowance is invariably made for "*reed space*"—*i.e.*, unoccupied space in the loom—which is practically a sliding scale of prices, and enables the weaver to earn about the same, whatever kind of goods he weaves, thereby adjusting the "piece-work" wages to the average "day-work" wages or standard of living.

If we examine the shoe trade we find the same unvarying law obtains; and while the average wages of shoemakers have grown in a direct ratio with the cost of living, the price per pair for making shoes has grown less and less in proportion as improved machinery has been adopted. The same is strikingly true in the watch and jewelry business. The price of piece-work for pivoting, burnishing, gilding, fitting, casing, etc., through the use of improved tools and machinery, is in many instances from fifty to seventy-five per cent less than it was formerly. Still, the real wages in these industries are not reduced, the price of "piece-work" being lessened only in proportion as the capacity to produce is increased. But while wages never rise in the same proportion with the increased power of production, the price of commodities always falls in that ratio; consequently, though the nominal wages of watchmakers, jewellers, shoemakers, and weavers are not proportionately higher, the prices of watches, jewelry, cotton-cloth and shoes are relatively lower. This explains the fact that the direct and immediate effect of improved machinery is always more strikingly seen in lower prices than in higher

wages, all of which is in strict accord with the doctrine that the price of labor always moves in direct ratio with the cost of living, and that of commodities in direct ratio with the cost of production.

It will thus be observed that wherever we go or to whatever industry we turn our attention, we find that the price of labor, either under "piece-work" or "day-work," is ultimately governed by the same law. Manifestly, therefore,

> Whether laborers work by the piece or work by the day,
> The cost of their living determines their pay.

CHAPTER IX.

ULTIMATE ANALYSIS OF THE LAW OF WAGES.

SECTION I.—*How the Standard of Living is Determined.*

WAGES being governed by the cost of living, whatever affects that must indirectly affect wages. Consequently, in order to fully understand the causes which ultimately determine wages, it is necessary to ascertain what governs the cost of living.

As already explained,* the cost of living is affected by two causes—viz., the *price* and the *quantity* of the commodities the laborer consumes. But while both of these affect the *cost*, only the latter affects the *standard* of living. Consequently, though they both affect nominal, only the latter affects *real wages*. And as it is only the changes in real wages that produce any permanent effect upon the material and social wellbeing of the masses, it is only with *real wages* that we are here concerned. The real question before us, then, is, How is the *standard of living* determined? †

The standard of living in any community will be high or low, according as the social life of the masses is simple or complex; or, in other words, as the number of the daily wants of the people is large or small. It is lower in Asia than in Europe, lower in Europe than in America, lower at Five Points than on Fifth

---

* Part II., Chapter I., Sec. IV.   † See Chapter II., Part II., p. 88.

Avenue, for the reason that the *wants* of the people in the former places are fewer and simpler than those in the latter. We may be told that " if wants give wealth, beggars would wear diamonds and paupers be millionaires." But such statements have more seeming than soundness. Indeed, it is not true, in any economic sense, that beggars *want* diamonds. If they had diamonds they would not wear them, but would be sure to exchange them for something else. When people reach the diamond-*wanting* point, they have long ceased to be beggars and paupers. The laborers of India and China do not *want* the conveniences and comforts enjoyed by the English and American laborers, nor do those of the latter countries *want* the luxuries and elegancies of the wealthy classes. We do not mean to say that beggars would not accept diamonds, nor that the laboring classes in Asia, Europe, and America do not envy the comfort and luxury of the wealthy classes ; but a mere willingness to accept a thing, or an indifferent desire for it, or even a desire for it strong enough to complain at not having it, is not economically a *want*. A *want*, in the true sense of the term, is such conscious need of an object that its absence will cause sufficient pain to induce the effort and sacrifice necessary to its attainment. Until a desire has become sufficiently intense to produce more pain by its non-satisfaction than will result from the labor and sacrifice involved in satisfying it, it is not a want, but merely an indifferent or non-effectual desire ; and, therefore, it is not an economic force, because the need to consume is too weak to impel the effort to produce.

Man has certain wants in common with the animals, and to that extent the same principle operates upon

both; and in proportion to the similarity of their wants are their efforts alike. The wants of the animal are exclusively physical, food, shelter, and self-protection being his only wants; consequently, it is only for these necessities that he takes risks and puts forth efforts.

But man is capable of other and higher wants entirely unknown to the lower animals. In fact, there is no conceivable limit to the extent and variety of the desires and wants of man's higher or social nature. In proportion as his wants are limited to his physical necessities does he remain brutal and barbarous, and according as the desires of his higher nature are intensified into *wants* does he become superior to the animals, and rise in the scale of intellectual and moral development. Accordingly, we find that the quantity of wealth produced is always the smallest and the scale of civilization the lowest in those countries where the wants of the people are the fewest. Nor is it possible that this should be otherwise; for the standard of living can never rise above that of the wants. Hence, whether we will put forth any effort, or how much effort we will put forth, to obtain an object, will depend upon the intensity of our want.*

Accordingly, other things being the same, we will put forth more effort to procure necessities than conveniences, and more to obtain conveniences than luxuries and amusements. If the wages of the sudra of India were suddenly increased to the level of those of the American laborer, that would not improve the

---

* "Those nations and those classes of a nation who stand highest in the scale of civilization are those whose wants, as experience shows us, are the most numerous and whose efforts to satisfy those wants are the most unceasing."—*Hearn's "Plutology,"* p. 20.

standard of his living. Instead of consuming more, he would simply work less and increase his dissipation and wastefulness.* This explains why production cannot be much in advance of consumption, and why the aggregate wealth of the world can never be permanently much in excess of the world's aggregate wants.

SECTION II.—*Social Wants—How they are Determined.*

If the standard of living is governed by the wants, the question that next arises is, what determines the wants?

Man is a twofold being. He has a physical and a social nature, and, consequently, he has social as well as physical wants. The latter arise from his animal existence, and the former from his social relations. Therefore his physical wants, like those of the lower animals, are few, and mostly hereditary, while his social wants are acquired and have no conceivable limit. As a mere physical being, however, man has no more economic existence than a tiger. It is only when he associates with and reposes confidence in his fellow-man that the division of labor and exchange are possible and economic forces can operate upon him. It is, therefore, with man as a social being only that political economy has to do. If man's only attainable wants are social, it follows that the causes which govern them must be sought for in his social conditions;

---

* "If by digging the ground a whole day he [the Chinaman] can get what will purchase a small quantity of rice in the evening, he is content."—"*Wealth of Nations,*" Book I., ch. 8, p. 55. See also Brassey's "Work and Wages," pp. 88, 89; Hearn's "Plutology," p. 20.

and if we examine the history of man we shall find that his wants are few or many, and high or low, according to the quality of the habits and customs of the society in which he moves. Habit, as a little observation will show, not only governs our social wants, but it exercises an important, if not a controlling, influence over our physical wants also.* While it does not determine whether or not we shall eat, it does decide what and how we shall eat, the clothes we shall wear, and the house we shall live in—nay, more, the language we speak, the morals we adopt, and the religion we profess are all determined by the habits and customs of those among whom we live. Whether we are Christians, Mohammedans, or Buddhists; whether we eat with chop-sticks or use knives and forks, and whether we live upon rice, wear wooden shoes and a cotton smock, eat black bread and dress in sheep-skins, or enjoy the comforts and luxuries of civilization, all depends upon what country we happen to live in.

Nor is this confined to the lower classes and most barbarous countries; with a few rare exceptions, the style of living, the personal bearing, the company, and travel of the most educated and cultured classes in the most advanced countries are unconsciously determined by the habits and customs of the society in which they move. Habits are formed long before the power to think is acquired; it is much easier to do as others do than to theorize about new methods.

"This aggregate of beliefs and predispositions to believe," says Grote,† "ethical, religious, æsthetical, social, respecting what is true or false, probable or im-

---

* Bastiat's " Economic Harmonies," p. 57.
† " Plato and Other Companions of Socrates," Vol. I., p. 249.

probable, just or unjust, holy or unholy, honorable or base, respectable or contemptible, pure or impure, beautiful or ugly, decent or indecent, obligatory to do or obligatory to avoid, respecting the status and relations of each individual in the society, respecting even the admissible fashions of amusement and recreation —this is an established fact and condition of things, the real origin of which is for the most part unknown, but which each new member of the society is born to and finds subsisting. It is transmitted by tradition from parents to children, and is imbibed by the latter almost unconsciously from what they see and hear around, without any special season of teaching or special persons to teach. It becomes a part of each person's nature—a standing habit of mind, a fixed set of mental tendencies."

In fact, habit is the strongest force in human affairs. It is more powerful than governments, armies, or the most absolute despotism. Governments may be changed and political institutions overturned, wars may be waged, the people may be plundered and even murdered with impunity, but if the most powerful monarch on the earth should attempt to suddenly reverse the habits and customs of his people, it would cost him his throne, and probably his head.

The power of habit over the wants and conduct of man has long been observed by the best minds, although its relation to economic movement has never been understood. The influence of custom upon necessities was observed by Adam Smith, who says:[*] "By necessaries I understand not only the commodities which are indispensably necessary for the

---

[*] "Wealth of Nations," Book V., ch. 2, p. 691.

support of life, but whatever the *custom of the country* renders it indecent for creditable people, even of the lowest order, to be without. . . . Custom, in the same manner, has rendered leather shoes a necessary of life in England. The poorest creditable person of either sex would be ashamed to appear in public without them. In Scotland, custom has rendered them a necessary of life to the lowest order of men, but not to the same order of women, who may, without any discredit, walk about barefooted."

"The circumstances and *habits* of living prevalent in England," says Torrens,* "have long determined that women in the laboring classes shall wear their feet and legs covered, and eat wheaten bread, with a portion of animal food. Now, long before the rate of wages could be so reduced as to compel women in this part of the united kingdom to go with their legs and feet uncovered, and to subsist upon potatoes, with perhaps a little milk from which the butter had been taken, all the laboring classes would be upon parochial support, and the land, in a great measure, depopulated."

Therefore, if, as we have seen, wages are regulated

---

* "Essay on the External Corn Trade," pp. 57, 58. See also Spencer's "Social Statics," pp. 102, 103; Draper's "Intellectual Development of Europe," pp. 5, 6, 7; Wade's "Political Economy," pp. 87, 88; Walker's "Wages Question," pp. 118, 119, 120; Rogers's "Six Centuries of Work and Wages," pp. 169, 170; Brassey's "Work and Wages," pp. 15, 16, 59, 60, 61, 70, 88, 89, 93, 95, 96, 105, 108, 163; *ibid.*, 2d ed., ch. 8, pp. 160, 161, 164, 165; Cairne's "Some Leading Principles of Political Economy," pp. 3, 10, 362; McCulloch's "Principles of Political Economy," Part III., sec. 7, p. 181; J. S. Mill's "Principles of Political Economy," Vol. I., pp. 250–258, inclusive; Ricardo's "Works," ch. 5, p. 52, 1881; Bastiat's "Harmonies of Political Economy," Vol. I., p. 51.

by the standard of living, and the standard of living is governed by the wants ; and if, as is generally agreed, wants are determined by habit, it follows that, in the ultimate analysis, the law of wages has its rise in the habits and customs of the people. The habits of man, which are simply his aggregate wants, constitute his real social character. Ultimately, then, social progress is neither more nor less than the change of human habits, or, in other words, the increase of human wants, which constitute the differentiation of social character.

Here we have the true source from whence the regulating principle in wages arises, and therefore the basis upon which all industrial phenomena can be scientifically investigated. Human character being the focal point upon which all economic and social influences affecting progress must operate, it is manifest that nothing can permanently affect real wages which does not operate upon and through the habits and customs of the people.*

Applying this test to economic phenomena, the failure of the thousands of legislative and other artificial attempts to fix wages, and otherwise arbitrarily regulate the production and distribution of wealth, at once becomes explainable. Legislation upon trade, transportation, money, mines, railroads, land, rents, profits, interest, wages, etc., is as powerless to permanently force wages up as the "Statute of Laborers," the "Allowance System," and the "Conspiracy Laws," enacted against trades unions, were in keeping them down. The wonder, however, is not that all such

---

* "No remedies for low wages have the smallest chance of being efficacious which do not operate on and through the minds and habits of the people."—*Mill's* "*Principles of Political Economy*," Book II., ch. 12, § 4, pp. 455, 456.

efforts should fail, but that intelligent people should ever have expected them to succeed.*

Here, then, we repeat, is the true standard by which the economic soundness of all methods of dealing with industrial conditions must be estimated. It is here we must look for the true answer to the question, "What type of social structure am I tending to produce?" Whether or not, or to what extent, any proposition or policy will affect wages, and, therefore, general prosperity, entirely depends upon whether or not, or to what extent, it will influence the wants, habits, and social character of the masses.

SECTION III.—*The Influences which Determine Social Character.*

If we take man at the time he enters the world we find his wants are very few, exceedingly simple, and exclusively animal; and whether he is in Asia, Africa, Europe, or America, or whether he is the son of a slave or a prince of the blood, makes little real difference. Wherever or whatever he is, his wants at this stage of his existence are about the same. Food, with sufficient warmth to sustain his physical organization, comprises the whole list of his requirements. Nor does his nationality, social status, or parentage make any real difference as to what that food shall be. Whether he is in savagery or civilization at this point, it will be substantially the same, and will consist of the natural milk of his mother, or a substitute as near like that as possible.

---

* Herbert Spencer's "Social Statics," p. 22.

This being the extent of man's wants when he enters the world, it is manifest that all his other wants, of whatever nature, are acquired afterwards. The acquired wants, which we have seen constitute the distinctive character of man, are therefore produced by causes which operate upon him after birth. These causes may be grouped under two general heads, as *internal* and *external*. The former includes those forces which arise from the inherent qualities of man's organization, such as temperaments and other hereditary tendencies. The latter includes all the influences which arise from his social environment. His wants and character being the result of the joint operation of these two sets of causes, in order to understand how wants can be increased, it is essential to ascertain which of them exercises the dominating influence in determining wants and social character.

Although the subject of temperaments and heredity is an unsettled one, there is a conviction among scientists, writers and thinkers upon this subject that certain qualities of organization exercise an influence in determining the general tendency of character. That is to say, other things being the same, the desires, wants, and character of individuals, nations, or races will naturally tend in a certain direction. It is not pretended that the internal power of hereditary qualities of organization cannot be modified or even reversed by the influence of external circumstances. But all religious, educational, and reformatory institutions are based upon the idea that environment is more powerful than heredity as a factor in determining the wants and habits of man. Indeed, it is only on the condition that the general environment remains unchanged, that it is claimed that the in-

ternal or hereditary qualities govern the tendency of character. All history testifies to the fact that a change in the surrounding circumstances of man will not only produce a corresponding change in his wants and habits, but that it will also, though in a less degree, cause a similar change in the hereditary tendency of his organization.

It will be observed, however, that what is thus transmitted is not *wants*, nor anything that constitutes wants, but merely the capacity for acquiring wants and character, if the opportunity for their acquirement presents itself ; or, in other words, it is simply a modification of man's susceptibility to the influence of external circumstances, of which it is itself a result. It is clear, therefore, that it is not the internal power or hereditary qualities of man's organization, but the pressure of external forces, that exercise the controlling influence in determining social character.* This being true, it follows that man's wants will be many and varied, or few and simple, according to the variety and intensity of the social influences by which he is more or less constantly surrounded.

Man is essentially a conservative as well as a social being, and only yields to changes when opposition becomes more painful than acquiescence. It is for this reason that his wants and character change slowly, and progress is by slow degrees.

---

* " Whatever, therefore, the moral and intellectual progress of man may be," says Buckle, " it resolves itself not into a progress of natural capacity, but into a progress, if I may so say, of opportunity—that is, an improvement in the circumstances under which that capacity after birth comes into play. Here, then, lies the gist of the whole matter. The progress is not one of internal power, but of external advantage."
—"*History of Civilization,*" Vol. I., ch. 3, p. 128.

The child, instead of tiring of his first diet and wanting a change, can only by the pressure of external influences be induced to accept anything else, as all weaning experiences demonstrate. By the constant presentation of the new food, however, he not only takes it, but comes to like it, and finally prefers it to his previous diet. By repeated gratification, the desire thus produced for the new food naturally grows stronger, and soon develops into a want, which by the force of habit ultimately becomes an imperative necessity, the non-satisfaction of which will cause as much pain as did the withholding of the milk.* Thus, by the pressure of external forces the child learns to like what previous habits have taught its parents to regard as best for it. What parental authority is to the child environment is to the adult. The changes are, of course, much less painful to the adult than to the child, because they are generally much less abrupt. If, however, the average American was suddenly compelled to live upon the diet of the Hindoo, his suffering would scarcely be less acute than that of the weaning baby, and it would last much longer, because his character is more firmly fixed. The same would be true if the Hindoo was suddenly forced to adopt the diet and manners of the American. In proportion as volition supplants arbitrary authority these changes naturally become less painful, because they are more gradual and insensible; but they are nevertheless produced by the same general causes. Not to eat, drink, and wear what is commonly accepted by those with whom we live or associate, or even frequently come in contact with, is to incur the criticism, disapprobation,

---

* Carpenter's "Mental Physiology," ch. 8, pp. 351, 361.

or even ostracism of society, which will be more or less severe, according to the degree in which we dissent from the traditional mode of living. The social nature of man is so strong that to be excluded from the society of his fellows is one of the severest punishments that can be inflicted upon him.

Indeed, excommunication has ever been the most effective weapon with which society could inflict pain upon its individual members. In order to avoid the pain thus inflicted—to a large extent unconsciously—man naturally tends to either adapt himself to the prevailing mode of living or to gravitate toward a social atmosphere more congenial to him. And upon the same principle, whether he will adopt the former or the latter course will depend solely upon which of the two changes will be the least painful to him.

For the same reason that the child, through the pressure of parental authority, learns to like that which its parents habitually use, the adult, through the less abrupt, though no less effective, pressure of social environment, acquires similar likes and dislikes to those with whom he is immediately and most constantly surrounded, and, consequently, we always find him living upon the same general diet and adopting the same general mode of life as the family, class, or country to which he happens to belong. Although habits and customs thus form, as it were, a granite wall of resistance to all changes and, therefore, to all progress, they also form the strongest defence against retrogression; for while habit will resist the advent of the new, it will also make a desperate struggle against losing the old. While it is only through the persistent battering of external forces that it consents to take a

step forward, it will fight "as unto death" against taking one backward.

Although the hesitating influence of habit, which constitutes the real conservative element in human character, compels progress to move slowly, it is also the most unfailing guaranty for its permanence. What is thus true of our primary wants is even more strikingly true of our higher social and intellectual wants. By both instinct and reason we endeavor to avoid pain and obtain pleasure—*i.e.*, we endeavor to move in the direction of the least resistance. We therefore naturally desire to obtain such things as make others happy and avoid those which make others miserable; and the more we see and understand them the stronger will be our desire to obtain or avoid one or the other. In proportion as the desire to obtain possession of any object strengthens, the pain arising from its non-satisfaction increases, until it finally becomes greater than that involved in the effort necessary to satisfy it. And according to the well-established principle, that the power of our faculties increases with use, the more frequently the desire for an object is satisfied the stronger it becomes, and the greater will be the effort put forth for its gratification. Thus desires, by repeated satisfaction, grow into tastes, and tastes into absolute wants, which ultimately become a part of the fixed character, or " second nature." *

---

* "It is a phenomenon well worthy of remark, how quickly, by continuous satisfaction, what was at first only a vague desire becomes a taste, and what was only a taste is transformed into a want, and even a want of the imperious kind."—*Bastiat's* "*Economic Harmonies,*" p. 52. "By the powerful influence of habit the desire becomes a taste, and the taste quickly passes into an absolute want."—*Hearn's* "*Plutology*," p. 14.

Nor is the influence of a want confined to its own satisfaction. In accordance with the principle that the strength of a desire increases with its gratification, does the complete satisfaction of a want tend to give rise to new desires. Each new want calls forth a new effort for its gratification, and thereby enlarges the field of experience, by making more frequent and various social intercourse necessary, from which new desires naturally arise.

This fact was clearly observed by Professor Banfield, who says : * " The satisfaction of every lower want in the scale creates the desire of a higher character. If the higher desire existed previous to the satisfaction of the primary want, it becomes more intense when the latter is removed. The removal of a primary want commonly awakens the sense of more than one secondary privation. Thus a full supply of ordinary food not only excites to delicacy in eating, but awakens attention to clothing. The highest grade in the scale of wants, that of pleasure derived from the beauties of nature and art, is usually confined to men who are exempted from all the lower privations. Thus the demand for and consumption of objects of refined enjoyment has its lever in the facility with which the primary wants are satisfied."

Nor is this all ; for it follows that, for the same reason that the satisfaction of the primary wants gives rise to new desires, must the new social influences with which one comes in contact, in the satisfaction of these desires, as they become transformed into wants, give rise to still more desires. Thus the gratification of present wants becomes the ever-increasing source of

---

* " Organization of Industry," 1844, 2d ed., pp. 11, 12.

new desires, and constantly tends to further development. Again, the larger the number of established wants, the larger will be the number and the greater the variety of the constantly-increasing *new desires*.

The reason for this is obvious : the more numerous our established wants, the wider will be the field of our experience ; and the more frequent and varied our social intercourse, travel, etc., the greater will be the opportunity for external objects to excite our admiration and create within us new desires. And as our desire for and efforts to obtain any object is governed by our estimation of its capacity to increase our happiness, it follows that in proportion as we are acquainted with the nature and influence of external objects, is our power of judging of their relation to ourselves and their suitability to our purpose increased, and, consequently, our capacity for desire enlarged. And, according as our capacity for desire enlarges, our social, intellectual, and moral character is developed, and thereby the power of satisfying our most numerous wants is increased. It is thus manifest not only that our wants are directly produced by the pressure of external circumstances, but that our capacity for desiring and acquiring new objects is also determined by the extent and variety of our opportunities for contact with social influences. In fact, there is no conceivable limit to the development of man's social wants and his ability to satisfy them, except those fixed by his opportunities.

"It therefore depends," as Professor Hearn observes,* "upon the *education*, in the *widest sense of*

---

* "Plutology," pp. 19, 20.

that term, of each individual and upon his *character as mainly resulting from that education, how many and what kind of objects, and with what persistency he desires.** . . . We know that the desires of educated men are more varied and more extended than those of persons without education. We know that the wages of educated men are higher and, consequently, the means of gratifying their desires greater than those of the uneducated."

The power of social influences in shaping man's desires, wants, habits, and character is everywhere manifest. It is the recognition of this fact that makes us so solicitous about what our children shall see and hear, or where they shall go, the school they shall attend, the company they shall keep, the amusements they shall have, etc. Even parents who are in the habit of frequenting saloons will forbid their children going to such places, and none but the most degraded will allow their children to see them do so.

Indeed, the whole history of the human race is one continuous stream of evidence of the universal operation of this principle. Wherever man's social opportunities have been the most restricted, his wants, tastes, and desires are the most limited, and his industrial and political character has made the least progress, and *vice versa*. For the same reason that the extent of man's wants and the development of his character is the measure of social progress, so, too, the extent of his opportunities to increase those wants and develop that character is the true measure of civiliza-

---

* The italics are our own.

tion. Therefore, how to increase the wants, develop the character, and consequently advance the wages of the laboring classes, ultimately resolves itself into the question, *How can the social opportunities of the masses be enlarged ?*

PART III.

PRINCIPLES AND METHODS OF SOCIAL REFORM.

CHAPTER I.

POPULAR REMEDIES FOR SOCIAL EVILS.

SECTION I.—*Industrial Progress the Cause, not the Consequence, of Political Freedom.*

THE various efforts to promote industrial reform have hitherto been put forth in three general classes of propositions. Among the first class are the propositions to improve industrial conditions by changing political institutions. All such propositions are unsound, and hence must fail to accomplish the desired end, because they are based upon the popular but inverted idea that material prosperity depends upon political liberty, whereas the very reverse is true. The history of human progress is one continuous train of evidence showing that, instead of political freedom being the cause, it has everywhere been the effect of industrial prosperity.

Freedom does not consist in the mere absence of legal barriers, but in the actual power to go and to do. The poor can never be *free* in any true sense of the term. Whoever controls a man's living can determine his liberty. Freedom means independence, which noth-

ing but wealth can impart. Even intelligence cannot give independence, except as it can give wealth.

The reason the greatest intellects in art, science, poetry, politics, and literature through the ages have for the most part been the slaves of royalty, the nobility, or the commercial aristocracy, is because the poverty of the former made the patronage of the latter indispensable to their life and labors. There is no power on earth that can give freedom to the poor. Poverty and freedom are incompatible with each other.

Whatever may be, theoretically, the form of government, the political *freedom*—real power and influence—of the masses is always proportionate to their industrial prosperity and progress. Thus, the political influence of the masses is far greater under the present European monarchies than it was under the ancient republics. And the political influence of the masses is greatest to-day in those countries where the industrial conditions—real wages—are the highest. The laboring classes possess more political influence and freedom in England under a monarchy with higher wages, than they do in France under a republic with lower wages; and there is still more real democracy with higher wages under a republic in America than with lower wages under a monarchy in England.

We repeat, therefore, that the popular idea that pervades the literature and forms the basis of the statesmanship of the period, which ascribes our superior civilization to our democratic institutions, and which has just been emphasized by an international monument in New York harbor, representing liberty as enlightening the world, is *radically and fundamentally false.* It is not true that our superior civil-

ization is due to our democratic institutions; it is not and never was true that liberty enlightens the world. On the contrary, our democratic institutions are the natural consequence of our industrial prosperity and superior civilization; and liberty, like morality, instead of enlightening the world, is the golden result of the world's being enlightened by the material and social progress of society. Were this otherwise, the industrial depressions which afflict the Old World would be unknown here. The notorious fact is that the frequency and severity of industrial depressions are as great under the democracies of France and America as under the monarchies of England, Germany, and Belgium.

When the advocates of woman suffrage demand the ballot for her on the ground that it will enable her to become the industrial or economic equal of man, they are logically and historically putting the cart before the horse. There is no logical reason why woman should not be permitted to vote on the same conditions as man. The mistake is not in claiming for her the right to vote on the same conditions that it is conceded to man, but in assuming that the industrial condition of either man or woman would necessarily be improved by their having that right. Woman is not industrially and socially inferior to man because she does not vote, but she does not vote because of her industrial and social inferiority; in a word, it is because she is poorer, and, consequently, less independent than man.

Her wages and general industrial conditions are governed by the same economic laws as those of man. Her condition, therefore, can only be improved by the same methods that will improve his. Woman is ma-

terially more dependent than man, for the simple
reason that she has had less opportunity for social
development than he has. Her material condition,
like his, is the result of her industrial and social environment,
and it can be changed only through changing
her relations with that environment. In other words,
the economic condition of woman, like that of man,
can only be elevated by increasing her opportunity for
more frequent and varied contact with new and more
complex social influences.

Therefore, as the social disadvantages of woman
arise from industrial causes, all attempts to improve
her social position by changing her political relations
are economically unsound and practically false and
illusive.

The same is true of all propositions for prohibition
and other sumptuary legislation. This class of reformers
act upon the idea that drunkenness is the cause
instead of the consequence of poverty and its degrading
influences. They talk and act as if men drink rum
because saloons are numerous, whereas the truth is
that saloons are numerous because men drink rum. It
is true that drunkenness, like pestilence, tends to increase
poverty, but the former, like the latter, can
exist only in the social and sanitary atmosphere which
poverty makes possible. Drunkenness is as much a
social disease as cholera and small-pox are physical
diseases. Indeed, they are both primarily due to the
same general economic causes—poverty and its consequent
degrading social and unwholesome sanitary conditions.
It is true that drunkenness becomes a quality
of human character, but character is the moral consequence—the
infallible register of the ethical influence
of social environment. Vital and criminal statistics,

the world over, show that crime and disease are most prevalent where poverty most abounds. The rumshop everywhere vies with the home. In the poorest quarters of our large cities, where the social influences and, consequently, the moral character is the lowest, the rumshops are the most numerous and degrading.

In the vicinity of the lowest class of tenement-houses, where whole families eat, sleep, and work in one or two rooms (of which there are thousands in New York City alone), the rumshops are unattractive, ill-appointed, and often filthy, their attendants are untidy, coarse, insolent, and not infrequently brutal in their bearing. But as we approach the localities where the material conditions of the bulk of the community are higher and their homes and social surroundings are better, we find the saloons become fewer in number and superior in quality. They become cleaner, more commodious, and better appointed; their attendants are correspondingly neater, more intelligent and attractive personally, and more courteous and gentlemanly in their attentions and bearing. When we reach the " Murray Hills," the " Back Bays," and the " West Ends," where the average material and social conditions are the highest, the saloon fails to compete with the general comforts and refinements of the home, and therefore it practically disappears.

In the lowest districts where wages are the smallest, the homes the poorest, and the rumshops the vilest, the man who gets drunk and abuses his family, or even is sent to the house of correction occasionally, does not lose his social reputation and character. He may be referred to as " a little unfortunate," but it in no way affects his social standing in the class to which

he belongs. Indeed, he would be more liable to be ostracized in such a social atmosphere if he did not get drunk occasionally. If we go into districts where the wages, homes, and social surroundings are of a higher grade and the rumshop is better, we find drunkenness less general.

A man there may, perhaps, be excused for getting drunk occasionally, but if he does it habitually, or disturbs the peace, or abuses his family, and if he should be arrested, he would lose caste with his neighbors, and soon become socially ostracized. And in the localities where material and social conditions are still better, and the general culture and refinement is greater, we find this social boycott automatically imposed on much smaller provocation. Here drinking will necessarily be conducted more cautiously; a man will take great pains to avoid being regarded as a tippler. If, through over-indulgence, he should fall into the hands of an officer of the law, great efforts will be made, perhaps bribes paid—as is commonly the case—to keep it out of the public prints, or from otherwise becoming known, in order to escape the loss of reputation and the social boycott necessarily consequent upon such conduct. And in the localities where the superior material conditions and social refinement have practically eliminated the grogshop as an institution, this social boycott on drunkenness and its accompaniments becomes still more summary and absolute in its influence.

It may be said that the rich have the wine in their cellars. This is true, but when, through the refining influences of superior material and social conditions, the wine is transferred from the saloon to the cellar, because that institution is incompatible with the pre-

vailing culture and social customs, drunkenness is surely in its last stages of elimination. When the wine has reached the cellar it is directly under the influence of the strongest social power in existence against its abuse or indiscriminate use. The presence of the family, especially the children, and the refinement of the home influences in such a social atmosphere, all directly tend to prevent its common or excessive use. It would be brought out only on special occasions, and dealt out with care, so that under such conditions drunkenness must necessarily become almost an impossibility.

In fact, when the material and social conditions of the masses have reached the point where the comforts and refinements of the average laborer's home are more attractive than those of the saloon, drunkenness will cease to pollute the moral atmosphere of the community.

Drunkenness, like all other social diseases, has its tap-root in economic conditions. Consequently, any attempt to abolish drunkenness by sumptuary legislation which does not operate upon and through the industrial and social conditions of the masses is necessarily unsound and impracticable.

SECTION II.—*Rent, Profit, Tax, and Money Reforms.*

Among the second class of propositions for promoting the industrial reformation of society are those which propose to improve the economic condition of the laboring classes by the arbitrary abolition or manipulation of rent, profits, interest, taxes, etc. These propositions are all based upon the very erroneous

assumption that if rent, profit, interest, and taxes were arbitrarily reduced, wages would thereby be correspondingly increased, which is a fundamental mistake. If these were all abolished to-morrow, there is no economic force by which the wealth thus saved would, *for that reason*, go to the laborer.

This error arises from an entire misconception of the economic law of wages. It is commonly assumed that wages are determined by rent, profits, etc., whereas, as we have elsewhere shown, the reverse is true, and instead of these determining wages, they are ultimately determined by wages—*i.e.*, by the economic ability of the masses to consume wealth, without which neither rent, profit, nor interest would be possible. Wages not being governed by profit and rent, it is futile to attempt to increase the former by any direct or arbitrary manipulation of the latter. Wages can only be permanently increased by dealing with the causes that govern wages, which, as already shown, are entirely outside of profits, rent, interest, and taxes.

Not that the question of taxation is of no importance. It is, of course, an important function of government to see to it that the revenues necessary for the administration of public affairs should be as equitably levied, as economically collected, and as wisely disbursed as possible. And it is for the best interest of the community that the methods which will accomplish this with the least amount of bureaucracy, favoritism, and waste should be adopted. But all this merely relates to the details of administration, to the wisdom or unwisdom of disposing of a very small portion of the wealth at present produced. It exercises no appreciable influence upon the total amount of wealth produced, nor upon the income of the laboring

classes, for the simple reason that it does not affect the causes which influence the production of wealth and the general rate of wages.

While a careful collection and an honest and wise disbursement of public funds is a marked feature of good government, the wise or unwise use of a few millions of dollars is of no sort of importance as compared with promoting the social influences which tend to increase the aggregate production of wealth and the daily income of the masses. Indeed, the promotion of the latter is the only sure way of securing the former. Public integrity and the wise administration of government can only be permanently secured by elevating the intelligence and social character of the masses, upon which the character of all government finally depends. No government can continuously dissipate the revenues or abuse the trust of an intelligent, well-informed people, and no power can prevent profligate waste, public corruption, and maladministration in the public affairs of a poor and ignorant people.

The same is essentially true of money. It is one of the functions of government to furnish a medium by which commodities can be easily exchanged. It is quite important that this money should be made of a material and issued in such form and quantities as shall best suit the industrial and social convenience of the people. This should be done on a scientific basis, so that a sudden change in the volume and value of the currency, to any considerable extent, could never occur. Beyond this there is no real economic importance to be attached to the money question. Any violent disturbance of prices, which a sudden change in the currency always involves, is invariably inimical to industrial interests. That it is the duty of good

government to devise a scientific financial system by which an unvarying medium of exchange be continuously issued, I freely admit, but if such a perfect system of finance were devised and universally adopted to-morrow, it could not possibly produce any important effect upon the general prosperity of the community, or upon the economic condition of the laboring classes. No industrial or social improvement could be produced by any change in the quantity or quality of the currency, for the obvious reason that money, as such, having no other function than a medium of exchange, sustains no important economic relation to the social forces which determine the amount of wealth produced or the amount of the laborer's income.

In fact, so far as the inherent economic and social influence of money is concerned, wages might forever remain at ten cents a day with the most perfect currency the world is capable of devising. Nothing can permanently affect wages that does not influence the social character of the laborer, which no system of finance, as such, however perfect it may be, is capable of doing.*

SECTION III.—*The Inadequacy of Socialistic Methods.*

The third class of measures which are proposed for the industrial improvement of society are those of a socialistic character, such as state socialism, colonization, co-operation, etc. These propositions are more plausible in theory, but are as futile in practice as those just considered. The fundamental error in these

---

* For a more thorough discussion of the money question, the reader is referred to the next volume.

schemes is that they are attempts to anticipate instead of to promote social evolution.

They are proposals for the remodelling of society on a high plane of intelligence and equity, without the first conditions upon which such a society can be possible. Like the effort to play Hamlet with Hamlet left out, they are conspicuous for the absence of the essential conditions upon which their success depends. All propositions of this nature are based upon the idea that not only the political government, but also the industrial and commercial enterprises should become the collective property and be under the control of the collective management of the community.

If the advocates of these schemes would content themselves with pointing out the fact that such is the goal toward which all social development is tending, and were willing to help to promote its natural movement in that direction, there could be little ground for taking exception to their position. Whether their conclusions as to the goal of human progress are correct or not, if the movement of society is accelerated along the line of its natural development, it will surely move in the direction of its true end, whether that be the one they have pointed to or not. The important function of the social philosopher is not to discover the extreme goal or final terminus of human progress, nor to decide what will be the precise social relations in the highest possible state of social development. This, at best, must necessarily involve considerable doubtful conjecture. The function of the true philosopher is to ascertain the laws by which the movement of society from the simple to the complex is governed. This being done, if we put ourselves in correct relation with those laws, whether that goal is

in accordance with our more or less fanciful speculations or not, we shall be sure to move toward the highest possible social eminence and perfection.

But this is precisely what the advocates of co-operation and state socialism do not do. They first satisfy themselves as to what an ideal state of society should and would be, and then instead of helping to promote industrial and social progress toward the point where such a state of society could be possible, they attempt to anticipate all necessary growth and preparation, and establish what they regard as a high state of society upon low industrial and social conditions. In other words, they want to arbitrarily inaugurate a high state of civilization upon the conditions which will barely sustain a modified state of barbarism; than which nothing can be more fallacious and impracticable.

A proposition for introducing an important change into social institutions is just as unsound, for all practical purposes, if it is incorrect in relation to time, as if it were incorrect in relation to principle. The first and indispensable condition to the successful establishment of an industrial and social democracy is intelligence and character, not only in the leaders, but in all, or nearly all, who participate in it, in order to understand and appreciate its principles, and harmoniously sustain its government in accordance therewith. If intelligence and character is not general among its members, the management and control of affairs must naturally soon fall into the hands of the most capable and successful members of the community. And these, in the very nature of things, will become the governing and, therefore, the fortunate and wealthy classes.

That this condition is conspicuously absent as yet,

not merely in the barbarous but in the most civilized countries in the world, is too obvious to need stating. Not only do the great mass of the laboring classes lack the material conditions and intellectual and social character necessary to sustain a truly industrial co-operative commonwealth, but no considerable portion of them are equal to any such an undertaking. This is demonstrated by the almost universal failure of industrial co-operative undertakings. It should also be remembered that these experiments have been undertaken by the most intelligent and enthusiastic portions of the community.

If we examine the history of co-operative or socialistic enterprises we shall find that their failure or success has been proportionate to the simplicity or complexity of their undertaking. Thus, even in England, where co-operative enterprises have reached their highest success, all attempts to establish a purely democratic form of industrial, not to say social, co-operation have completely failed. There is scarcely a single industrial enterprise in Europe or this country that was started on the democratic plan which, in less than twenty years, and generally in a quarter of that time, has not been forced to assume the aristocratic— "property qualification"—mode of government, or go out of existence. In other words, they all failed as democratic industrial undertakings, and either became joint-stock companies or disappeared altogether.

Another and less democratic and less complex form of productive co-operation, known as "profit-sharing," has been more widely adopted, and has been somewhat more successful. That is to say, the experiments have lasted longer in most cases where rich employers, while keeping the management of the business in their own

hands, have divided a portion of the profits among their employés, than in cases of purely democratic co-operation, where the laborers shared equally in the control of the business as well as in the profits accruing from it. But while the experiments of profit-sharing have been more general and continuous than those of industrial co-operation, pure and simple, they also have, with a few exceptions, proved failures. The few successes like Leclaire, in Paris, and Godin's Familistere, at Guise, stand almost alone amid the numerous failures along this line, not only on the continent, but in England and this country.

Furthermore, the success of these few, as the history and methods of the enterprises clearly show, is mainly due to the character and *personnel* of the individual capitalists undertaking them.

Again, profit-sharing is impracticable as a general scheme, because it is only the most successful or advantageously situated employers* who have any considerable amount of profits to divide. A large proportion of employers, instead of having any large amount to divide among the laborers as profits, as is generally supposed, are struggling on the verge of insolvency. If, by any force of law or custom, profit-sharing should become general, so that all employers were virtually compelled to adopt it, one of two things would necessarily follow—*viz.*, either the general rate of stipulated wages would fall or the price of products would rise in the same ratio, and the actual income of the laborer would, in the long run, be practically the same. In-

---

* Such, *e.g.*, as those who have large capital, most improved machinery, situated near to the general market, or have some other monopolistic advantage over the bulk of those engaged in the business.

deed, it is impossible that it should be otherwise, for the obvious reason that the capitalist can only divide profits when he has profits to divide, which a large portion of employers have not.

Profits can be increased only in one of two ways: either by raising prices or reducing the cost of production. A rise of prices would be a virtual reduction of wages, and any division of profits by such means would be simply "taking away with one hand in order to give with the other." The cost of production can only be permanently reduced by the use of large capitals or labor-saving appliances, which implies a larger aggregate production, and, consequently, an increase in the general consumption of wealth. And this, as we have fully explained elsewhere,* is governed by the standard of living or social character of the masses, which no amount of profit-sharing can materially affect. In fact, whatever would enable the employer to give the laborer a bonus in the form of profits would enable him to raise wages, and, for the same reason, whatever would make it necessary to reduce wages would render it impossible to divide profits.

It is a law in economics, which all industrial history proves, that the income of the laborer is proportionate to his social wants; and if it is derived from one or from several sources it will ultimately be substantially the same. Accordingly, when the English laborer received parish allowance in addition to his wages, his income from both sources was no greater than from wages alone, after the former was abolished. And so it is to-day. Where the laborers have perquisites, such as the privilege to keep a cow, small allotments

---

* Chapter II., Part I.

of land, etc., in addition to their wages, the rate of wages is correspondingly lower than where their whole income consists of money. It is notorious that in those industries where the income of the laborer's family includes the earnings of the wife or children, the wages of the man are, on the average, proportionately lower than in those where the sustenance of the family depends entirely upon his wages.* For the same reason, if the income of the laborer was made up of wages and profits, ultimately the two would be no more than wages alone.

If we turn from productive to what is commonly called distributive co-operation, where the business is simpler and more direct, where the industrial subtleties and commercial fibres are less intricate and complex, where the business is all done with the members, and, therefore, a little bad judgment is less likely to prove disastrous, a much larger per cent of successes is to be found. And among these, much the largest portion of successful undertakings is to be found in the retail grocery trade, where the variation of prices, qualities, and styles of goods is at the minimum, and, consequently, where the smallest possible amount of business skill, sagacity and shrewd financiering is necessary. Again, if we examine the associations of the laboring classes, such as trades unions, where still less of these qualities of character are required, and where the whole purpose of the association is centred upon one or two simple, though important, objects, such as

---

* "For the same reason it is found that, *cæteris paribus*, those trades are generally the worst paid in which the wife and children of the artisan aid in the work."—*Mill's* "*Principles of Political Economy*," Book II., ch. 14, § 4, p. 488. See also Chapter VII., Part II., pp. 167–175.

watching for the timely moment to demand an increase of wages, a reduction of the hours of labor, or other direct improvements in their industrial conditions, the undertakings are far more numerous and the percentage of successes is much greater. All experience thus shows that industrial co-operation has failed just in proportion as the higher qualities of character became necessary to its success

It may be urged that this is no argument against co-operation, *per se*, because all the failures are due to the inexperience and incapacity of those undertaking them, and not to the principle itself. And the fact that it is feasible in a few cases proves that it could be a universal success, if the people were sufficiently intelligent to carry it out. This may all be true, but its universal failure conclusively demonstrates that this indispensable condition is conspicuously wanting among the great mass of the laboring classes to-day. Therefore, co-operation, whatever would be its merits in a more highly developed state of society, as a means of abolishing the evils arising from our present industrial and social conditions, must be practically inoperative and hopelessly inadequate.

"Yes," replies the advocate of state socialism, "but that does not apply to our proposition. What we ask for is not that the most intelligent and capable members of the community should band themselves together in order to improve their own condition, regardless of that of those below them. That is only what capitalistic corporations are doing, which tends to increase rather than lessen the burdens of the poorest and weakest classes. What we want," he adds, "is that all industrial co-operation shall be undertaken by the state for the whole people. All the

means of production, in the phrase of Marx, should be in the hands of the government." And, as a sample of the marvellous powers of state socialism, we are referred to the phenomenal success of the governmental management of the Post-Office.

Well, let us see. In the first place, the Post-Office Department has not been a financial success—that is to say, it has not been self-sustaining, and its deficiencies have had to be made up from time to time out of the general taxes. If any private enterprise was in that condition, instead of being called a great success, it would be regarded as bankrupt. But, it may be asked, could letters be sent across the continent for two cents by private enterprise? Certainly! Why not? What does the government do toward making it possible to send a letter three thousand miles for two cents? Nothing, positively nothing! All the government does in the mail service is to collect, assort, stamp, and bag the outgoing and deliver the incoming letters, give out and receive money-orders, and render a correct account of the business done. All of this is purely clerical work, which, after being once systematized, is simple and even monotonous. There is nothing in it which calls for exceptional skill or rare business capacity, such as is required to successfully manage large business enterprises, with their close competition and ever-varying subtleties and complications, where a slight error of judgment might involve a loss of thousands of dollars, and perhaps cause the ruin of many persons. When the letter-bags leave the door of the Post-Office to start on their flying trip across the continent, they enter into the hands of private enterprise. It is the great railroads and steamship companies that make it possible for the letter to

go three thousand miles for two cents. The cheap methods of travel and transportation which carry the mails are in no way due to state influence, but entirely to private enterprise. In fact, they are the natural outcome of the industrial and social progress of the community.

Thus it is seen that all the important work in the cheap and rapid transmission of the mails is due to the social development of the people under the impetus and control of private enterprise; and that portion of the mail service which is entirely in the hands of the state, unlike all private enterprises of a similar character, such as express companies, etc., is a complete monopoly, being entirely free from competition, and almost free from responsibility; at least so far as its relation to the individual is concerned. If I send a package through the United States mail, and it is lost, I have no redress, whereas if I send it by any express company they are responsible to me for the full value I set upon it when it is delivered to them. And where the railroads are owned or the tariffs controlled by the state, as on the continent, they are more expensive, less efficient, and the rates of transportation are higher and the wages of labor are much lower than in this country, where they are all managed by private enterprise.

Manifestly, then, there is nothing connected with the management of the Post-Office or in the experience of governmental control of railroads to sustain the claim that state management of industries, especially in the more complex branches of production, is necessarily superior or even equal to those of private enterprise. Indeed, such a supposition is illogical and contrary to all known facts. If the most select and en-

lightened members of the community lack the necessary intelligence to sustain co-operative or socialistic enterprises, except of the most simple character, what right have we to assume that the whole community, with a much lower average intelligence, could more successfully manage the most complex and difficult economic undertakings ? It is simply absurd.

To this it may be replied that if the industries of the country were in the hands of the state, the same class of persons would have charge of them as now, the only difference being that they would then be managers for the people instead of their being owners of the plant, and managers for themselves, as at present. But there is no reason to believe, and every reason to disbelieve, that the same class of business capacity and enterprise which now prevails in economic affairs would be put in charge under state socialism to-day. In fact, with the present state of average intelligence, such a result would be practically impossible. Democracy seldom elects the very best capacity to any office ; nor, in the nature of things, can that be expected. Socialism, which means the broadest kind of democracy, must necessarily be governed by representation through popular election and not by limited or qualified selection. By this means public officers cannot be drawn from the most capable nor from the most incapable classes. The laborers would not vote for a Vanderbilt, Gould, or a Field for railroad managers, although they are the most competent men on the continent for the business ; nor could an east-side laborer obtain the votes of Fifth Avenue for any public position. In order to obtain the popular vote in a broad democracy, the representative must reflect in the main the ideas, capacity, and character of the great

mean average of the community, which will always be better than the poorest, and considerably inferior to the best.

This explains why our legislative and executive offices, with a few rare exceptions, are always filled by men of the most commonplace type, the highest order of executive and enterprising capacity being devoted to trade and industry. Consequently, we find public business is conducted with notoriously less economy and ability than are private enterprises.

Thus, from whatever point of view we consider industrial co-operation or state socialism, we find them wholly inadequate as a means of reforming the present industrial and social conditions. They must necessarily fail as a *means* toward establishing an ideal social state, because they are the very ideal state (so claimed) which we need the means to establish. It is because " industrial co-operation," " association," or " socialism" implies a high social state that they require a high grade of intellectual and social development in the people in order to sustain them. It is this very weakness and incapacity among the laboring classes, arising from their poverty and its social disadvantage, so fatal to the establishment of " industrial association," which makes industrial reformation necessary. Therefore, while " mutual association" or " co-operation" may prove to be the most equitable, convenient, and harmonious industrial system to adopt when sufficient progress has been made to sustain it, manifestly it can never be successfully adopted as a means to that end.

There is another objection to this class of schemes which is fatal to them as a means of reforming society, and it applies with equal force to profit-sharing, land

nationalization, co-operation, and all industrial phases of socialism, as well as to efforts to arbitrarily manipulate interest, profits, rents, wages, etc. It is that they are efforts to enrich one class at the expense of another, which is wholly uneconomic. Nothing can permanently improve the economic condition of one class in any industrial community which does not tend to improve that of all classes. No change, however equitable, in the distribution of the wealth now being daily produced could make any important difference in the well-being of the masses. There is nothing more delusive than the rose-colored dreams about the social advantages that would result from transferring the profits, by means of profit-sharing, co-operation, etc., from the capitalist to the laborer. The advocates of these propositions, which have included some of the most careful economists, both in England and on the continent, as well as in this country, appear to be unwittingly captivated by the delusive coloring of their own picture. This delusion arises partly from the mistake of estimating the amount capable of being divided upon the basis of the profits of the most successful enterprises, which constitute but a very small per cent of the employing class. It would be just as correct to estimate the profits of all newspaper enterprises on the basis of the earnings of the New York "Herald," "World," and "Sun," or all railroads upon that of those of Vanderbilt and Gould; and it is partly due to the fact of viewing the amount that can be thus divided in the aggregate, instead of in the weekly amount it would give to each laborer.

We have occasionally heard of ten, twenty, and even fifty thousand dollars being divided among the laborers by some exceptionally fortunate experiments

at profit-sharing and other forms of co-operation. These amounts have an imposing appearance to the abstract theorist, who sees them only in the aggregate. It has no such rose-colored seeming to the laborer, however. He is interested not so much in that large-sounding aggregate as he is in the portion of it which will reach him, and that, from such sources, is always very small, seldom amounting to more than a few cents a week. Suppose it should be announced that, in 1887, the employing classes in this country would divide one hundred million dollars among the laborers. Imposing as that amount may seem in the aggregate, and important as it might be in reducing the cost of commodities if employed as capital in improved methods of production, it would be of very little importance to the laborer, as it would give him less than twenty cents a week, or about three cents a day, equal only to a rise of about two per cent in wages. And because the laborer does not evince a disposition to abandon his trades union and forego all efforts to increase his wages, and otherwise improve his condition, for the privilege of participating in the present profits at the rate of two or three cents a day, he is berated as an economic blockhead. Even Professor Jevons, one of England's most scientific economists, took this view. In his chapter on profit-sharing* he cites the experiment of the Briggs Brothers, which was one of the most successful of its kind in England. He shows that the laborers received in profits from two to five pounds a year, according to their wages, and still they finally went on strike, and broke up that beautiful arrangement.(?) If we look at the case from the laborer's

---

* "Problems of Social Reform."

standpoint, which is the true economic view, it appears quite different. While a very few of the highest-paid employés received five pounds (twenty-four dollars), the bulk of them did not get more than three pounds (fourteen dollars and forty cents). But suppose they received four pounds—which they seldom did, more frequently getting less than half that amount—that would be less than six cents a day. Thus while the distribution of that amount to each employé may be regarded as an exceptionally generous act on the part of the Briggs Brothers, economically it was a matter of small moment to the laborer, being about one-third less than a permanent advance of ten per cent in his wages would have given him. The same is true of the nationalization of the land.*

It is not surprising, therefore, that the laborers, who, though they have never entertained very sound theories on economics, have always displayed a much greater degree of practical common-sense in regard to industrial affairs than most social theorists, should prefer to rely upon the traditional means of bringing about an increase in their wages. The failure of this and hundreds of other similar experiments are not due to a lack of mutual good feeling between the employer and employed, as is so often affirmed, nor lack of generosity and sacrifice on the part of the capitalist, but it is due to the economic impossibility of attaining the desired end by such means. Indeed, the material condition of the masses can never be appreciably improved by any possible amount of generosity or sacrifice on the part of the few. The poverty of the laborer is not due to the inequitable distribution of the pres-

---

* See Introduction, p. 5.

ent wealth, but to the fact that the aggregate wealth produced is too small. In fact, it is a universal law in economics,* that the greater the aggregate amount of wealth produced per capita in any community, the more equitable its distribution.

It is equally true that there are no economic means by which the material condition of the masses can be permanently improved which do not tend to increase the aggregate production of wealth per capita. And this, as we have repeatedly shown, can only be brought about by increasing the influences that develop the social wants and economic demands of the masses. The first and indispensable condition for the permanent development of character is *increased social opportunities*, which is precisely what the class of propositions we have been considering does not tend to furnish.

---

* See chapter on Profit, Vol. II.

CHAPTER II.

HOW TO ENLARGE THE SOCIAL OPPORTUNITIES OF THE MASSES.

IN the foregoing chapters we have seen that industrial, social, and political progress primarily depends upon the social character of the laboring classes. They constitute what Lasselle tritely termed "the fourth estate," whose well-being underlies and includes that of the whole community. It is upon *their* consumption, as determined by their habits and character, that all economic movement in the production and distribution of wealth depends; and it is by *their* character, as mainly resulting from their social opportunities, that the progress of civilization is ultimately determined.

The question, therefore, for the science of social economics to solve, is not how to abolish rent, how to reduce profit, prohibit interest, regulate the currency, diminish taxation, manipulate tariffs, control liquor traffic, etc., but how it is to enlarge the social opportunities of the masses. Let this question be once clearly settled, and all such minor issues, which are more the consequence than the cause of the laborer's social condition, will as surely be economically solved as that savagery recedes before advancing civilization.

But before a satisfactory answer to the above question can be given, it is necessary to understand what constitutes social opportunity. In the sense that the

expression is here used, opportunity, like freedom, does not consist of the mere absence of legal or arbitrary limitations. A man is not *free* to go and to do, simply because statute law does not forbid him, nor even by virtue of its expressed permission to do so. The man whose livelihood depends upon the will of another has no more freedom than if he were bound by statutory enactment. Whoever controls a man's living *can* control his liberty. To be restricted, by whatever means, to choosing between obedience to the will of another and starvation, is not freedom. The worst form of chattel slavery that ever existed could not prohibit the slave from choosing between obedience and death. The *freedom* to do implies not only the right, but also the *power* to do. To simply remove imposed restrictions, to make access to certain places and things legally possible, is not necessarily creating opportunity. In India both law and caste forbid social intercourse between the sudras and Brahmins, but the absence of these conditions in China does not constitute an opportunity for social intercourse in that country. The fact that there are no class distinctions in our educational institutions does not constitute an opportunity for the masses to receive a college education. It would be just as correct to say that every citizen has an opportunity to be President of the United States, because there is no law forbidding it.

Social opportunity may be defined as contact with an increasing variety of social influences, and this will be effectual in proportion as it becomes general, which, in turn, will entirely depend upon the incentives for bringing it about. The mere authoritative permission or legal right of the masses to travel, mingle with refined

society, to acquire education and general culture, does not necessarily constitute an adequate motive or incentive for them to put forth the necessary effort to obtain such objects. The amount of effort devoted to the accomplishment of any object is governed by the intensity of the desire to be gratified, and the intensity of the desire is proportionate to the extent of the contact with the influences which stimulate it.

Therefore, as contact with more complex environment involves additional effort, and the expenditure of effort is governed by the desire, it follows that contact with new social influences (opportunity) can only become frequent and general according as they arise from efforts devoted to the gratification of existing wants and desires.* In other words, nothing but the force of present desires can sustain the effort necessary to encounter the pressure of new and more complex environment. The only natural means, therefore, by which the laborer's opportunities can be enlarged is through increasing his *economic necessity* for more frequent contact with an increasingly differentiated social environment. In other words, to automatically increase the complexity of his social relations.

Here, then, is the economic fulcrum upon which the lever of statesmanship must be placed, in order to effectually raise the industrial and social condition of the masses. No change of political institutions or industrial conditions which is not based upon this principle can produce any permanent improvement in the economic and social condition of the laboring classes. Therefore, in dealing with the social problem, the im-

---

* "We teach not by lessons, but by going about our business."— *Emerson.*

portant question for the statesman to ask is, What political, industrial, or social change, if any, will naturally call into operation the forces that will unconsciously and automatically differentiate the higher social relations of the industrial classes. According as any change, of whatever nature, tends to do this, will it tend to develop the laborer's character—increase his wants—raise his standard of living—advance his wages—increase the consumption and production of wealth—dispel industrial depressions, and promote the prosperity and progress of the community. But while no measure can be efficacious in improving the laborer's condition in any country or state of society which does not operate upon and through his industrial and social environment, it does not follow that the particular change which would most effectually tend to increase the social opportunities of the masses under one set of industrial conditions would necessarily do so under all industrial conditions. For instance, what would tend to enlarge the facilities and increase the incentives for more complex social relations among the laborers of America, England, or in the more advanced continental countries, might prove inoperative or even injurious to the Patagonian, the Jamaica negro, or the mass of laborers in Asia, Africa, and South America. For while the general law governing economic and social evolution is universally the same, the special measures necessary to accelerate its movement may vary according to the existing industrial and social conditions to which it is to be applied.

The industrial system with which we are at present concerned is the *wages system*. Therefore, in considering the question, How can the opportunities of the masses be enlarged? we must always be understood

to mean the masses in wages-paying countries, especially in those where the division of labor and the use of machinery most generally prevails.

It is important at the outset to recognize the fact, which we have so often emphasized, that consumption is the economic basis of production, and that the laborer is as important a factor in the one as he is in the other. This being the case, it follows that the development of the laborer's capacity to consume wealth is as important economically, not only for his own interest, but for that of the capitalist and the community, as it is to increase his power to produce.

The laborer's ability to produce is derived from the influence of a very different set of circumstances than those which develop his capacity to consume. His ability to produce, which depends upon the skill and dexterity with which he can manipulate the material and implements for producing commodities, is the result of frequent contact with the means and conditions of production. His ability to consume, which consists of his wants, habits, and character, is the effect of frequent contact with an increasing variety of social influences.

Now, so long as nearly all the laborer's time not occupied in eating and sleeping is devoted to the former, as at present, no commensurate development of the latter is possible. Therefore, the first condition for increasing the opportunity of the masses to develop their social character, and thereby increase their natural capacity to consume wealth, commensurate with their power to produce it, is *more leisure*. By leisure, however, we do not mean merely unoccupied time. Enforced idleness is unoccupied time, but it is not leisure. The masses, the world over, have a great deal of unoccu-

pied time, but it is mainly in the form of idleness, and not that of leisure. Though idleness and leisure are both unoccupied time, the economic and social influence of the one is directly opposite to that of the other. Idleness tends to impoverish, dwarf and degrade, while leisure tends to enrich, develop, and elevate character. It is very important, therefore, to distinguish clearly between leisure and idleness. Nor is this difficult to do if we observe their essential characteristics.

As much of the argument in the following pages will be devoted to a consideration of propositions for the promotion of social progress through increasing the leisure of the working classes and reducing their idleness, it may be well to digress a moment, in order to define more clearly the meaning of the terms leisure and idleness as they are here employed.

Whether unemployed time will become leisure or idleness entirely depends upon the circumstances under which it occurs. There are two conditions necessary to render unemployed time leisure : (1) It must be time that is not necessary to obtain a living, and (2) it must not be in excess of the capacity to utilize it to social advantage. Leisure, therefore, may be defined as unemployed time capable of being devoted to industrial and social, and, therefore, intellectual and moral, improvement. On the other hand, all unemployed time which lessens the power to obtain a living, or which, for whatever cause, cannot be appropriated to social advancement, is *idleness*, and is inimical to progress. Idleness, however, may be properly divided into two kinds, *natural* idleness and *enforced* idleness. The former is unemployed time, the use of which is not necessary to obtain a living, but which cannot,

under existing conditions, be utilized for social development, and is exhibited by the two extremes of society—barbarian and aristocratic. The latter is unemployed time, the use of which is indispensable to the maintenance of the prevailing standard of living, and applies to the wage-receiving classes.

While all idleness is inimical to progress, the influence of enforced idleness is far more disastrous to civilization than that of natural idleness. True, the idleness of the Esquimaux, Patagonian, or Jamaica negro, like that of the sons of the aristocracy, is injurious to their social development, but it does not directly inflict nearly so much hardship and degradation, either on the individual or the community, as does the enforced idleness of the wage-receiving class. This is explained by the fact that the idleness of both the former classes consists of unemployed time which is not required to obtain the means of subsistence; consequently, they are not directly impoverished by it. In the case of the privileged aristocracy this is due to the fact that their income, or means of subsistence, does not depend upon their own effort, and in that of the barbarian to the fact that the number of things made necessary by his simple mode of life is so small and easy to procure that a few hours' labor a day is all that is required to supply them.

This is not the case, however, with the wage-laborer; his idleness comes in a different way, is of a different kind, and produces a very different economic and social effect upon society. Having, through the more highly complex state of industry, lost the power to employ himself, the wage-laborer is compelled to work for others, whose sole object is to obtain from him the maximum amount of effort for the minimum reward.

Consequently, when he is employed he is compelled, for the most part, through circumstances entirely in the hands of the employer—except when limited by law or public opinion—to work as hard and as long as his physical and nervous energies will endure. This being the only condition upon which he can, under the wages system, obtain a livelihood, when idleness is forced upon him all his means of living are cut off.

The *enforced* idleness of the modern laborer, unlike the *natural* idleness of the barbarian and the aristocrat, does not consist of time that is unemployed, merely because it is not necessary for the gratification of his wants, but it consists of time, the use of which is indispensable to his very existence, except as he becomes a pauper or a criminal.

Again, the inability of the wage laborers to obtain a living according to the accepted social standard of their class is not only inimical to prosperity and progress, but it is more dangerous to property and democratic institutions than is that of the barbarians. (1) Because he is living in a more highly complex state of society, he does not, like the barbarian, produce directly for his own consumption, but he produces what others consume, and consumes what others produce. Thus the consumption of the masses becomes the basis of the market for the wares of the whole community, from whose transactions the income of all the other classes is derived. Consequently, the failure of the wage-receiving classes to consume—which enforced idleness implies—does not, as in the case of the barbarian, impoverish the laborer alone, but undermines the prosperity of the whole community—so frequently exemplified by indus-

trial depressions. (2) The privations of the modern laborer are more dangerous to society than those of the barbarian. This is because, having reached a higher state of social development, he is more sensitive to the needs and conscious of the rights of his industrial and social relations ; and, being more intelligent, he is naturally more powerful in producing a social and political tornado, if the means of gratifying his established and recognized wants are cut off. When the barbarians fail to obtain the means of supplying their meagre wants, they will die of hunger and disease, as they have frequently done by the tens of thousands, while the modern laborers, when, through enforced idleness, they are deprived of the means of satisfying their much more complex wants and desires (unless supplied from the wealth of the upper classes), they will endanger the safety of life, property, and government itself. (Witness the political revolutions with which the history of every so-called civilized country is replete.)

It will thus be observed that while the natural idleness of the barbarian tends to stereotype his environment and arrest his progress, the *enforced* idleness of the wage-receiving classes threatens the very existence of civilization. It may be laid down as a law in social progress, that the evil effects of enforced idleness increase in direct ratio with the advancing complexity of industrial and social relations. Enforced idleness, therefore, is the most serious evil with which modern society has to deal. If enforced idleness can be prevented, natural idleness will surely be gradually eliminated as civilization advances. Enforced idleness arises from the failure of the masses to increase their economic capacity to consume wealth commensurate

with their power to produce it,* which is due to their lack of opportunity for social development.

This condition of things is the natural consequence of the popular economic heresy of regarding the laborer as a factor in production, and ignoring him as a factor in consumption ; which, in turn, naturally led to the mistaken policy of absorbing the greatest possible amount of the laborer's energy and time in the former ; consequently, seriously restricting, if not destroying, his opportunity for developing the latter. In this way the growth of consumption has been limited, and that of enforced idleness—the greatest of all social evils—has been promoted. While all social opportunity may not be leisure, all leisure is social opportunity.

As enforced idleness is the greatest barrier to leisure, and leisure is the economic solvent for enforced idleness, whether or not the social opportunities of the masses can be increased turns upon whether leisure or idleness shall prevail. If we do not increase the former we cannot escape from the latter, with all its consequences.

The immediate and most important question, the answer to which is necessary to enable us to take the first correct step toward preventing enforced idleness, is, how to wisely and permanently increase the *leisure time* of the laboring classes. To this question we are now in a position, on the basis of sound economic principles, to give a definite and emphatic answer, which is—REDUCE THE HOURS OF LABOR.

---

* See chapter on business depressions, Vol. II.

CHAPTER III.

THE ECONOMIC EFFECT OF REDUCING THE HOURS OF LABOR.

SECTION I.—*The General Situation Stated, and the Line of Opposition Indicated.*

BEFORE entering upon the consideration of the subject, let me say, once for all, that in proposing a reduction of the hours of labor as the indispensable *first step* toward promoting industrial and social reform, we do not say that it is the only means that will, under any and all conditions, tend to promote that end. But what we affirm, and in the preceding chapters have endeavored to show, is, that under all conditions, without regard to race, climate, or state of development, the universal principle—the first essential condition upon which the permanent progress of society depends—is the *enlarged social opportunities of the masses*. Under the wages-system, which includes, if not the largest, the most advanced portion of the race, upon whose progress that of the remaining portion largely depends, the safest, the most general, and, consequently, the most effectual means for increasing the social opportunities of the masses is by a general reduction of the hours of labor.

While there are other more or less effectual means of promoting the same end, such as education, free

lectures, public libraries, parks, museums, and art galleries, these are, and must necessarily remain, practically ineffectual, so far as lifting the community from its present industrial and social mire is concerned, unless the *leisure time* of the *masses* is increased.

Having said this much by way of explanation, let us without further delay proceed to consider what would be the *economic* effect upon the community of a general reduction of the hours of labor. Society is economically divided into three general groups or classes, as laborers (wage-receivers), capitalists (employers), and land-owners. The incomes of these groups take the form of wages, profits, and rent, respectively. Instead of recognizing the universal law that the top is necessarily sustained by the bottom, and that the incomes of the upper or profit and rent-receiving portions of the community finally depend upon the prosperity of the great mass of wage-receivers, it is commonly but wrongly assumed that the economic interests of these groups are not only distinct, but often antagonistic to each other.

Accordingly, any proposition to increase the social opportunities of the masses, by reducing their hours of labor, has always encountered the united opposition of the profit and rent-receiving classes. Nor is this due, as is commonly charged, to an abnormal amount of selfishness on their part, but it arises from a gross misconception of their economic relations to the community, and especially to the laboring classes. This misconception, as we have already shown, is mainly due to the false teachings of political economy. Having been taught that profits move inversely with wages, "rising as wages fall, and falling as wages

rise," * it is not surprising that they should regard every effort to improve the laborer's economic condition—which always finally involves an increase of his real wages—as inimical to their interests. This inverted position in relation to reducing the hours of labor has been further strengthened by the fact that hitherto the proposition has always been presented on sympathetic and philanthropic, rather than upon economic grounds. The capitalists have been asked to grant this boon, not as an act of wise and broad statesmanship, but out of sympathy for or charity toward the "unfortunate classes," especially "the women and children." To this they have, with some degree of consistency, replied, that "factories are economic and not charitable institutions;" that they prefer to keep their business and their charities separate, making the extent of the latter dependent upon the success of the former. Under the influence of these views, they have vigorously resisted all efforts in this direction, as being what they regard as attempts to make them give something for nothing, in wanton violation of all their rights as free citizens.

We shall doubtless be told by the impersonal and irresponsible "*we*" of journalism that such a proposition would be a violation of the rights of contract; that profits, which are now so small that ninety per cent of all who enter business fail, would be so reduced as to bring ruin to the capitalist and disaster to the community. And in order to show its special guardianship over the interests of the "unfortunate

---

* " Thus we arrive at the conclusion of Ricardo and others, that profits depend upon wages, rising as wages fall and falling as wages rise."—*Mill's* " *Principles of Political Economy*," Book II., ch. 15, §7.

classes," we shall be assured that the prosperity of the laborer depends upon the profits of the capitalist, and that as the laborer is paid according to what he produces, especially where piece-work prevails,* a reduction of the hours of labor would naturally involve a corresponding reduction of wages. Thus, to the employing class this measure is presented as containing nothing but smaller profits and bankruptcy, and for the laborer lower wages, more poverty, and social degradation.

In anticipation of this double line of opposition, we shall consider what the economic effect of reducing the hours of labor would be upon each of these groups separately as follows: (1) What would be its effect upon wages? (2) What would be its effect upon profits? (3) What would be its effect upon rent?

First, then, what would be its influence upon wages —*i.e.*, upon the general rate of *real* wages? The correct answer to this question largely depends upon the extent to which the hours of labor are reduced. That is to say, it will depend not so much upon the number of hours per day the laborer shall work as upon the extent to which his unemployed time shall be increased.

SECTION II.—*The Principle which should Govern the Reduction of the Hours of Labor.*

Before entering upon the consideration of the main question, we will digress a moment to call special attention to this point. We do this because the failure to recognize its logical and economic importance has

---

* See chapter on Piece-work.

led the well-meaning and often uneconomic friends of short-hour legislation to urge it for sympathetic but untenable reasons, and thereby expose the movement to objections which would otherwise have been too inexcusable and absurd to be injurious. For example, according to the humanitarian and "ideal equity" point of view from which this question has hitherto been presented, it is held that the hours of labor should be reduced the most where the labor is the hardest and the working day the longest.

Now, this is just the reverse of being correct, and, like nearly all conclusions induced by sympathy and ideal conceptions of an "ought to be" social state, it is an economical and philosophical inversion. The error involved in this idea is of the same character, and arises from the same source as that which impels the endeavor to plant high morality in extreme poverty and to inaugurate ideal co-operation amid the social conditions of barbarism. It should always be remembered that unemployed time, like wealth, will prove to be an advantage or a disadvantage according to the capacity or incapacity of persons to wisely employ it.

Although we have repeatedly emphasized the fact that wealth is an indispensable condition to progress, we have more than once pointed out that even wealth cannot with any permanent advantage be distributed in advance of the social need or general capacity of the people to wisely consume it. Were it possible to arbitrarily double the wealth (wages) of the laboring classes to-morrow, it would not increase the average comfort and well-being of the masses, simply because, as before explained, such a sudden increase of wealth in advance of the natural development of the social

wants and character necessary for its wise consumption would inevitably lead to reckless waste, dissipation, and vice in a thousand forms. But four times or even four hundred times as much wealth can be safely distributed among the masses, if it comes in response to, instead of in advance of the social need and ability to nominally consume it. In short, whenever the dollar precedes the want, it means waste and dissipation; but when the dollar is preceded by the want it means wise consumption and social progress.

In the same way and for the same reason unemployed time will prove to be idleness that injures and degrades, or leisure that develops and elevates, according to the capacity to socially utilize it; and this, in turn, depends upon the simplicity or complexity of the existing social condition of the people. And, as repeatedly explained, the wants and desires, or the social character, of a people are always commensurate with their social opportunities. Accordingly, we find that where the laborer's employment is physically the most exhausting, and the normal work day the longest, his social opportunities are the smallest, his life the simplest, and his character the lowest and weakest; and, consequently, his ability to wisely utilize unemployed time the smallest.

Thus the American laborer can with advantage to himself and the community consume from two to five dollars a day, while the sudra of India would be surfeited and demoralized by half that amount.* For

---

* Sir Thomas Brassey referring to his father's experience with the coolies of India, and the effect of a sudden rise of fifty per cent in their wages during the building of railroads in that country, observes: " The Hindoo workman knows no other want than his daily portion of rice, and the torrid climate renders watertight habitations and

the same reason, the laborer in Russia, who is employed from thirteen to seventeen hours a day, subsisting chiefly upon black bread and water, could not at once employ to social advantage as much unoccupied time as the laborer of America, England, France, and Germany, whose opportunities and material conditions have been better, and whose social character is correspondingly higher.

Obviously, therefore, to make the greatest reduction in the hours of labor where the work is the hardest and the working day the longest, is to give the greatest amount of unemployed time where there is the least capacity to use it to personal or social advantage, and thereby defeat the prime object of the measure. In truth, a reduction of the hours of labor, in order to be economically and socially effective, must be applied inversely in degree with the industrial and social degradation of the masses. In other words, its application must be governed by the principle that the ability to utilize new advantages of whatever kind is proportionate to the extent of previous social opportunities and character. That is, "to him that hath shall be given," not as a matter of favoritism, but simply because he only can appreciate and use, and hence derive any advantage from having it. A clear understanding of this principle will not only prevent the friends of short-hour legislation from exposing the movement to many unnecessary attacks, but it will also forever explode that stale, illogical, and superficial objection, "that if twelve hours' labor a day is better than four-

---

ample clothing alike unnecessary. The laborer, therefore, desists from work as soon as he has provided for the necessities of the day. Higher pay adds nothing to his comforts; it serves but to diminish his ordinary industry."—"*Work and Wages,*" pp. 88, 89.

teen, then six must be better than twelve, three better than six ; and that even none would be still better." It might with equal force be said that because moderate eating is more wholesome than gluttony, to abstain from food altogether would be even better than moderate eating. Indeed, if there were any sense in such talk it would follow that sixteen hours' labor a day must be better than fourteen, and eighteen or twenty still better than sixteen. Therefore, the surest way for the masses to obtain wealth and comfort is to work the whole twenty-four. Although the utter imbecility of such reasoning when carried to its logical conclusion is apparent to the dullest mind, it has been for more than a quarter of a century one of the stock arguments of the opponents of short-hour legislation.*

Now, to recapitulate, we have seen, (1) That increased social opportunities tend to increase alike the wages of the laborer and the wealth and progress of the community. (2) That leisure time constitutes social opportunity. (3) That unoccupied time is leisure only proportionate to the existing capacity to socially utilize it. (4) That under the wages (or fac-

---

* The New York *Evening Post*, one of New York's most respectable dailies, which takes special pride in the soundness of its economic reasoning, on the 1st of May, 1886, in an editorial over a column in length, devoted to a criticism of an article of mine on the eight-hour question in the April number of the *Forum*, employed the above argument in the following language : " It is sufficient, therefore, to suggest that the principle that we have considered may eventually lead to the entire extinction of the primeval curse of labor. We know of no reason why, if a reduction of the hours of labor infallibly leads to an increased production of wealth, the condition of the race should not be infinitely improved by the general cessation of tiresome exertion." And this editorial was reprinted entire in the New York *Nation* for May 8th, 1886.

tory) system of industry, the most feasible way of increasing the leisure and, therefore, the social opportunities of the masses is by a general reduction of the hours of labor. (5) That while a reduction of the hours of labor is the only practical means of increasing the laborer's leisure, whether the unoccupied time given to him by such a measure will tend to increase his leisure or add to his idleness, will depend upon whether or not the extent of the reduction is in excess of the capacity of the average laborer to use it to his personal and social advantage.

It will thus be observed that while the principle here laid down is universally sound, if it is unscientifically applied the result may not only prove to be not beneficial, but it may be positively injurious to the best interests of the community. Manifestly, therefore, the extent to which the hours of labor are reduced must be an important factor in determining the economic effect of that measure upon the community.

SECTION III.—*How much can the Hours of Labor be Safely and Wisely Reduced ?*

If we were called upon to answer that question for the Patagonian, the Jamaica negro, or the coolie of India, where hand labor and "natural idleness" prevail, we should probably find that larger social opportunity for them lies in the direction of a closer contact with the industrial whips and spurs of the wages or factory system, with its machinery and division of labor, and even by an increase instead of a reduction of the hours of labor. And if we were considering the question in relation to the laborers of Russia, Turkey,

or Austria, where the wages system exists only in its first and most barbarous stages, and where the laborers work from thirteen to sixteen hours a day, living mainly on black bread and broth, amid the social conditions but slightly removed from those of the Middle Ages, a reduction of the hours of labor to ten per day would probably give them all the unoccupied time they could safely be trusted with.

But we are not considering the question with reference (except indirectly) to the laborers in the lowest, but to those in the highest stages of civilization—not in relation to those whose social opportunities have been the most limited, but with reference to those whose opportunities have been the greatest, and whose social character is accordingly the most highly differentiated. If this proposition can be successfully applied in a few of the most advanced countries—as the United States, England, France, and Germany, and, perhaps, Belgium and Switzerland—nothing can prevent it from extending to the less developed countries as fast as they adopt improved methods of production and become a part of the modern industrial system.

We will consider the question, then, with special reference to its effects in the United States, England, France, and Germany. For while these countries are politically distinct, and in some respects quite different, economically they may be regarded as practically all one. They all employ the same methods of production, pursue the same industrial policy, and very largely buy and sell in the same markets. In fact, the present means of transportation and communication are such that a change of a half cent in prices in any one country is felt almost simultaneously

in them all. And despite superficial perturbations resulting from discriminating tariffs and other local causes, the remarkable uniformity of industrial depressions * clearly shows that the industrial prosperity of all these countries is governed by the same general economic causes. It is not only true that for all the purposes of economic reasoning and for industrial legislation these countries are one, but whatever will dispel the industrial and social chaos in those four countries will redeem all Christendom, and give civilization such momentum that even in Asia and Africa the days of barbarism will be numbered. What are the hours of the average working day in those countries, and how much can they be safely—economically—reduced?

In this country, outside of Massachusetts,† except in a few limited trades, the hours of labor range from eleven to thirteen per day. Although data for ascertaining the exact average for the whole country is difficult to obtain, it may safely be placed at eleven and one half hours. But in order to be sure of under rather than overstating the case, we will put it at eleven hours.

In England they are fixed by statute at nine and one half, in France at twelve, and in Germany, while there is no law regulating the hours of labor, custom has limited the nominal working day to twelve hours.‡

---

* See First Report of United States Commissioner of Labor, 1886, p. 290.

† Since writing the above, a ten-hour law has been adopted in Rhode Island, and bills have been introduced into the Legislature in Maine and New Hampshire for that purpose.

‡ In many parts of Germany the hours of labor are thirteen and fourteen per day. See Young's "Labor in Europe and America," p. 573.

Thus, in these countries, taken all together, the average working day is about eleven and one eighth hours a day. How much, then, can these hours be safely reduced—*i.e.*, how much can they be reduced without promoting dissipation, instead of improvement, among the great mass of the laborers in those countries?

It should ever be remembered in this connection that wise statesmanship can never do more in economic and social affairs than influence the direction of general tendencies, and also that it is the character of the great mass—the seventy or eighty per cent of the community—that determines the direction and moulds the character of the social and political institutions.

In the light of experience, to which we shall hereafter refer, and the present highly complex industrial conditions in the above-named countries, there can be no doubt as to the economic and social safety of reducing the normal working day for adults to eight hours, and that of children under sixteen years of age to half time.

SECTION IV.—*The Direct and Immediate Effect of an Eight-Hour System.*

What would be the natural effect upon wages of the general adoption of an eight-hour system in the United States, England, France, and Germany? In order to understand the proposition clearly, we will consider, first, its effect upon wages if it were adopted only in this country. According to the last census (1880), the total population of this country was 50,155,783. Of this number, 36,761,607 were over ten years of age, and 17,392,099, or nearly one half, of

those over ten years of age were engaged in the various occupations. Of these, 1,017,034 were engaged in the various professions, as lawyers, physicians, clergymen, teachers, journalists, actors, etc., and 1,479,634 were manufacturers, merchants, bankers, traders, clerks, etc., leaving 14,895,431 who properly came under the head of laborers. Of this number, however, 4,347,617 are farmers and others engaged in agriculture, who work for themselves, and hence they cannot be strictly classed as wage-laborers, although a large per cent of them work for wages a considerable portion of the time, and would be directly affected by an eight-hour system. The remaining 10,547,814 are exclusively wage-receivers. In other words, thirty-four per cent of the whole population actually participate in industrial pursuits. Twenty per cent of the whole population—sixty per cent of those engaged in all occupations—and seventy four per cent of all engaged in industries, outside of agriculture, work for wages. If we exclude from this number the 1,075,655 domestic servants, there are still 9,472,159 persons actually engaged in productive industries who work exclusively for wages. The general adoption of this measure would properly include the whole 14,895,431 ; but, in order to avoid captious objections, we will consider its economic effect upon the laboring classes, if only applied to the 9,472,159 who work exclusively for wages. This number consists of 8,353,803 adults of both sexes and 1,118,356 children under fifteen years of age.

All considerable industrial and social changes produce two effects. One is immediate and more or less temporary, and the other secondary and permanent, in its character. Whether the latter is in harmony or conflicts with the former depends upon the economic

soundness of the measure adopted. Most legislation, especially upon industrial questions, has been adopted with special reference to its immediate effect, and often in utter ignorance of the natural tendency of its permanent influence; and not infrequently the latter has proved to be the mere reaction and its effect to be the opposite of the former. Such has been the case with all abnormal expansions and contractions of the currency, and, indeed, with all attempts to regulate wages, profits, interest, rent, etc., or to otherwise improve society by means which do not first operate upon and through the social opportunities and character of the people.

The adoption of an eight-hour system, however, would be an exception to this rule. Its immediate effect, which is all that has hitherto been recognized, would, as we shall soon see, be in perfect harmony with its ultimate and permanent economic influence. The first and immediate effect of the general adoption of this system would be to reduce the working time of the 8,353,803 adult laborers three hours a day, or about twenty-seven per cent, and that of the 1,118,356 children seven hours a day, or sixty-four per cent. This would withdraw 25,061,409 hours of adult labor and 7,828,492 hours of child labor from the market without discharging a single laborer. The industrial vacuum thus created would be equal to increasing the present demand for adult labor thirty-one per cent, and that of child labor fifty per cent. In other words, without increasing either our home or foreign market, but simply to supply the present normal consumption, besides creating a demand for 1,118,356 children under sixteen years of age to work the other half day with those already employed, it would create employment

for 3,552,059 new laborers. In order to do this, about twenty per cent more factories and workshops would be needed, besides setting all our present idle machinery in operation. This, it is needless to say, would create a further demand for labor in the mines, quarries, forges, furnaces, iron works, and other industries that contribute to the building and equipment of the new factories and workshops.

Now, enforced idleness is the greatest obstacle to social progress. All careful students of social economy have come to recognize the fact that nothing can permanently improve the condition of the laboring classes which does not dispel that industrial terror, enforced idleness, which is exactly what the uniform adoption of this measure would succeed in doing.

According to the report of the United States Commissioner of Labor (1886 *), there are in this country bout one million unemployed laborers, or about five and one half per cent of the whole number engaged in all occupations. This, it will be observed, is only a little over one fourth (twenty-eight per cent) of the number of new laborers that would be required by the general adoption of this system. There are no exact data as to the number of unemployed in England, France, and Germany. It may be safely assumed for

---

* The exact language of the report is as follows : " Applying the percentage arrived at (seven and one half per cent), we obtain a total of 998,839 as constituting the best estimate of the possibly unemployed in the United States during the year ending July 1st, 1885 (meaning by the unemployed those who during the time mentioned were seeking employment), that it has been possible for the Bureau to make. It is probably true that this total (in round numbers 1,000,000), as representing the unemployed at any one time in the United States, is fairly representative, even if the laborers thrown out of employment through the cessation of railroad building be included," pp. 65, 66.

THE NUMBER OF UNEMPLOYED.

general purposes, however, that, on the whole, the proportion to the number actually engaged in the various occupations is approximately the same as in this country.

According to the latest returns, the total number of persons engaged in the various industries in the above-named countries is as follows:

Countries.	Persons Employed.	Per cent of Population.
France	14,996,998	43
Germany	18,986,494	42
England and Wales	11,187,584	$43\frac{1}{16}$
Scotland	1,606,984	43
Total	46,778,060	

Assuming the unemployed to constitute five and one half per cent of this number, as in this country, there are in those countries 2,572,793, which, added to the 1,000,000 in this country, makes a grand total of 3,572,793, being only 20,734 more than the number of new employments created by this measure.

It is thus clear that the general adoption of an eight-hour system for adults and half time for children under sixteen years of age in the United States alone would nearly absorb all the unemployed laborers in America, France, Germany, and England, including Scotland and Wales. This, we repeat, is not a fanciful speculation, based upon an imaginary expansion of our home or foreign market, but it is what would necessarily result from the natural operation of economic forces in the effort to supply the present normal consumption. The employment of nearly four millions of new laborers would necessarily increase the number of consumers, and

thereby enlarge the market for commodities to that extent. That such a result would tend to increase wages is very clear. Although wages would not necessarily rise in the same proportion that enforced idleness was reduced, all the influences would be in that direction.

By the absorption of the unemployed and the consequent diminution of competition among the laborers for employment, the power of the direct influences that tend to promote the rise of real wages would be increased. In other words, the power of natural forces to raise wages increases as the opposing pressure of enforced idleness is diminished. Manifestly, therefore, the adoption of the measure under consideration, by absorbing the enforced idleness and able-bodied pauperism in this and the three leading countries in Europe, would at once tend to reduce poverty, increase the consumption of wealth, and raise wages.

If this would result from its application in the United States alone, what, it may be asked, would be the effect of its adoption in England, France, and Germany at the same time? Let the facts answer.

The number who work for wages in those countries, according to the most recent data upon the subject,* is in France, 8,700,515 ; Germany, 10,970,845 ; England and Wales, 9,317,374, and in Scotland, 1,324,077, making a grand total of 30,312,811. Of this number there are of both sexes engaged in domestic service, in France, 739,544 ; Germany, 938,294 ; England and Wales, 1,803,810, and in Scotland, 176,565, making a

---

* The official returns in the respective countries as given in J. Scott's latest "Statesman's Year-Book" for 1886.

total of 3,658,213, leaving, exclusive of domestic servants, 26,654,598 who work for wages. Exactly what proportion of this number is composed of children under sixteen years of age I am unable to ascertain.

Fortunately, however, we have those facts for this country, which will serve as a safe basis for an approximately correct general estimate.

In 1880 there were in the United States 1,118,356 children under fifteen years of age employed in the various occupations, being at that time about eleven and eight tenths per cent of the whole number working for wages in productive industries. Assuming the same proportion of those who work for wages—exclusive of domestic servants—in Europe are children under that age (which is a very low estimate), the 26,654,598 wage laborers consist of 23,509,256 adults and 3,145,342 children under fifteen years of age.

Now, to reduce the working time of the adults to eight hours each day, and that of the children under sixteen years of age to half time, would withdraw from the market 92,545,162 hours' labor each day without discharging a single laborer. But in order to put the children now at work on half time would necessitate the immediate employment of 3,145,342 additional children to work the other half day with them. This would take 12,581,368 hours a day, leaving a net withdrawal of 79,963,794 hours' labor a day, which would be equal to creating employment for 9,995,474 adult laborers. This number added to the 2,627,434 days' work created by its adoption in this country makes a grand total of 12,622,908 created in the four countries by a general adoption of an eight-hour and half-time system.

It may be objected by the opponents of this propo-

sition, that it cannot be successfully applied to agricultural laborers. To avoid this objection—although it is untenable, especially where modern machinery is used—we will eliminate agricultural laborers as well as domestic servants from the calculation.

The number working for wages in the four countries referred to is 11,931,525. Three hours a day for this number equals 4,474,321 days' labor. Deducting this number from the grand total of 12,622,908, leaves 8,148,587. Or, to state the case another way, the simultaneous and uniform adoption of this proposition in the United States, England, France, and Germany (exclusive of agricultural laborers and domestic servants), besides giving half-time employment to 4,263,698 children, and absorbing all the unemployed laborers and able-bodied paupers in the above countries, would create a demand for more laborers than the total number now working for wages in productive industries in Belgium, Holland, Norway, Sweden, Switzerland, Portugal, and Ireland combined. If it would only do half this, it would more than absorb all the enforced idleness and able-bodied pauperism in this country and Europe to-day.

But even if it only created sufficient employment to absorb the 3,572,793 unemployed laborers referred to, which we have seen would be accomplished by its adoption in this country alone, it would increase the demand for general products equal to adding to the present market the entire consumption of the wage-receiving classes of Belgium, Holland, and Switzerland, which, it is needless to say, would make a proportionately larger production; and, consequently, more laborers would be necessary.

That a measure which would do this, without arbitrarily molesting vested interests, invading the rights

of property, or disturbing the prevailing methods of trade, commerce, or industry, would tend to advance wages and improve the condition of the laboring classes is too obvious to need discussing. For while, as already observed, wages would not rise proportionate to the diminished relative supply of labor, the removal of enforced idleness would enable the influence of social forces to push wages up to the maximum, instead of being forced down, as at present, to the minimum rate consistent with economic and social safety.

If anything approximating to such results could be shown on a scientific basis, for any form of state socialism, land nationalization, tariff, or currency reform, it would be deemed sufficient to warrant, if necessary, the overthrow of existing institutions for their accomplishment.

SECTION V.—*The Permanent Economic Effects.*

Thus far we have considered the proposition only with reference to its immediate and perhaps temporary effect. What would be its secondary and permanent influence? is the next and still more important question.

A little consideration will show that while this would be more gradual, permanent, and far-reaching in its nature than the first, its tendency and influence would be in the same direction and in perfect harmony with it. Indeed, it is in the gradual and permanent effect—for which the first merely clears the way—that the real economic and social importance of this proposition consists. Were it otherwise, its economic soundness would be questionable, and its adoption, to say the least, an act of very doubtful expediency.

It is a well-established principle in political economy that the extent of the demand for commodities determines business prosperity. It is equally clear, though less understood, that this demand is governed by the habitual consumption of wealth by the masses. Nor is it any less evident that the consumption of wealth in any community is finally determined by the general standard of living in that community. It is the essence of economic law that whatever tends to develop the wants, raise the standard of living, and elevate the social character of the masses, necessarily tends to promote the advance of real wages.

The first condition necessary to the development of character is social opportunity, which, under present conditions, more leisure alone can give. This indispensable condition for social progress is what the measure before us is specially designed to furnish. Simultaneous with the immediate effects referred to, over thirty-six millions of laborers would leave their work each day less exhausted, mentally and physically, and have three hours' extra leisure time on their hands, which means so much positive opportunity for family life and general social intercourse. With more leisure and less exhaustion the laborer, from various motives, will be continually forced or attracted into new and more complex social relations, which is the first step toward education and culture, in the broadest sense of the term. In short, it means his gradual introduction to a new social environment, the unconscious influence of which would necessarily awaken and develop new tastes and desires for more social comforts. He would desire more wholesome and better appointed homes, more travel, literature, entertainment, etc. Not to speak of the intellectual,

moral, and political influence to result therefrom, which we shall consider hereafter, the purely economic effect of this would be little short of a revolution. In proportion to the frequency that the new desires were gratified, the development of which, under such conditions, no power on earth could prevent, would they crystallize into urgent wants and necessities, the satisfaction of which would become an essential part of the standard of living, demanded by the social habits and character of the people.

The accepted standard of living being the economic law of wages, to raise the standard of living of the masses is necessarily to increase the rate of wages. By the *accepted* standard of living, we mean the standard of living which the consensus of that class or country has determined is requisite to material comfort and social decency, and below which one cannot permanently go without incurring social disadvantage. A few laborers in any class or community may adopt a standard of living considerably above or below that generally adopted by the great mass or general average of that class, but the standard of living thus adopted by exceptional individuals does not determine the general rate of wages, nor even their own wages. Wages, like all economic elements, are governed not by individual, but by general social forces.

Some slight perturbations in wages may be determined by the individual character and capacity of the laborer himself, but the sphere in which those oscillations can occur is absolutely determined by the social character of the great mass. For example, the wages of a certain class of laborers in China may oscillate between seven and twelve cents a day, according to ability, necessity, etc., but from the sphere of

thirty or forty cents a day, he is absolutely debarred. Indeed, to attempt, for any personal reasons, to obtain such wages would simply exclude him from employment altogether.

If he comes to this country the sphere of these oscillations is entirely changed. Here it will probably be between forty and sixty cents a day, instead of from seven to twelve cents, as in China. This difference is wholly due not to his individual character, but to that of the community, which he has taken no real part in determining. It is not the character of the ten or twenty per cent, but those of the eighty or ninety per cent, that determines the socially accepted standard of living in any class or country. It will be seen, therefore, that if an eight-hour system only applies to a small fraction of the laboring class, it might not produce any permanent effect upon the general rate of wages, or even appreciably change that of those who are directly affected by it.

But if it was applied to the whole nine and one half millions of laborers in this country, or, as we propose to do—apply it to the whole thirty-six millions, who with their families embrace nearly all of the lower half of the entire population in this country, France, and Germany—it would generate a social force, the full economic influence of which it is impossible to contemplate.

The influence of the change here proposed would be even greater upon the children than upon the adults for two reasons: (1) Because the character of children under the age of fifteen is much more susceptible to social influences than that of older persons. (2) Because the children will be under the elevating influences of educational institutions a portion

of each day. By this means, within a single decade every laborer of twenty years of age, both in this country and in Europe, would have had five, and many of them seven or eight years' daily contact with the educational, moral, and social influences of school life. It is clear, therefore, that the necessary consequence of the general adoption of the half-time school system alone would be not only to greatly improve and elevate the home, but to almost revolutionize the domestic and social atmosphere of the masses within a single generation.

The advance of the general rate of wages, consequent upon a higher standard of living, would produce a corresponding increase in the general demand for commodities in the four greatest wealth-consuming nations in the world. The satisfaction of these new wants would create a permanent international market for new products more than equal to that of the entire population of this country, which would, in turn, create new industries and, therefore, new employments, and further increase the demand for labor. But, it may be asked, will not this increased demand for labor and rise in wages involve a corresponding rise of prices? We answer No! Indeed, that would not be a rise in real wages, because if the prices of commodities increased in the same proportion that wages rose, the laborer would obtain no more wealth for a day's work than formerly, and therefore would be economically and socially no better off. But, it may be replied, "you laid it down in a previous chapter, that prices were determined by the cost of production, and that the controlling element in the cost of production is wages. If this be true, does it not follow that an increase of wages involves a rise of

prices?" Paradoxical as it may appear, we again answer No!

It is true that we laid it down that prices are determined by the cost of production, and that the cost of production is governed by wages, and that if wages were arbitrarily and locally increased, it might and probably would, temporarily at least, tend to raise prices. It will be remembered, however, that we also explained that the increased consumption of wealth accompanying a general rise of real wages tends to promote the use of improved machinery—or a greater concentration of capital in production, and in that way therefore cheapens the cost—which always tends to reduce prices, and is the same as a still further increase of real wages. The larger the market the lower the price, is one of the best-established principles in political economy, as well as one of the best-attested facts in economic history. The successful use of improved machinery, which is the only means of permanently reducing the cost of production and lowering prices, is possible only with the use of large capitals and extensive production. It is equally true that the use of large capitals and extensive production is compatible only with a large aggregate consumption of wealth, which *nothing but a high standard of living can sustain.*

Obviously, therefore, whatever tends to increase the aggregate consumption of wealth per capita necessarily tends to reduce the cost of production and lower prices. This explains why the comforts and luxuries of life are cheaper in England now, with labor at five shillings a day, than they were in the Middle Ages, with labor at less than sixpence a day, and why wealth can be produced cheaper in America at two dollars a day than in China at ten cents.

It becomes clear, then, that the uniform adoption in the United States, England, France, and Germany of an eight-hour system would rapidly abolish enforced idleness and able-bodied pauperism, tend to continually extend the consumption and production of wealth, increase the comfort, education, and culture of the masses, and permanently advance real wages, without arbitrarily disturbing existing institutions.

13

CHAPTER IV.

THE EFFECT OF AN EIGHT-HOUR LAW UPON PROFITS.

IF it were true, as taught by orthodox economists, that "profits fall as wages rise," the fact that a reduction of the hours of labor would tend to increase wages would be a sufficient reason why the employing class should oppose it, as they almost invariably have done. The logic of this theory is that the economic interests of the wages and profit-receiving classes are necessarily antagonistic to each other. This doctrine, like all error, cuts more than one way. While it has served its obvious purpose in supplying the employing class with a defence for their almost universal endeavor to keep down wages, it has at the same time laid the foundation and furnished the arguments for that most erroneous belief among the masses that the profit-receiver is their natural economic enemy; hence, to foil or despoil him, by whatever means, is to promote their interest.

This unfortunate view, which has been so fertile in promoting the use of the most uneconomic means for social and industrial reform, has led the more modern economists to give a somewhat modified rendering of the doctrine, asserting that "capital and labor are *allies, not enemies.*" While this presentation has a more satisfactory seeming, upon examination it will be found to contain the real error of the Ricardo-Mill theory. For, although it affirms, correctly, that

the laborer and employer are natural allies, whose economic interests are inseparable, it is always upon the presumption that the success of the alliance primarily depends upon the prosperity of the capitalist or employer. Whereas, the reverse is true, and, as elsewhere explained,* the prosperity of the employing and mercantile classes ultimately depends upon that of the laboring class—upon the economic capacity of the masses to consume wealth.

There is a certain sense in which the Ricardo-Mill theory has, at least, a plausible appearance of truth. For example, if it cost in raw material, building machinery, etc., sixty cents a pair to manufacture shoes, and they could be sold at one dollar, clearly forty cents a pair would remain to be divided between the laborer and his employer. In whatever proportion this surplus is divided between wages and profits, if all other things remain the same, Mr. Ricardo's statement that a rise of wages is a fall of profits, and *vice versâ,* would be correct. Assuming each received twenty cents a pair, it is a mere matter of mathematics to see that, if wages rose to twenty-five cents, profits must at the same time and for that very reason fall to fifteen cents a pair. Consequently, if wages could be reduced to five cents a pair, profits would rise to thirty-five cents a pair. This appears plausible, and even conclusive, and has been generally accepted as unanswerable.

It will be remembered, however, that, clear as all this seems, it is true only provided that something else is true—viz., that all other things remain the same —*i.e.,* if the same number of shoes could be sold at

---

* Chapter II., Part I.

the same price. This, however, is a condition which never is and never can for any considerable time exist. If the shoes were exclusively consumed by a community which had no economic relations with that which produced them, this would be possible. If, for instance, all the shoes could be consumed by the people of another planet, or by a people who are so remote, geographically and socially, from the scene and conditions of production that the wages of the laborers who made them formed no part, directly or indirectly, of the market in which they were sold, such a condition might prevail.

This, however, is almost an economic and social impossibility. If the laborer was merely a factor in production and exercised no influence upon consumption, as he has been so commonly regarded, all this might be true; but as the consumption of the laboring classes constitutes the preponderating element in the general market for commodities—and as the laborer is constantly increasing as a factor in consumption and decreasing as a direct factor in production, as fast as improved machinery is adopted—the possibility of "other things remaining the same," when wages are reduced, is constantly becoming more and more out of the question. In other words, the quantity of shoes that can be sold and the price that can be obtained for them —the extent of the market—is becoming to depend more and more upon the consumption or wages of the laborer. Therefore, a reduction of wages directly tends to limit the market for commodities.

If the demand for shoes is lessened, the manufacturer is soon forced either to sell fewer shoes or sell them at a lower price. In either case, the actual amount of profit he will receive, as well as the rate per

dollar invested, will be reduced. Therefore, to say that a reduction of wages, "other things being the same," means a rise of profits, is essentially false, because the only condition upon which such a result can follow is one that is never present, in any general sense.

The error involved in this doctrine appears to arise mainly from the mistake of regarding wealth as a fixed instead of a varying quantity. If the question of wages and profits was a matter of the division of a given amount of wealth already in existence, the distribution of which had no influence upon future production, this theory might have some force. But when it is a question of the distribution of wealth, the amount of which in the future depends upon how that now existing is distributed, as it always does in an industrial society, the case is very different. One is a question of arithmetical division, and the other one of economic law. It is only with the latter that economic science is concerned and in which the community is interested. Clearly, therefore, as profits depend upon the extent and continuity of the demand for commodities, which, in turn, depends mainly upon the consumption or wages of the laboring classes, a fall of wages cannot in any general sense tend to promote a rise of profits. The concern of the laborer is not so much as to whether he shall have one or three dollars a day, but as to the actual amount of wealth he can finally obtain for a day's labor. For the same reason, the manufacturer has no special interest in a high rate of profit. What he really wants is a large actual income. On the other hand, the community has no special interest in reducing the actual income of the manufacturer. Its only concern is to increase its own. This result, however, is compatible only with an increase in the gen-

eral rate of real wages. Low wages involve a relatively small aggregate consumption, which always implies slow methods of production, and slow methods of production make a high rate of profit inevitable, even to obtain a small income.

Suppose a manufacturer of shoes, in order to live according to the accepted standard of his class, was forced to charge a profit of ten cents a pair; and if, by using improved machinery, he could make the same shoes for one third less, and be enabled to sell twice as many, he could reduce the price of the shoes to the consumer, and actually obtain more wealth per day for himself at a profit of six cents a pair, than he had previously done with his small production at a profit of ten cents a pair. It will be observed that this can only occur according as the aggregate demand for commodities (real wages) is increased; which is precisely what has always taken place just in proportion as wages or the demand per capita of the population has increased. This explains why the manufacturer of to-day is actually richer with a profit of two cents a pound on cotton cloth than he was fifty years ago with a profit of more than double that amount.

Thus it is clear that by the increased aggregate production, consequent upon the larger general demand for commodities (higher wages), all classes would become actually richer. The laborer would get more wealth through his increased wages—the general consumer would obtain more through lower prices—and the manufacturer, while receiving a smaller per cent of the total product in profits, will actually obtain a greater quantity of wealth through the larger productions and extended business.

This principle is fully illustrated by the experience of

England, where the hours of labor are shorter and the wages higher than in any country in Europe ; and the increase in the use of capital and the production of wealth per capita is greater than in any country in the world.* Instead of English products being undersold by those of the long-hour and low-paid continental laborers, it is to protect themselves against the competition of the products of the nine and one half hour laborers of England that the high tariffs are imposed in every country on the continent, and in this country as well. *We* are not afraid to compete with the products of the thirteen to sixteen-hour labor of Russia, Austria, and Italy, but it is the products of England, where the hours of labor are the least of those in any country in the world, that we are most anxious to exclude.

The fact that a diminishing per cent of the total product goes to profits is not an economic disadvantage to the capitalist, for the reason that while a smaller per cent of the aggregate wealth will go for profits, the relative size of the profit-receiving class is diminishing in a still greater ratio. Hence, the capitalists are becoming both absolutely and relatively richer and relatively fewer in number as the aggregate wealth increases.

This being the natural result of a general rise of wages, which in the last chapter we have seen would be the logical consequence of the adoption of an eight-hour system, it follows that the economic effect upon profits by the adoption of that system would be to diminish profits relatively to the aggregate wealth and population, and to increase them actually and relatively

---

* See Chapter VIII., Part III., pp. 336, 338.

to the number of the profit-receiving class. In other words, it would tend to reduce profits in proportion to the wealth and number of those by whom they are paid, and to increase them in proportion to the number by whom they are received.

Obviously, therefore, *it would tend to improve the economic and social condition of the laboring classes without injuring that of the capitalist.* In order to procure the full advantages of this measure without incurring the temporary disadvantages incident to all social changes, two conditions are necessary, both of which are attainable : (1) That its adoption be general, and (2) That it be gradual.

The adoption of this measure should be general, because all its important economic effects to which we have referred arise from its influence upon the general social character of the masses, which, to be effectual, must necessarily be general ; at least, it must be sufficiently so to be national. Not that it would be entirely useless to reduce the hours of labor in a single city, industry, or state, but the temporary disadvantages would be greater, and the permanent benefits arising therefrom would be not only very much less, but very much less in proportion to the number affected by it. Thus, *e.g.*, if it were adopted simultaneously in America, England, France, and Germany, it would permanently affect the social atmosphere of the masses over the best part of the civilized world. The economic effect of so extensive an influence would probably be ten times greater than if it were only adopted in any one of those countries. And if it were applied to the whole ten millions of wage laborers in this country, the economic advantages

would be proportionately very much greater than if it were only applied to one million of laborers.

As the economic and social benefits of an eight-hour and half-time system, to all classes, increase in proportion as its application is extended, it is clearly to the interest of the employing classes to use their social and political influence to secure its general uniform adoption. By so doing they would eliminate much of the class feeling from the social controversy, destroy the excuse for revolutionary methods, and help the masses to take the first step in true social reform, by means of which the economic condition of all classes would be permanently promoted without injury to any.

(2) Its adoption should be gradual.

The charge that an abrupt reduction of three hours a day would be inimical to business, and hence to profits—at least temporarily—is the most valid of any objection that is urged against this measure. It is a well-established fact in economics that any sudden disturbance of industrial relations, however sound in principle it may be, would, for the time being, have an injurious effect upon business. Witness financial panics, sudden inflation, contraction of the currency, etc. Some such result might be temporarily produced by the sudden adoption of a general eight-hour system. But this can easily be avoided by providing that it go into operation gradually—say half an hour a day every six months. By this means it would take three years to get the measure in full operation, during which time industrial relations would naturally be adjusted without serious inconvenience or injury to any class in the community.

CHAPTER V.

WHAT WOULD BE ITS EFFECT UPON RENT?

RENT, as we have elsewhere explained, sustains substantially the same economic relation to wages as do profits.* Therefore, for all practical purposes, the real answer to the above question is given in the preceding chapter, and need detain us but a few moments here.

The value of land is governed by the same general causes as that of commodities. Consequently, rent is subject to the same social and economic influences as profits. Indeed, in the strict sense of the term, it is profit. For the same reason that the laborer will not devote his efforts to production without wages, and the capitalist devote his capital without profit, will no one pay rent for land, either for the purposes of agriculture, manufacture, or commerce, unless it will reimburse him for his outlay, and afford him something for his trouble.

Whether land, for whatever purpose it is used, will do that, depends upon the social character and wealth-consuming capacity of the community. No matter how fertile, or conveniently situated for manufacturing or commercial purposes, land may be, it will yield no rent unless the results of its use or cultivation

---

* For a full consideration of the question of Rent and Profits, the reader is referred to the next volume, where a chapter is devoted to each subject.

are demanded in sufficient quantities and at such prices as will pay for all the labor, risk, and enterprise devoted to its production.

And this effective demand, as we have so often pointed out, is finally determined by the wants or socially accepted standard of living of the people. In other words, rent, like profit, primarily depends upon the consumption of wealth per capita of the population, or the real wages of the masses, actually rising and relatively falling as wages are increased. This explains why the actual rent-roll of the community increases as civilization advances. Nor is this inimical to the interests of the laborer or the community, as is so commonly claimed by the leading socialistic reformers and their confiding followers.

The statement persistently proclaimed by Henry George, on the one hand, that a rise of rent implies a fall or prevents a rise of wages, and that of Karl Marx, on the other hand, that extreme wealth at one pole of society implies extreme poverty at the other, are both essentially false. As we explained in the last chapter in relation to profit, these claims would be true if it were a question of a mere division of a fixed quantity already in existence. If we were considering the division of a given estate among a fixed number of people, or the apportionment of the booty in a community of brigands, there would be considerable force to this claim, because in such cases it would be a mere matter of mathematics. Consequently, the more one portion obtained of the estate or booty, the less there would be for the others. Whether the wealth thus obtained should be wasted or wisely consumed would not affect the amount received, for the reason that it is procured by gift or plunder. This, however,

could not be true in any industrial community, where wealth is produced as the economic consequence of consumption or the effectual demand, and distributed through the natural equity of exchange, under the free operation of social and economic forces. Indeed, it could be possible only where wealth is obtained by the process of taking something for nothing. We are often referred to the history of Rome as an illustration of the truth of the affirmation, that the increase of wealth among the upper classes necessarily involves an increase of the poverty of the lower. Probably Rome is the strongest case that could be cited in support of that position, and at first sight it seems convincing. A moment's reflection, however, will suffice to show that instead of sustaining the conclusion of either Marx or George, it affords a complete confirmation of our own view. Rome was notoriously a military and not an industrial State. She obtained the bulk of her wealth not by productive industry, but by organized brigandage. The most pronounced trait in the Roman character was contempt for industry. Nothing could be more degrading in the eye of Roman society than to be engaged in an industrial or commercial pursuit.* Those who produced wealth received nothing but social contempt, while those who were most successful in confiscating the property of others received all the honors and emoluments of the state. The little wealth that was produced was wrung from slaves under such debasing and brutalizing conditions that they were unable to reproduce their kind

---

* Augustus is said to have pronounced the sentence of death upon Senator Ovinius for "having so degraded himself as to engage in manufacture."

as fast as they died off, and their numbers could only be kept up by the enslavement of the people whose countries they had conquered and whose wealth they had confiscated. In short, Rome was economically a colossal highwayman, who lived mainly upon the plunder and forced tribute from her neighbors. For these reasons, it is true that to the extent that the wealth of Rome was the result of military instead of industrial effort, the opulence of the rich did increase the poverty of the poor. To that extent did it tend to promote waste, dissipation, and social and moral degeneracy among the upper classes, and weakness and disloyalty among the lower classes. Hence, when the confiscable wealth of the neighboring countries began to diminish, the fall of her power became inevitable.

Thus, while under Rome it was to a considerable extent true that extreme wealth at one pole of society implied extreme poverty at the other, it was due to the fact that Rome was a military instead of an industrial society, because she obtained her wealth by plunder instead of by production. Consequently, its distribution was not the result of the free operation of social and economic forces, but of arbitrary apportionment by authority, which is just what state socialists are demanding to-day. Economically, Rome may be said to have had very little in common with modern society. Therefore, instead of the history of Rome serving as an illustration of the necessary consequence of present industrial tendencies, it much more correctly foreshadows what might naturally be expected from the arbitrary inauguration of state socialism.

In fact, the assumption that the increase of the wealth of the modern capitalist is tending to produce

the same economic and social results as did that of the Roman patrician, implies the inability to distinguish between the effects of arbitrary division and that of economic law, the social influences of which are as opposite as those of industry and piracy.

The fact that the aggregate rent-roll of a country is increasing does not necessarily imply that the wages and profit rolls are diminishing, nor even that their increase is lessened on that account. But, on the contrary, in an industrial community an increase in the aggregate rent-roll always implies an increase in that of wages and profits also.

Economically, rent can no more precede profits than profits can precede wages. For the same reason that the laborer cannot continuously devote his effort to any purpose which will not yield him a living (wages), will the enterpriser or capitalist refuse to pay rent for land, the use of which will not yield a profit, or, at least, secure him against the ordinary risks of losing his capital.

It follows, therefore, that a permanent increase in the aggregate rents of a community is impossible without a previous increase in the aggregate profits. An increase in the aggregate profits is equally impossible without an extension of the general market, which, in turn, depends upon an increase in the general consumption by the masses. Moreover, the socially accepted standard of living, which constitutes the bedrock of the general rate of wages, being an inseparable part of the civilization of the community, cannot be lowered without a disruption of society. Indeed, a general permanent reduction of real wages is an economic impossibility. Therefore, an increase in the aggregate rents of a community is impossible with-

out an increase in the aggregate production of wealth.

Thus, from whatever point we approach this subject, we are forced to the conclusion that the actual increase of rents is only compatible with higher wages—*i.e.*, the increase in the economic ability of the masses to consume wealth. Hence, instead of the general rise of real wages being inimical to the interests of the rent-receiving classes, it is the only means by which their aggregate incomes can be increased with safety to themselves and advantage to the community.

Again, the principle that economic law always operates to the ultimate advantage of the great mass, and not to that of a small class of the community, is just as true of rents as it is of profits. The actual increase in the aggregate rent-roll, arising from the causes to which we have referred, takes a constantly diminishing per cent of the total wealth produced. Thus, while rents absolutely rise, they relatively fall with the increased consumption of wealth (real wages), because the aggregate products are increased in a much greater ratio.

The truth of this is demonstrated in the history of every industrial community in the world. The merely nominal rent of the country merchant or manufacturer takes a much larger percentage out of his small business than does the apparently fabulous rents paid in New York City. The simple reason for this is that the latter, being in close proximity to a much larger consumption, does a larger business per dollar invested than the former. This explains why nearly all manufactured products are cheaper in the city, where the rents are actually the highest, than in the country, where they are the lowest. In other words, the rents

which are actually the highest are relatively the lowest—*i.e.*, they take the smallest per cent of the wealth of those who pay them.

If we compare the aggregate product per capita of the population with that of the rent-roll at different periods in any industrial community, the operation of this law will at once be manifest. There is, perhaps, no country where the question of rent has been so widely discussed and where the income of the landowner has been regarded so inimical to industrial and social progress as in England ; and there is, outside of the United States, certainly no country where real wages and the aggregate production of wealth have increased to so great an extent. Indeed, it is to that country, above all others, to which Mr. George most delights to refer as especially illustrating the truth of his often-repeated but most fallacious statement, that rent swallows up the whole gain of increased productive power, and, consequently, poverty and pauperism increase with progress.* Now, if we compare the rent-roll with the aggregate wealth produced in that country at different periods during the last two hundred years, we shall find that it completely illustrates the operation of the law we have laid down.

Just before the close of the seventeenth century, according to the best authorities of that period (Davenant and Gregory King), the total agricultural produce, including pasture and forest land, was estimated at twenty-one million and seventy-nine thousand pounds, and the total rent at nine million four hundred and eighty thousand pounds,† a little over forty-five per cent of the whole produce.

---

* "Progress and Poverty," pp. 11, 12, 162, 163.
† Davenant's Works, Vol. IV., p. 70.

About a century later (1779), according to Arthur Young,* the total produce was estimated at seventy-two million eight hundred and twenty-six thousand eight hundred and twenty-seven pounds, and the gross rental at nineteen million two hundred thousand pounds, or about twenty-six and one half per cent of the produce.

Sixty-three years later (1842–43), McCulloch † estimated the total produce at one hundred and forty-one million six hundred and six thousand eight hundred and fifty-seven pounds, and the total rent-roll at thirty-seven million seven hundred and ninety-five thousand nine hundred and five pounds, or twenty-five and one tenth per cent of the whole produce. And in 1880, thirty-eight years later, Mulhall estimated the total agricultural produce at two hundred and seventy million pounds, and the aggregate rental at fifty-eight million pounds, or a little less than twenty-two per cent of the whole. Thus, while the rent-roll has increased six hundred per cent, the product from which it is paid has increased twelve hundred and fifty per cent. In other words, the proportion of the total agricultural produce paid in rent has diminished during the last two hundred years from forty-five to twenty-two per cent, or over one half.

If we include the land used for manufacturing and commercial purposes, which pays the highest of actual rents, we shall find the same law holds true. According to authorities already referred to, at the close of the Revolution (1689) the annual produce of all kinds was put down in round numbers at forty-three million

---

* "Political Arithmetic" (1779), Part II., pp. 27–31.
† "Statistical Account of the British Empire," 3d ed., p. 553.

pounds, and the total rent-roll at ten million pounds,* or a little over twenty-three per cent of the whole produce of the country. In 1882 the total produce was estimated at one billion two hundred million pounds,† and the total rental at one hundred and thirty-one million four hundred and six-eight thousand two hundred and eighty-eight pounds, or about eleven and ninety-five one hundredths per cent of the whole product of the country.

Thus, while the aggregate rental has increased about thirteen hundred per cent, the total product has increased within a fraction of twenty-eight hundred per cent. In other words, while rents have absolutely increased over thirteenfold relatively to the wealth produced, they have fallen about fifty-five per cent.

From this it is evident that in proportion as the standard of living of the masses has risen—the general consumption and consequent production of wealth increased—the land-owning, like the profit-receiving class, has become actually richer, but, at the same time, it obtains a smaller per cent of the total wealth produced. This being true, it follows that the economic effect of the rise of wages, which we have seen would result from the general adoption of an eight-hour system, is positively favorable to the interests of both the profit and rent-receiving classes.

From whatever point of view the proposition for a general reduction of the hours of labor is considered, it will be seen that its economic effect is to promote the industrial progress, not merely of the laboring

---

* Davenant's Works, Vol. IV., p. 71.

† This estimate was based upon Mulhall's figures for 1880, which put the total product at one billion one hundred and fifty-six million pounds.—" *Balance Sheet of the World,*" p. 33.

class, but of the whole community. Indeed, were it otherwise, it would not be a real reform. There can be no permanent improvement in the economic and social condition of any one class which is obtained at the expense of another. That is why true social improvement can never be promoted by any method of redistribution of existing wealth, however well intended or seemingly equitably apportioned it may be. Redistribution is necessarily arbitrary, wasteful, and unjust. In fact, it is one of the best-established principles in economic science that wealth can never be economically, and, therefore, equitably and wisely distributed, *except in the natural process of its production.* It is equally true that no progress can be real and permanent which does not tend to ultimately improve the condition of all the economic elements in the community; and this obviously necessitates an increase in the aggregate quantity of wealth produced.

There are two conditions essential to any proposition for the promotion of the industrial and social welfare of the masses : (1) *That it must operate upon and through the subtle and unconscious influences of economic law;* and (2) *That it must automatically tend to increase the total production of wealth.* Unlike all propositions for the arbitrary manipulation of industrial interests, the measure we have proposed completely conforms to both of these conditions. It involves no arbitrary disturbance of any socially recognized vested interests, nor would it precipitate any sudden change in the prevailing industrial and social institutions. It is directed to and relies wholly upon the automatic but unrestricted operation of economic and social forces. All that it asks is that the laborer shall have a little more leisure time, by means

of which, as we have shown, he not only *could*, but necessarily *would*, gradually be brought into more frequent contact with an increasing variety of social influences. The natural, and therefore necessary, tendency of this would be to eliminate enforced idleness and able-bodied pauperism—the gradual but general development of the wants and standard of living of the masses—the increased consumption of wealth, and, consequently, the use of improved machinery—the use of large capitals and the larger aggregate production of wealth, yielding higher wages to the laborer and lower prices to the consumer—a larger aggregate but smaller rate of profit to the capitalist and rent to the landowner—thus naturally improving the economic condition of all classes in the community without injuring that of any.

CHAPTER VI.

THE FEASIBILITY OF SHORT-HOUR LEGISLATION.

SECTION I.—*History of Factory Legislation in England from* 1800 *to* 1840.

AFTER all, the question of adopting an eight-hour system must turn largely upon its feasibility. Its economic and social advantages previously pointed out being conceded, if the obstacles to its practical application were such as to ultimately neutralize its benefits, as its opponents would fain have us believe, its importance as a measure of social reform would be destroyed. Fortunately, however, the answer of experience confirms in full its feasible character. A uniform reduction of the hours of labor, the regulation of the labor and education of working children, and the sanitary and other conditions of mines, factories, and workshops, is not an untried experiment. This system does not introduce any new principle into society, but it is only the scientific application of one which, though never understood, experience has demonstrated to be indispensable to social progress. It has been adopted more or less extensively in different countries, and wherever its application has been sufficiently general to exercise any appreciable economic or social influence, the effect has always been of the most encouraging character.

A ten-hour law, with half-time schools for working

children, has been in operation to a limited extent in England for forty years, and, without half-time schools, for thirteen years in Massachusetts. Although in both countries it was adopted for humanitarian and not for economic reasons, despite the pessimistic prophecies of its enemies, after having been tried for nearly half a century in the former and more than a decade in the latter, its beneficial effect upon the material, educational, and social conditions of the masses is unqualifiedly attested to in the official public documents of both countries. Indeed, it is the only kind of industrial legislation that has ever stood the test of experience. Wherever it has been adopted, to any considerable extent, its success has more than sustained the claims of its most sanguine friends. Its good effect has not only completely answered the objections and exploded the false predictions of its enemies, but in many cases it has converted them into its ardent friends.

England was the cradle of the factory system. It was there that the spinning-jenny, the spinning-frame, the power-loom, and the steam-engine were brought into existence. It was there that machinery was first brought into general use, and the division of labor became possible. It was also there that the political economy originated out of which grew the blind industrial policy of sacrificing human beings to produce and save wealth, instead of using wealth to save and improve human beings. Hence, it was naturally there that the evils growing out of the excessive toil of women and children in the polluting atmosphere of the factory and workshop first forced themselves upon the attention of statesmen.

In the name of humanity and decency, legislation

upon the hours of labor began to be demanded at the very commencement of the present century—indeed, as soon as the factory system had become fairly organized. At that time (1800) before any legislation reducing the hours of labor, providing half-time schools for working children, or in any other way increasing the social opportunities of the masses had been adopted, the social condition of the factory operatives in the north of England was very little, if any, better than that of the agricultural laborers of the south.*

The conditions under which the factory population in England at that time lived and labored was such that I have no power to adequately describe it. In the earlier years of the factory system, before steam-power was much used, factories were driven by water, and had, therefore, to be located on the banks of streams, mostly in the country. The inventions of Hargreaves and Arkwright made it possible to employ a large number of children and women in productive industries. The opposition of the spinners and hand-loom weavers to the use of the new machines, which they regarded as their deadly enemy, was such that for a time it was difficult to obtain a sufficient number of children, minors, and women to run the machines, especially as the factories were, for the most part, located in sparsely-populated districts. Accordingly, the apprentice system, which had been in vogue since the early days of Elizabeth, in all the branches of artisan labor, was applied to the factory operatives.

Under these circumstances, in order to keep down

---

* Rogers thinks the condition of the factory operative was even worse than that of the agricultural laborer at that time. See "Work and Wages," p. 495.

the "poor rates," the inmates of the poor-houses were forced into the factories. The poor-law authorities transferred (practically sold) pauper children to distant manufacturers, whose only responsibility was to furnish such food, clothing, and shelter as was indispensable to keep them in working condition.

With this almost absolute power over the laborers, the manufacturers were enabled to compel the operatives to work under whatever conditions and as many hours as they chose, without let or hindrance. According to the testimony taken before Parliamentary committees, and from other official statements upon the subject at that time, women and children, from seven years of age and upward, were compelled to work under the most unwholesome and immoral conditions from fourteen to sixteen hours a day, and in some cases more, often forcing the children to work part of the day on Sunday.* The debasing consequence of these conditions was such that, in 1802, Sir Robert Peel, who was one of the largest cotton manufacturers in England, introduced a bill into Parliament reducing the time of labor for apprentices in factories to twelve hours per day. This bill, which was regarded as very radical, if not revolutionary, provided : (1) For the washing and ventilation of factories. (2) For the proper clothing of the apprentices. (3) For the

---

* " Every Sunday children are employed in cleaning the machinery. Their orders are to work from six to twelve at noon. I have known children to work for three weeks together from five in the morning till nine or ten o'clock at night, with the exception of one hour for meals. I have frequently found the children asleep on the mill floor."—*Testimony of John Moss, a manager of mill apprentices at Backbarrow, before Sir Robert Peel's Committee*, 1816. See Grant's " History of Factory Legislation in England," p. 10.

limitation of their labor to twelve hours per day. (4) For the instruction of apprentices in reading and writing during the first four years of their apprenticeship. (5) For the separation of the sexes. (6) For Sunday instruction for apprentices and attendance at divine service. (7) For justices at quarter sessions to appoint persons to visit such factories. This bill became a law, and, although its provisions relating to the sanitary condition of the factories, the education of the apprentices, etc., were never enforced, it accomplished one important result: it practically reduced the working time of the operatives about two hours a day, and greatly reduced, if it did not abolish, Sunday and night work for women and children.

Simple and limited as this law was, its beneficial effect upon the operatives soon became apparent, as the testimony of physicians, overseers, and others before Parliamentary committees conclusively show.*

This kind of legislation at that time, as it has ever since, met with the bitterest opposition from the manufacturing and employing classes. Consequently, every opportunity was taken to defeat or evade it. A few years after the passage of this law a circumstance occurred which greatly favored the designs of the manufacturers to escape from what they regarded as the

---

* "Having the assistance of Dr. Percival and other eminent medical gentlemen of Manchester, together with some distinguished characters both in and out of Parliament, I brought in a bill in the forty-second year of the king (1802) for the regulation of factories containing such parish apprentices. The hours of work allowed by that bill being fewer in number than those formerly practised, a visible improvement in the health and general appearance of the children soon became evident, and since the complete operation of the act contagious disorders have rarely occurred."—*Speech of Sir Robert Peel before the Committee of the House of Commons,* May 21, 1816.

terrible hardships this legislation imposed upon them. The improvement of the steam-engine by James Watt, which had adapted it to the production of rotary motion, and its application to the driving of the new machines, including the power-loom, finally became practicable in 1806, and relieved the manufacturer from his dependence upon the water-wheel and the country stream for his motive power.

With this improvement in motive power, it became possible for the first time to build factories in the midst of populous towns and drive them by steam. The factory was thus brought to the door of the mass of the laboring population. It now became possible for children to work in the factories and live at home with their parents, and thereby avoid the necessity, and with it the hardships, of the apprenticeship system. Much as the manufacturers wanted the absolute control over the children which that system gave them, they had a still stronger desire to get from under the jurisdiction of the law, which prevented them from working children more than twelve hours a day, and prohibited their employment nights and Sundays. Accordingly, as the factory system extended—and it grew very rapidly at this period—the factories became centred mainly in the large towns.

By this means the employers were enabled to obtain the labor of children without apprenticeship conditions. They could also procure a larger number of them than were to be had in the rural districts. Thus the master succeeded in getting entirely outside the purview of the factory law, at the same time avoiding all responsibility for the food, clothing, shelter, health, and education of the working children. The consequence was that, with something of the zest that

the cannibal devours the flesh of his fellow-man, the manufacturers returned to the long-hour, Sunday, and night work system, with all its barbarities.*

Fortunately, however, sufficient time had elapsed before the return to the old system could become general to enable the advantages of the reduced hours to be established beyond doubt. This was clear to all except the manufacturers, who, like their brethren of to-day, erroneously believed their interests to be on the side of long hours and oppressive conditions for the laborers.

The employers had now escaped even the little responsibility for the life and physical condition of the children imposed by the apprentice system. A few years of real *laissez faire*, however, was sufficient to demonstrate the evils of the unlimited-hour system.

For the same reason that to be remanded back into slavery is more galling than to never have been free, to return to the unlimited-hour system, after having had a taste of the advantages of a short-hour factory law, seemed even worse than the old *régime*. The greater speed of the steam machinery became an increased tax upon the energies of the operatives. The effect upon the physical condition, to say noth-

---

* "Large buildings are now erected, not only, as formerly, on the banks of streams, but in the midst of populous towns, and, instead of parish apprentices being sought after, the children of the surrounding poor are *preferred*, whose masters, being free from the operation of the former act of Parliament, are subjected to no limitation of time in the prosecution of their business, though children are frequently admitted there to work thirteen to fourteen hours per day at the tender age of seven years, and even in some cases still younger. I need not ask the committee to give an opinion of the consequences of such a baneful practice upon the health and well-being of these little creatures."—*Speech of Sir Robert Peel before Parliamentary Committee*, 1816.

ing of the moral and social state of the operatives, especially the children and women, was such as to challenge the attention and enlist the sympathy of the most indifferent classes. Despite the fact that England was then engaged in a deadly war with Napoleon, upon the result of which the fate of civilization itself seemed to hang, the cries of the factory children were distinctly heard, and the demand for a reduction of the hours of labor for women and children again forced itself upon the attention of statesmen.

Accordingly, in 1815, Sir Robert Peel again came to the front as the champion of short-hour legislation. In that year he introduced into the House of Commons a motion for the appointment of a committee to "inquire into the expediency of applying the apprenticeship act to children of every description." This committee continued to take evidence upon the subject for three years, the result of which may be found in the reports of Parliamentary proceedings for 1816, 1817, and 1818. The effect was that, in 1819, a law was passed extending the provisions of the apprenticeship act (of 1802), not only to all children employed in cotton factories, but also prohibiting the employment of children altogether under nine years of age, and limiting the labor of all under sixteen to twelve hours a day, or seventy-two hours a week, exclusive of meals.

The beneficial effect of this measure upon the operatives soon became so manifest that it greatly strengthened the efforts of its friends, and modified the opposition of its enemies.* This was clearly

---

* " Meagre as were its provisions, there was soon a sensible improvement in the health and appearance of the children, and both masters

shown by the fact that after passing four amendments to this act, in order to make it more valid and effective in its operations, in 1825 another law was passed still further reducing the hours of labor.

The measure, which was known as "Sir John Hobhouse's bill," reduced the working time of the operatives from twelve to eleven and one half hours a day, or to sixty-nine instead of seventy-two per week. The constant improvement in the laborer's condition and the absence of injury to the capitalists which accompanied this legislation was so marked that although, with a few exceptions, it was bitterly opposed by the political economists and manufacturers, it steadily grew in public favor. Encouraged by this fact, the friends of reform began to renew their efforts for a more extensive application of this legislation. Accordingly, in 1829, the work was vigorously taken up by the Manchester "Short-time Committee." Such was the popular response to the work of the committee, that in 1831 Sir John C. Hobhouse introduced a measure embodying their claims, which was seconded by Lord Morpeth. This bill proposed: (1) That the hours of labor should be reduced to eleven per day, or sixty-six per week. (2) That it should include all minors under eighteen years of age, instead of sixteen, as formerly. (3) That night-work should be abolished for women and all persons under twenty-one years of age; and (4) That its operation, together with that of all previous factory legislation, should be extended to woollen, worsted, linen, and silk, as well as cotton factories.

---

and men became more reconciled to factory legislation."—*Grant's* "*History of Factory Legislation in England*," p. 14.

This raised a degree of opposition among the woollen, linen, and silk manufacturers hitherto unprecedented. They organized, held public meetings, and drew up a series of fourteen resolutions appealing to the public, and Parliament in particular, to save them from the calamities which would befall them and the whole industrial community if this measure should become a law. They dolefully set forth, as they do now, that to lessen the hours of labor would reduce the wages and increase the hardships of the poor. They also predicted that it would raise the price and diminish the sale of manufactured products, thereby destroying the profits of the manufacturers and driving capital from the country, the result of which would be to afflict the people with all the ills in the calendar of industrial calamities.* The consequence was that they succeeded in defeating that clause of the bill which extended its application to woollen, linen, silk, and other industries.

This was a serious blow to the measure, but it still reduced the working time in the cotton industry from eleven and one half to eleven hours per day, and was applied to all under eighteen instead of sixteen years of age, and also prohibited night-work for all under twenty-one years of age.

Having secured this much, the friends of reform decided to make another effort to obtain the lost portion of their measure. The benefit of each instalment of social opportunity thus acquired was so manifest in the improved condition of the operatives, that it steadily gained in its hold upon the sympathy and

---

* See Grant's "History of Factory Legislation," pp. 22, 23, 24, 25, 26.

support of the public. The movement had now reached the point where it had the endorsement and active support of several prominent persons among the wealthy classes, foremost among whom was Lord Ashley (afterward Earl Shaftesbury).

In 1833 Lord Ashley introduced a bill to reduce the hours of labor for women and minors in manufacturing establishments to ten per day. In order to avoid the passage of what they regarded as a radical and dangerous measure, the Government promised a bill dealing with the whole subject. The result was that Lord Althorpe, then Prime Minister, finally introduced a bill reducing the hours of labor for children to eight per day, with two hours' schooling each day. This act also provided that its own provisions and those of all previous factory acts should be applied to all textile industries except silk, and accomplished the object of Mr. Hobhouse's act, which the manufacturers defeated two years before. This was a greater step forward in short-hour legislation than its friends were then prepared to admit. While it did not make a very material reduction in the working time of operatives in cotton factories, its extension to the woollen, worsted, and flax mills greatly increased the number of operatives to whom this legislation applied. Thus to a very large number of workers it was a reduction of working time two hours a day. The extent to which such legislation is applied is often more important than the degree in which the hours are reduced.

The fact, however, that the last-named act reduced the working time of the children to eight hours a day, while all the others were working eleven, created a disproportion in the working time, which was very

inconvenient to the manufacturers. This was made a pretext on the part of the employers for the starting of a movement to repeal the law.

Meantime, however, a very much larger portion of the laboring people had begun to receive the actual benefits of the reduced hours of labor, and the good effects of the law were so obvious as to be admitted by all classes in the community, except manufacturers and political economists, who were never-failing in their opposition.

Accordingly, the mere mention of an attempt to repeal the law was the signal for a simultaneous outburst of indignation throughout the manufacturing districts. Instead of consenting to a plan for equalizing the hours of labor by increasing those of the children, as demanded by the manufacturers, the operatives proposed to accomplish that result by reducing the hours of the adults.

Two opposite movements were now set on foot, one for the repeal of the law reducing the working hours of children, and the other to extend it. The former was supported by the wealth, intelligence, and social influence of the manufacturers, and the latter by the zeal and earnestness of the factory operatives, led by Lord Ashley and a few men of means and character in Lancashire and Yorkshire. The community constituted the jury to which the case was submitted. The masters' side consisted mainly in prophesying that industrial depression, poverty, social degradation, and national dishonor would speedily befall the country if the children were not permitted to work eleven hours a day. On the other hand, the operatives pointed to the results of factory legislation in the past. They triumphantly referred to the fact that each re-

duction of the hours of labor, even when it was confined to cotton factories, was followed with marked benefits to the operatives and without injuring the employers. When it was extended to the woollen, flax, and other industries, the benefits were even more than proportionately greater. Thus, while the claims of the advocates of short-hour legislation had been approximately sustained in every instance, the evil prophecies of their opponents had as frequently proved to be nothing but the ghosts of their short-sighted and selfish fears.

As the agitation progressed, the cause of the operatives gained power in Parliament and popularity in the country. In 1839 Lord Ashley, as the leader of the people's cause in Parliament, introduced a bill extending the Factory Acts to silk mills, which had hitherto been exempt. After a protracted debate, the Government, which had always stood for the employers, was beaten by a majority of eleven.

SECTION II.—*History of the Half-Time Law of 1844 and the Ten-Hour Law of 1847.*

In 1840 Lord Ashley introduced a motion to appoint a committee to investigate the condition and the employment of children in coal and iron mines, foundries, brick-yards, and other industries not affected by the Factory Acts, with the view of bringing them under the influence of such legislation, which was also adopted.

From this and other similar experiences, it became clear to the leaders of the "masters'" movement that the opinion of the jury, both in and out of Parliament,

was steadily tending toward the side of the operatives, and that unless the case was brought to an early close the verdict would be to grant their whole claim.

In order to prevent this result, an effort was made to check the operatives' movement by depriving it of its most powerful leaders. To this end, in 1841, Sir Robert Peel, son of the author of the first factory bill, offered Lord Ashley a seat in the cabinet, that being regarded as the most effectual mode of disposing of a powerful antagonist. His lordship, however, true to the cause he had espoused, would accept it only on condition that the Government would introduce his *Ten-Hour Bill.* This being the very thing his entrance into the cabinet was intended to avoid, this offer was, of course, declined, and his lordship refused the office and its honors, and continued his work as a commoner on the floor.

It now became clear that the only way to avoid the granting of the whole of the operatives' demands, and pass a ten-hour law, was to offer a compromise. Accordingly, in 1843, Sir James Graham, then Home Secretary, promised that if Lord Ashley would desist in pressing his bill, the Government would introduce a measure dealing with the subject.

After several postponements and delays, on the 6th of February, 1843, Sir James Graham introduced a bill reducing the working hours of women, which had hitherto, like those of men, been unlimited, to eleven per day. It also reduced the working time of children from eight hours a day to half time, compelling attendance at school the other half. The objections raised to the previous law—that making irregular working hours disturbed the business—were entirely obviated by the provisions of this act.

Reducing the working hours of children to half time, and prohibiting the employment of a child any portion of both forenoon and afternoon in the same day, reduced the employment of children to a simple and uniform basis. All that was necessary, in order to have the time fully occupied, was to employ two sets of children, one to work in the forenoon and the other in the afternoon—each attending school the alternate half day.

This measure contained two elements which tended to make its operation smooth and automatic : (1) The attendance of the children at school being made an indispensable condition of their employment, tended to secure the aid of parents to enforce the school law. Even those parents who were the most ignorant and indifferent to the education of their children now became very eager to keep them constant in their school attendance, because it was the only means of securing their meagre earnings. (2) Two children being employed, each to work half of the time, no child could be employed a whole day without depriving another of half a day's employment. To do this would inflict the loss of half a day's wages upon the other child, which would be vigorously resisted. The violation of the law would thus be exposed, and, indeed, made practically impossible, by the self-interest of the operatives themselves. In other words, its operation was substantially automatic. These features, together with the fact that the law applied to children in all the leading industries, outside of agriculture, made this the most important labor measure that had ever been adopted. It provided a greater degree of social opportunity for the masses than the world had ever before seen. From this time every work-

ing child in England was spending as much time in school as in the workshop. In this way over-cramming in the former and overwork in the latter were safely guarded against.

The foundation for a degree of intellectual and social development among the masses was thus laid that had never before been dreamed of. It is from the passage of this law that the educational and social progress of the English laboring classes really dates. The extraordinary benefits this measure conferred upon the children soon conclusively established the economic and social expediency of short-hour legislation. Accordingly, instead of serving as a compromise to head off Lord Ashley's ten-hour bill, as the Government had supposed, this law had the opposite effect, and made its long delay an impossibility.

Having secured this great boon for the children, the efforts to obtain a ten-hour law, at least for women and minors under eighteen years of age, were now redoubled. The manufacturers had grown more and more bitter and vindictive in their opposition. In their almost fanatical enthusiasm for the repeal of the corn laws—the agitation for which was then at its height—they made great pretence of sympathy for the hardships of the poor ; yet they sneered at, ridiculed, and often personally abused all who favored the demand of the operatives for a ten-hour law.*

---

* The extent to which this bitter opposition was carried is shown by the fact that even John Bright, the Quaker and much-lauded reformer, was so unrelenting in his opposition to the ten-hour bill (he was a large manufacturer), and became so personally abusive in his attacks on Lord Ashley (whose motives and character were always above suspicion) for his advocacy of that measure, that in the House of Commons he was compelled to publicly apologize for his ungentlemanly conduct. See Grant's "History of Factory Legislation," p. 75.

The manufacturers and free-traders generally, led by Cobden, Bright, Roebuck, and others, backed by all the prominent political economists, who were advocating cheap bread that they might obtain cheap labor, again indulged in their doleful predictions of the calamities that would befall the laborers and the community if this bill became a law. If that measure were passed capital would leave the country, manufactures would decline, England's power and prosperity at home and her influence abroad would diminish, and she would fall from her high place among nations to that of a third or fifth-rate power in Europe. In short, all the evil prophecies which had been repeated on every occasion since 1802—not one of which had been fulfilled—were again proclaimed with as much vigor as if they involved a new discovery or a special message of warning from heaven. Professor Senior's argument—which was invented to defeat the extension of the elder Sir Robert Peel's apprentice law to factory children in 1819—"That all the profit of the manufacturer was made in the last hour," which if taken off would ruin him—was urged with increased vigor and emphasis.*

Fortunately, however, the result of the various reductions in the working time during the previous twenty years was such that the operatives and their friends had good reason to remember it, as Lord Ashley in his speech (1845) conclusively showed. In this speech, which was, in many respects, one of the most remarkable orations ever delivered in Parliament, his lordship, by data obtained from manufacturers' books, pay-rolls, and other authentic sources, exposed the

---

* See Hansard's "Parliamentary Debates," 1842-47.

fallacies of these sham prophecies. He proved that wages had not fallen, profits had not been lessened, production had not been diminished, and business prosperity had not been injured. On the contrary, he showed that wages had advanced, profits had risen, prices fallen, and production greatly increased ; and, instead of capital leaving the country, "we see gentlemen, brokers, merchants, doctors, lawyers, drapers, tailors, etc., leaving their respective professions and trades, and see them building mills in almost every town in Lancashire." Referring to the Senior "last-hour" subterfuge, his lordship declared : " It has always been urged, and has never been verified, and yet experience should go for something in these great considerations. It was broached in 1816, repeated and enforced in evidence before committees in speeches and pamphlets in 1817, 1818, and 1819, and utterly refuted by the whole subsequent history of the cotton trade from that day to the present. You had no diminution of produce, no fall in wages, no rise in price, no closing of markets, no irresistible rivalry from foreign competition, although you reduced your hours of working from sixteen, fourteen, thirteen to twelve hours in the day. What change has there occurred so mighty as to prevent a similar result in 1845 ?"*

While this speech did not convert the Brights and Cobdens, it diminished the influence of their oratory in the community against the ten-hour movement. Although it was then defeated by a majority of sixty-

---

* Hansard's " Parliamentary Debates," 1844. See also Grant's " History of Factory Legislation," pp. 95, 96, 97 ; Hodder's " Life of Earl Shaftesbury," 1886, and *Edinburgh Review*, April, 1887, p. 366.

two, in 1847, only two years later, and three years after the passage of the half-time law, it was adopted after seven divisions, in each of which it was carried by an average majority of over two to one.*

This completed the reduction of the working time during the twenty-eight years (1819 to 1847) from sixteen to five hours per day for children under thirteen years of age, and from sixteen to ten hours per day for women and for minors from thirteen to eighteen years of age. What the effect of this was upon the industrial and social condition of the masses we shall see in the next chapter.

---

* Grant's " History of Factory Legislation," p. 138.

CHAPTER VII.

THE PHENOMENAL EFFECT OF THE TEN-HOUR LAW AND HALF-TIME SCHOOLS IN ENGLAND.

SECTION I.—*The Striking Success of these Laws Converted Sir James Graham, Mr. Roebuck and Other Opponents.*

THE ten-hour law of 1847, which did not go into full operation till the first of May, 1848, was more complete in its construction and more extensive in its application than any previous legislation upon the subject. Factory inspectors were appointed to see to its enforcement, with heavy penalties for its violation. Hence, notwithstanding the ingenious devices of mill managers to evade the law, and the skill of the legal fraternity to wrench the virtue out of it, by strained interpretations in their defence, it was more literally and uniformly enforced than any previous act had been. Therefore, the effects of this law, together with that of 1844, for half-time schools, which have been in continuous operation ever since, may fairly be taken as the test of the economic and social tendency of short-hour or *opportunity-creating* legislation.

The industrial history of England from that time to this conclusively shows that, instead of verifying the pessimistic predictions of its enemies—the Cobdens, Brights, and Roebucks—it more than justified the claims of its most ardent supporters. The working

children in the leading productive industries were now for the first time receiving an education as the condition of employment. And within a single decade it became a rare thing to find an operative of either sex under twenty years of age who could not read and write.

By this means the general intelligence of the laboring classes was rapidly developed. What the schooling did for the children the increased social intercourse —for that, in its broadest sense, is social education—did for the adults. The increased leisure, with diminished exhaustion, increased the opportunity and inclination of the laborer for a greater variety of social life. This, in accordance with the principles we have laid down throughout this work, naturally tended to stimulate and enlarge his social tastes, desires and wants, raise his standard of living, and advance his wages. It also brought about, as a necessary consequence, an increase in the consumption and production of wealth ; it promoted the use of improved machinery, and thus reduced prices without lessening the income of the capitalist, thereby advancing the material prosperity and also the intellectual, moral, social, and political progress of the whole community.

And this is what the industrial history of England since 1850 shows has taken place. The marked improvement in the material and social condition of the laboring classes in all industries affected by this legislation, especially among the factory operatives, that immediately followed these two last-named measures —the half-time law of 1844 and the ten-hour law of 1847—was such that within less than a decade and a half it had not only sustained the claims of its friends, but it had completely silenced, and, in many cases, converted its most bitter enemies into positive advocates.

In 1859, eleven years after the final passage of the latter act, Mr. Barker, chief of the factory inspectors, read a paper on the condition of the factory operative before the Social Science Congress, held at Bradford, in which he said: "I have thus given you not only the result of my own experience, but the local testimony of gentlemen who weekly visit mills which employ in the aggregate upwards of seventy thousand persons, of whom upwards of forty thousand are females and forty-five hundred are children, and who all testify to the same fact—*viz.*, the almost entire disappearance of deformity and the non-appearance of any other disease specific to factory labor. And it is exceedingly gratifying to find that an experiment which had many opponents when it was about to be tried has been productive of such great benefit to the working classes, without, I believe, an atom of either personal, commercial, or national wrong. I venture to make this statement on three grounds: *First*, Because, although the hours of work have been very much diminished, *wages* have increased in some cases forty per cent, and generally about twelve per cent, and therefore the means of providing home comforts by the people have been multiplied. *Secondly*, Because it has not diminished any kind of textile production, and, therefore, it has not injured our national prosperity."

In support of this he quoted the immense increase in manufactured products and commercial prosperity, showing that the volume of business had nearly doubled from 1844 to 1858, a fact which has been fully sustained by all subsequent investigations.*

---

* Mulhall, in his " Progress of the World in the Nineteenth Century," p. 539, shows that the commerce of Great Britain not only

In support of his statement that the social condition of the masses had been greatly improved, he pointed to the great increase during the same period of schools, lectures, public gardens, and other sources of pleasure, "refinement, and civilization, which," he adds, "only take their date from the possession of the privileges which restricted labor conferred upon the people." *

In 1860 a bill was introduced to extend the Factory Acts to print works, whereupon, on March 21, Mr. J. A. Roebuck, who, it will be remembered, was one of the bitterest antagonists the half-time and ten-hour bills had to encounter, rose in the House of Commons, publicly apologized for his opposition to those measures, and supported the bill. In his speech he said: "I am about to speak on this question under somewhat peculiar circumstances. Very early in my Parliamentary career Lord Ashley, now the Earl of Shaftesbury, introduced a bill of this description. I, being an ardent political economist, as I am now, opposed the measure, . . . and was very much influenced in my opposition by what the gentlemen of Lancashire said. They declared then that it was the last half hour of the work performed by their opera-

---

actually doubled during that period, but that, including Ireland, it has doubled per capita of the population. In 1841 the commerce of Great Britain was six pounds and three shillings per head of the population, and in 1861 it was twelve pounds and ten shillings. Thus, from three years before the passage of the half-time act to two years after the time Mr. Barker made the above statement, commerce had increased six pounds and seven shillings per capita. In other words, the volume of trade increased from 1841 more than twice as fast as the population, while from 1801 to 1841 it had hardly kept pace with it. See also his "History of Prices," p. 34, London, 1885.

* Grant's "History of Factory Legislation," pp. 148, 149.

tives which made all their profits, and that if we took away that last half hour we should ruin the manufacturers of England. I listened to that statement, and trembled for the manufacturers of England [a laugh] ; but Lord Ashley persevered. Parliament passed the bill which he brought in. From that time down to the present the factories of this country have been under state control, and I appeal to this House whether the manufacturers of England have suffered by this legislation. [Great cheers.] But the honorable member for Manchester [John Bright] still I find makes the same objection. He gets up and prophesies all sorts of evil if we interfere now ; but he has kept out of view the evils for the prevention of which we are now about to interfere. [Cheers.] . . . But I will read some facts from Mr. Tremenheere's report, and will then appeal to the House of Commons, to the fathers and the brothers of English women and children, if they will not interfere to put down this tremendous evil. . . . I, at least, will not be a party to the perpetration of any such atrocities as I find recorded, and I do hope that the gentlemen of England will not be parties to them, either. . . . Having prevented this misery in the one case, let us interfere to prevent it in the other." [Great cheering.] *

Sir James Graham, who, it will be remembered, was a no less persistent opponent to short-hour legislation than Mr. Roebuck, on one occasion even threatening the resignation of the ministry if Lord Ashley's bill was passed, at once congratulated Mr. Roebuck,

---

* Hansard's "Parliamentary Debates," 1860. See also Grant's "History of Factory Legislation," pp. 149, 150.

and said: "I am glad that you have read your recantation, and I will read mine to-morrow." *

On the ninth of May, when the bill came up for a third reading, Sir James rose in his place, and said: "I am sorry once more to be involved in a short-time discussion. I have, however, *a confession to make to the House.* . . . Experience has shown to my satisfaction that many of the *predictions formerly made against the Factory Bill have not been verified by the result*, as, on the whole, that great measure of relief for women and children has contributed to the well-being and comfort of the working classes, while *it has not injured their masters.* The enactment of the present bill ought to approach as nearly as possible the Factory Act. . . . *By the vote I shall give to-night, I will endeavor to make some amends for the course I pursued in earlier life in opposing the Factory Bill.*"

Sir Thomas Bazley, a prominent manufacturer in Manchester, also rose and testified to the great and unexpected advantages which had resulted from the Factory Acts.

In a speech in the House of Commons, March 7, 1864, Mr. Gladstone added his testimony to the virtues of this measure, and said: "You have prohibited by your Factory Acts the employment of children beyond a certain number of hours, and the employment of young persons beyond a certain number of hours. . . . *It may be said that the Legislature is now almost unanimous with respect to the necessity which existed for undertaking it, and with respect to the ben-*

---

* This statement of Sir James Graham's was publicly repeated by Mr. Roebuck in a speech in the Mechanics' Institute, Sheffield, May, 1864, and was reported in the London *Times*.

eficial effect it has produced both in mitigating human suffering and in attaching important classes of the community to Parliament and the Government."

The success of this measure was not only sufficient to disarm the opposition of the average editor, politician, and manufacturer, and convert the leading statesmen from antagonists to advocates, but it also silenced the opposition of the political economists, and forced from the more candid of them a public endorsement of its economic and social soundness. Although every political economist in England who wrote before 1850 was uncompromisingly opposed to short-hour legislation, not one who has written since 1865, even of the most ultra *laissez faire* type, has ventured to announce his opposition to the Factory Acts. In fact, the ablest and most influential of them, such as Professor Newmarch, John Stuart Mill, Professors Rogers, Cairnes, Jevons, Mr. Thornton, and others, have frankly admitted the economic expediency of these measures, while those of the more modern school, especially on the continent and in this country, who have never been committed to ultra *laissez faire*, are quite pronounced in approval of their economic influence.

The social benefits arising from these measures are still further shown by their constantly growing popularity with all classes in the community, which is unmistakably indicated by the fact that in 1850, 1853, 1861, 1864, and 1867 measures were passed further extending the principle of the ten-hour law of 1847 to other industries, and in 1874, while all her commercial competitors, both on the continent and in this country, were working from eleven to fourteen hours a day, England, after thirty years' experience with a

half-time industrial system for children, and twenty-seven years with a ten-hour law for adults, further reduced the working time of the operatives *to nine and a half hours per day.*

SECTION II.—*Social Progress Shown by the Rise of Wages, the Fall of Prices, and the Diminution of Illiteracy, Pauperism, and Crime.*

If we turn from personal testimony to the unconscious economic and social data, we shall find that the answer is no less emphatic and conclusive. An examination of the economic and social condition of the laboring classes from 1850 to the present time will show that in proportion as the increased leisure and social opportunity consequent upon fewer hours of labor and half-time schools became general and permanent in their influence, the social well-being of the masses increased. This is shown (1) By the general and steady rise of wages. (2) By the increased production of wealth per capita of the population. (3) By the fall in prices. (4) By the increased general intelligence of the masses. (5) By the decrease in pauperism. (6) By the diminution of crime.

First, then, as to wages. There has never been anything like an approximately complete statistical statement of the rates of wages in the different countries from year to year, or decade to decade. Indeed, we are only just beginning, even in the most civilized countries, to recognize the importance of industrial statistics. Hence, industrial data have hitherto been meagre and fragmentary. Instead of the rates of wages being uniformly taken for all industries at the

same time, as we now take the census, the work has been undertaken in one industry or locality for some special purpose by a public-spirited person ; at another time or place by a board of trade or chamber of commerce ; at another by a labor organization or scientific or statistical society, or at another by a parliamentary committee. For this reason, while statistics have been taken in all industries, and are, for the most part, quite reliable, it is difficult to obtain them for all industries at any one date, especially up to twenty years ago.

As wages are governed by social influences, it is safe to assume, except in case of some special local disturbance, which, in relation to the general rate, would never be more than a perturbation, that their tendency in those industries not recorded was the same or similar to that of those which were.

I must beg the indulgence of the reader for a moment's digression here to correct what I regard, to say the least, as a misleading method of using statistics, especially in relation to wages. It is literally true that "figures do not lie," yet they may be, and often are, so used as to warrant the statement, so often made, "that nothing lies like figures." The percentage of a rise or fall in the rate of wages will infallibly indicate the extent of the movement in either direction from a given point. But the same percentage of rise or fall in wages at different times and places will not necessarily indicate the same actual variation in each case, unless the point from which they moved was identical. For this reason, at one time and place a small actual rise may show a large percentage of increase, while at another a much larger actual rise may show a very much smaller percentage of increase. Whether a given ac-

tual increase or diminution in wages will show a large or small percentage of rise or fall will entirely depend upon whether the amount at the point from which the variation took place is large or small. Thus, while it is true that a rise in real wages always indicates an improvement in the social condition of the masses, the extent of that improvement is not always adequately expressed by the percentage of the rise, but it is always infallibly indicated by the *absolute amount of the increase.* This is especially important in comparing the relative progress (social well-being) of the masses in different periods, countries, or industries. For instance, a rise of one hundred per cent in the wages in England in 1350 (three pence a day) would have increased the laborer's wealth less than would a rise of ten per cent in 1887. And for the same reason, to-day an increase of five per cent would give the American laborer as much additional wealth as in China a rise of one hundred per cent would give to the Mongolian. A pound of flour or a pound of beef, whether it represents one or fifty per cent of the laborer's wages, only represents the same amount of wealth or well-being. Social progress, therefore, actual or relative, is more correctly expressed in the actual amount of increase in acquisition of wealth than in any presentation of percentages. This is an important fact that should never be lost sight of in wages comparisons, and we shall rely upon the reader to keep it in mind throughout this discussion.

To resume, then. Robert Giffen, President of the British Statistical Society, estimates that during the fifty years previous to 1883 the operatives' wages in woollen manufacture rose, on an average, including women and children, one dollar and ninety-eight cents

per week, and those of artisans, two dollars and thirty-eight cents * per week, showing an average rise for the whole of two dollars and eighteen cents per week. By the returns of the Manchester Chamber of Commerce for 1883, we find that the wages of the cotton operatives (medium quality), all departments taken together, from 1850 to 1883, rose two dollars and forty-eight cents per week. Those in fine quality of goods rose one dollar and fifty-two cents per week; in bleaching, two dollars and twenty cents per week; in the building trades, two dollars and two cents per week, and in coal-mining, one dollar and ninety-two cents a week. Taking all the above industries together (and they embrace nearly one hundred different occupations outside of agriculture and the London trades), we find that from 1850 to 1883 the wages of men, women, and children have, on the average, increased two dollars and ten cents a week.†

The foregoing results are fully confirmed by Mulhall, who shows ‡ that during the forty years prior to 1875 wages in England, exclusive of agriculture, rose on the average two dollars and sixteen cents a week.

---

* This difference is partly due to the fact that there is a much larger number of children in the former than in the latter occupations.

† It is not pretended that these figures are literally correct, but when we remember that they are drawn from nearly one hundred different occupations and by expert statisticians of the highest reputation, who have such exceptional opportunities for obtaining the necessary facts as are open to the President of the British Statistical Society and the President of the Manchester Chamber of Commerce, who had free access to the pay-rolls of the leading concerns throughout the country, they may be safely accepted as approximately correct and quite reliable, and as indicating the general industrial and social conditions of the masses.

‡ "Progress of the World," p. 142, London, 1880.

And in a later work * he further shows that the wages of artisans (including London trades) and factory operatives, taken together from 1840 to 1884 (being one decade more than was covered by the estimates of Messrs. Giffen and Lord), wages rose two dollars and forty-nine cents per week.

These conclusions are thoroughly sustained by the investigations of Leone Levi,† who by distinct and, in some respects, quite different means arrives at substantially the same results. He shows that the income of the average family among the wage classes (which, he says, comprise seventy per cent of the population), from 1851 to 1880, increased from fifty-two pounds to eighty-three pounds per year, or two dollars and eighty-six cents a week per family. This embraces agricultural as well as artisan laborers in both England and Ireland, who have not been under the influence of the short-hour legislation (except as they have been indirectly affected by the improved social and industrial condition of artisan and operative classes in the towns, a fact which should not be ignored). Accordingly, the wages of agricultural laborers have only risen about seventy-two, or, at most, seventy-five cents a week. If we eliminate the agricultural laborers, who constitute twenty-three per cent, we find the rise, on the average, amounts to three dollars and thirty-seven cents per week per family.

Now, the proportion of earners to families, all taken together, are 1.57 to 1 ; according to which Mr. Levi's figures show that the wages of all classes of laborers taken together (exclusive of agriculture), from 1851 to

---

* " History of Prices," 1885, p. 125.
† " Wages and Earnings," London, 1885.

1880, have risen two dollars and fifteen cents per week, being substantially the same as given by Messrs. Giffen, Lord, and Mulhall.*

From the above facts, the general consistency of which, without pretending to literal accuracy, is sufficient to establish their approximate correctness, it is quite safe to conclude that during the last thirty-five years the general rate of wages in all industries (outside of agriculture) has actually increased from two dollars and ten cents to two dollars and twenty-five cents per week, or fully fifty per cent. But not only have nominal wages advanced under the *régime* of less hours of labor and increased social opportunities for the masses (which it was confidently predicted would bring industrial disaster), but real wages have increased to a still greater extent. The English laborer now not only receives fully fifty per cent more money than he did before the passage and the adoption of the ten-hour and half-time system, but, through the fall of prices, each dollar he receives to-day will procure him fourteen per cent more wealth than did that of 1850, and, leaving out house-rent, it will give him twenty-one per cent more. It is true that the price of meat and dairy products has risen during the period referred to, but that of wheat, clothing, furniture, and almost everything else has been greatly reduced. All investigations, without regard to the method of

---

* See also the investigations of Mr. Chadwick, as published in the journal of the Statistical Society, Dr. Wall in the "Encyclopædia Britannica," Dudley Baxter on the "National Income," Professor Young's "Labor in Europe and America," and Brassey's "Work and Wages." While these authorities deal with but a portion of that period, so far as they go they all sustain the conclusion given in the text.

computation employed, establish this fact. Mulhall, whose investigations have probably been the most extensive and come down to the most recent date,* shows that the general price level for Great Britain in 1884 was fourteen per cent lower than that of 1850—*i.e.*, what is called the "purchasing power" of money had increased fourteen per cent since the latter date.

Nor can the increase in house-rent, which Mulhall puts at about eleven per cent of the laborer's income, be properly put down as a rise in the price—*i.e.*, a rise in the price of houses of the same quality, which is what is always implied by that expression.

While it is true that the average rent paid for houses by the laboring classes in England has doubled since 1850, the quality of the average house occupied by that class, if not twice as good to-day, is certainly very much better than it was in 1850. Indeed, the kind of houses inhabited by a very large portion of the wage classes in England in 1850 are now prohibited from being used as human habitations at any price. Hence, while the laborer pays more rent to-day than he did in 1850, he gets a very much better house, which is the same as saying that he pays more money, but gets more wealth.

But assuming that the increase in house-rent is all sheer rise of price for the same quantity and quality of wealth—which obviously it is not—the rise in the money price of labor and the fall in that of commodities shows that real wages (the amount of wealth given for a day's work) in England have increased since the passage of the ten-hour law fully sixty-five per cent, or two dollars and forty cents a week.

---

* "History of Prices," 1885.

Now, according to the principle we have laid down and frequently emphasized throughout this work—that the progress of mental and moral development and of social, religious, and political freedom are the consequence of, and therefore commensurate with, the permanent increase in the consumption of wealth per capita of the laboring population—we have a right to expect, with such a permanent rise in the general rate of real wages, to find a higher standard of intelligence and general culture, and a greater degree of political power among the masses; and a diminution of ignorance, pauperism, and crime in the community. Indeed, if the evidences of the latter were wanting, the genuineness of the former might well be doubted. Fortunately, however, the indications of the intellectual, moral, and political advancement of the English laborer during this time are no less manifest than are those of his economic improvement.

The progress of the general intelligence of the masses during that period is clearly indicated by the fact that from 1840 (four years before the passage of the half-time school law) to 1870, twenty-six years after, the proportion of the adult population who could read and write increased thirty-five per cent.* In 1840 the number of children who attended school, both private and public, was nine per cent, in 1850, twelve per cent, and in 1877, seventeen per cent of the population; and in 1840 the number of children that went to the *public schools* (which are almost exclusively attended by the children of the working classes) was only 1 in 57 of the population, and in 1877 they constituted 1 in 9 of the population.† That is to say, the

---

* Mulhall's " Progress of the World," p. 167.
† *Ibid.*, pp. 89, 167.

number of adults who could read and write, from 1840 to 1870, increased thirty-five per cent faster than the population, and from 1840 to 1877 the number of children who attended school (all kinds) increased about seventy-five per cent faster than the population. During the same period the number of children who attended the *public schools* (workingmen's children) increased eight hundred per cent faster than population.

The marked growth of general intelligence among the masses is also shown by the great increase in the number of letters written by the common people. The post-office returns for the last decade of the period referred to (1867 to 1877) show that the number of letters sent through the mails rose from twenty-seven to thirty-five per head of the population,* or about thirty per cent, and the amount of newspaper reading increased to a still greater extent.

Criminal statistics for the same period afford equally conclusive evidence of the growth of the moral character of the masses. According to the official returns, the number of persons convicted of crime in Great Britain in 1840—four years before the adoption of the half-time school system—was 1 in every 780† of the population; in 1850 it was 1 in every 870;‡ in 1860, 1 in 2071; in 1885, 1 in 3272,§ being a diminution of crime in proportion to population of seventy-five per cent since 1840 and seventy-three per cent since 1850.

But this marked reduction of the criminal calendar is far from being the only evidence of the moral prog-

---

* Mulhall's " Progress of the World," p. 94.
† *Ibid.*, p. 167.   ‡ *Ibid.*, p. 89.
§ First Report of the United States Commissioner of Labor, 1886, p. 431.

ress among the masses during this period. If we examine the matter of the consumption of alcoholic drinks, we shall find that the facts all point in the same direction.

Indeed, we might well marvel were it otherwise, for the simultaneous decrease of crime and increase in the use of alcoholic drinks, if not impossible, is very improbable. Professor Leone Levi, in an exhaustive analysis of "the consumption of alcoholic and non-alcoholic beverages," has shown * that from 1867 to 1883 the consumption per head of the population of the former has steadily diminished, while that of the latter has greatly increased. From Professor Levi's figures it appears that the amount per capita of the population expended in spirits in 1867 was four dollars and ninety-four cents, and in 1883 was four dollars and eighty-eight cents. The amount per capita spent in wine in 1867 was one dollar and eight cents, and that in 1883, one dollar and six cents. The amount spent on beer—the beverage of the masses—in 1867 was ten dollars and seventy-two cents, and that in 1883, nine dollars and sixty cents per capita. It will thus be seen that while the amount spent per head of the population for all kinds of intoxicating drinks has diminished 7.27 per cent, the reduction is mostly on the consumption of beer—*the laborer's beverage*. While the amount spent upon wine and spirits decreased fourteen cents per head, or less than two per cent, that spent upon beer was reduced one dollar and twelve cents per head, or 11.66 per cent, clearly showing that the change is in the habits and character of

---

* "Wages and Earnings of the Working Classes," London, 1885, pp. 59–69.

the laboring classes, and not in those of the upper classes.

It may be further added that the decrease in the amount spent by the masses upon alcoholic drinks is not due in any degree to a change of prices, by which the same amount of liquor can be obtained for less money, but it is due to a *bona fide* diminution of the actual amount consumed per head of the population. Whatever influence the change of prices has had in that direction, which is very slight, has related to the wines and spirits of the upper classes, and not to the laborer's beer, as the following facts clearly show:

Beverages.	Gallons per Head. 1867.	Gallons per Head. 1883.	Actual Increase or Decrease per Head.	
			Increase, Gallons.	Decrease, Gallons.
British Spirits......	0.71	0.83	0.12	
Foreign "	0.28	0.23	....	0.05
Total..........	0.99	1.06	0.07	
Wine.............	0.45	0.40	....	0.05
Beer.............	29.66	27.10	....	2.56

It will be observed from the above that, taking the wine and spirits separately, the consumption of the latter has increased seven one hundredths of a gallon, and that of the former has fallen five one hundredths of a gallon per head, showing a net increase in the aggregate consumption of wine and spirits of two one hundredths of a gallon per head per annum, while that of beer—the laborer's drink—has diminished during the same period two and fifty-six one hundredth gallons for every man, woman, and child in the community.

Nor is this marked reduction in the use of intoxicating drink among the masses due in any sense to their inability to obtain it, because, as we have seen, real wages have steadily increased simultaneously with the gradual diminution in the consumption of alcoholic beverages. Were further evidence of this needed, it is abundantly supplied by the fact that during the same period that the use of alcoholic drinks has declined, that of non-alcoholic beverages has greatly increased. From 1867 to 1883 the consumption of tea per head increased 30.43 per cent, and that of cocoa, which is, hygienically, one of the most wholesome of all non-intoxicating beverages, increased 157.14 per cent, while the use of coffee, which is admitted to be the least hygienic of the non-intoxicants, has declined 14.42 per cent. The use of milk and sugar per head has also greatly increased. The most recent revenue returns also fully sustain these facts. The British Chancellor of the Exchequer, in his speech in the House of Commons, introducing the national budget last year (1886), called special attention to the fact that while the revenue from alcoholic beverages had fallen off, that from the wholesome necessaries of life had more than correspondingly increased.

From the above, three important facts are conclusively established : (1) That the diminished expenditure per head for intoxicating beverages correctly indicates a *bona fide* decrease in the use of those beverages, because the quantity per head actually consumed has diminished in about the same ratio as the amount expended upon it. (2) That this decrease is wholly confined to the beverages mostly used by the masses, and is therefore clearly due to the diminution in their habitual use of them. (3) That the use of in-

toxicating drink and the perpetration of crime among the laboring classes have both actually and relatively decreased in proportion as their wages and social opportunities have increased.*

As the natural result of higher wages, lower prices, greater intelligence, and purer morals, we naturally expect and do find a decrease of pauperism. According to the official returns in 1850,† the number of paupers in Great Britain was as 1 to every 18 of the population. In 1860 ‡ it was as 1 to 34 of the population. And in 1885 it was only as 1 to every 46 of the population, showing a relative decrease of pauperism to population of sixty-one per cent.

These facts furnish a complete answer to, and should forever silence, that shallow and flippant libel upon the laboring classes which, for more than half a century, has been constantly repeated, but never sustained— that " the reduction of the hours of labor tends to lower wages, increase idleness, dissipation, drunkenness, and vice."

We do not refer to these facts to give the impres-

---

* In presenting some important statistics showing the " moral effects of high and low wages," Professor Levi says : " It has been alleged that high wages only lead to extravagance and folly. I see no reason for such a proposition. As a rule, and in the long run, scarcity, low wages, and scantiness of food go hand in hand with high mortality, drunkenness, and crime ; while abundance, high wages, and full consumption go hand in hand with low mortality, temperance, and good behavior."—" *Wages and Earnings of the Working Classes,*" 1885, p. 35. Mulhall also gives some striking facts upon this point. See " Progress of the World," p. 103.

† Mulhall's " Progress of the World," p. 89.

‡ Statement prepared by Sir John Lubbock from the official statistical report of Great Britain, quoted in the first report of the United States Commissioner of Labor, 1886.

sion that the English laborer has reached the social millennium—not by any means.

The social state of a people where twenty out of every one hundred adults are still unable to read and write—where, on the average, every man, woman, and child annually consumes 1.46 gallons of wine and spirits and 27.10 gallons of beer—where 1 in every 46 of the population is a pauper, and 1 in every 3272 is a criminal—is not only very far from ideal perfection, but it can hardly be said to have reached more than the threshold of civilization. Our reason for calling attention to these facts is to show the important economic and social lesson they contain—that the elimination of poverty, ignorance, pauperism, intemperance, crime, and their accompanying evils move parallel with, and proportionate to, the *social opportunities* of the laboring classes.

The advocates of *laissez faire* will doubtless be ready to ascribe England's remarkable progress during the above period to her free-trade policy; but those who take that position will be called upon to explain how it is that, while England's free-trade policy applies to her whole people, it is only in those portions of the country where short-hour legislation and half-time schools obtain that this progress is to be found. They must explain how it is that the laboring classes in those sections of the country not affected by this legislation have made little more progress during that period than the same class of laborers in other European countries—they will have to explain how it is that since 1850 the wages of the mechanics and artisans have increased two dollars and forty-three cents a week, while those of the agricultural laborers have only risen about seventy-two cents a week. They will also have to explain how it is that the homes of

the English agricultural laborers to-day are very little better than those of the continental peasantry, while those of the Lancashire and Yorkshire operatives are far superior to those of the laboring classes of any other country, outside of America.

The good results of this policy are not only to be seen in the improved material condition of the masses, but in their intellectual and moral condition as well. Public opinion and legislation on the side of freedom and human progress have been practically moulded and directed by its effects. Every important reform that has occupied the public mind in England during the last quarter of a century—industrial, social, political, or religious—has originated in and received its main support from the people in those parts of the country where the influence of short-hour legislation and half-time schools has prevailed. It is notorious that the backbone of opposition to all popular reforms has been found in the representatives from the agricultural districts and the landed aristocracy. Even the enfranchisement of the agricultural laborers themselves was not the result, in any appreciable degree, of their efforts, but was mainly due to those of their brethren in the towns, who had long since procured that privilege for themselves.

Nor has the influence of this legislation upon progress been limited to England. We in America owe more to the moral results of these measures than we have yet learned to recognize. During the dark days of the Rebellion, when the success of the Union arms was very doubtful, and the English Government stood ready, as we then feared and still believe, to give aid and comfort to the enemy, the one bright spot above the horizon was the public opinion created by the

workingmen in the manufacturing districts in the north of England. Although the cotton industry was prostrated there for years, and thousands of operatives were out of employment, many of whom were on the verge of starvation, as the result of our war, they not only bore it without a murmur, but they turned England into a hot-bed of agitation by monster open-air meetings, from one hundred thousand to five hundred thousand strong, unanimously declaring for the freedom of the slave and the success of the Union, and instructing their representatives in Parliament to oppose every effort of the Government to recognize or assist the Rebellion. In the face of this popular force, the ministry did not dare do more than wink at the building of the Alabama.

I repeat, it was not from the agricultural districts that this declaration against slavery came. Not a single meeting was ever held nor a voice heard, in or out of Parliament, from those parts of the country on this question. No! It was from Birmingham, Manchester, Leeds, Bradford, Halifax, Oldham, Bolton, Stockport, Rochdale, and the manufacturing districts of the great north, that, as the first fruits of the seed of progress that had been planted by the ten-hour law and half-time schools, there arose a popular power, which, at an opportune moment, stayed the hand of the British Government, and helped us to save the republic.

The effect of similar legislation in Massachusetts is equally encouraging. The results there are not so pronounced as in England, because the ten-hour law has only been in operation a few years, and it affects much smaller proportion of the population. But, notwithstanding this fact, its elevating influence upon

the masses is so apparent that it has become very popular among all classes in the community ; so much so, that many of those who strongly opposed its adoption would now, with equal force, object to its repeal. In 1880, six years after the passage of the ten-hour law in that State, as the result of an argument made before the Legislative Labor Committee by a prominent free-trade advocate, Edward Atkinson, who has always been an active opponent of the law, on the ground "that its operation was injurious to the workingmen, as they had to work for one eleventh less than similar laborers in other States," the legislature ordered the Labor Bureau to investigate the hours of labor and the wages paid in Massachusetts and in the other New England States, and also in New York. This was done, and the result, which appeared in the Bureau Report for 1881, was as follows :

State.	Average Hours.	Average Wages per Week.
Maine	66¼	$7.04
New Hampshire	66⅜	7.44
Connecticut	65¼	7.81
Rhode Island	66	8.61
New York	65¼	7.57
Massachusetts	60	8.32

It will be seen from this investigation, which was instituted by the enemies of the law, that in the States of Maine, New Hampshire, Rhode Island, Connecticut, and New York the average working time is sixty-five and one half hours per week, and the average wages of labor seven dollars and sixty-seven cents per week ; while in Massachusetts, with only sixty hours a week,

the average wages are eight dollars and thirty-two cents per week, or sixty-three cents a week more for five and a half hours a week less labor. That is to say, the laborer in Massachusetts works twenty-two hours, or over two full days, less, and receives two dollars and fifty-two cents per month more wages than do similar laborers in the other States referred to.

There never was any legislation adopted in any country in the world that has yielded such good economic fruit! It operates alike under a monarchy in Europe and a republic in America. In fact, it is the one species of industrial legislation that has never failed, and its results have only been limited by the extent of its application.

CHAPTER VIII.

THE RELATIVE INDUSTRIAL PROGRESS IN ENGLAND AND OTHER COUNTRIES SINCE 1850.

SECTION I.—*England and Continental Countries Compared.*

IN the last chapter two important facts were established : (1) That the reduction of the hours of labor and half-time schools for working children is a practical and feasible proposition ; and (2) That it has not only not been inimical to the economic interests of either the laborer or the capitalist, but that under the influence of the leisure and social opportunities created by it, the material, social, and political progress of the masses has been phenomenal—such, indeed, as the world has never before seen. While it is not pretended that all the social advancement that has taken place in Great Britain since 1850 is due to her short-time industrial policy, that a very considerable portion of it is the result of this legislation can be easily shown. To do this, it is only necessary to compare the progress of the social well-being of the masses in England and other countries during the period under consideration. The most infallible test of the social well-being of the masses in any community is the general rate of *real* wages.

In instituting a comparison between the rate of wages paid in England and in other countries, it should be remembered that the question is not whether

330   *WEALTH AND PROGRESS.*

or no wages are higher in England than elsewhere, but whether the actual increase in the amount of wealth obtainable for a day's wages has been greater in England than in this country or on the continent since 1850.

Nor can the comparative industrial improvement be ascertained by the percentage of increase in the wages in the different countries, because, for reasons already explained,* the highest percentage of increase may sometimes indicate the smallest actual rise in real wages, and *vice versâ*. We shall, therefore, always take the actual amount and not the percentage of the increase in the quantity of wealth received as the measure of the material progress.

From the most reliable sources, we have already seen that the general rate of nominal wages in England, exclusive of agriculture, from 1850 to 1883, at the lowest estimate, has actually increased two dollars and ten cents per week. Now, according to Mulhall,† the average wages of artisans in France, from 1850 to 1880, only rose one dollar and forty-one cents per week, and the official returns for eighteen leading industries in the principal cities in France, from 1853 to 1882,‡ show an average increase of one dollar and sixty-three cents per week.§ The mean

---

* Chapter VII., Part III.   † " History of Prices," 1885, p. 124.

‡ See tables in First Report of United States Commissioner of Labor, 1886, p. 237.

§ It will be observed that these returns do not cover exactly the same dates as Mulhall's, going back three years less and coming down two years later. This will doubtless explain at least some of the difference, as the same tables show that from 1853 to 1881 the rise was only $1.60. Had they gone back to 1850 and only come to 1880 the result would probably have been very similar to Mulhall's. This is important only as showing the similarity of two different investiga-

average of these would be one dollar and fifty-two cents per week; but to give France the benefit of the most favorable returns, we will call it one dollar and sixty-three cents. Taking the official returns for nineteen industries, including spinners, weavers, winders, carders, firemen, laborers, machinists, carpenters, joiners, masons, etc., in the Rhine District of Germany, which are complete for every year from 1855 to 1885,* we find the average rate of wages has increased one dollar and fifty-four cents per week. Among the many other investigations for different portions of this period, all of which tend to show the general accuracy of the above, may be cited the elaborate tables given by Edward Young. In addition to a vast amount of statistical data relating to the wages and industrial conditions in Germany, Professor Young gives a very full table † of the average wages paid in eighty-four different industries from 1860 to 1868, inclusive. During the nine years covered by these tables, it appears that wages rose a fraction less than forty-six cents a week. If they had risen at that rate throughout the whole thirty years (1855–1885), the increase would have been exactly one dollar and fifty cents a week. This is only four cents a week less than is shown by the returns quoted above, which may therefore be regarded as substantially correct. As to the other continental countries, I have been unable to obtain reliable data as to actual wages for a sufficient portion of the period under consideration to warrant fair com-

---

tions of the same facts, which is the best internal evidence of their general correctness.

* See tables in Report of United States Commissioner of Labor, 1886, pp. 238, 239.

† " Labor in Europe and America," 1875, pp. 525, 526.

parisons, but there is ample data of other kinds just as conclusive (as we shall soon see), showing that the actual increase of wages in Italy, Spain, Austria, Russia, etc., since 1850 has been much less than in France and Germany. Therefore, taking the most liberal estimates for France and Germany, and the most moderate ones for England, the facts in relation to the rise in weekly wages may be stated as follows :

Countries.	Amount of Increase per Week.	Hours of Labor per Week.
Germany	$1.54	75*
France	1.63	72
England	2.10	60†

From the above it will be seen that the increase in the average wages in England since 1850 has been forty-seven cents a week more, with two hours a day less (and for children under fourteen seven hours a

---

* This is, if anything, too low. So far as I know, there is no law limiting the hours of labor for adults in Germany, but the prevailing practice appears to be thirteen or more hours a day. "Throughout nearly the whole of Prussia," says Professor Young, "artisans and apprentices work regularly in summer from 5 A.M. to 12, and from 1 P.M. to 7, and even later; and in winter from daybreak, sometimes 6 A.M. to 8 or 9 in the evening. The hand-weaver frequently sits in his loom, employed at monotonous labor, for sixteen hours in the day. The agricultural laborers have to work hard for twelve hours a day out of harvest-time, and during harvest-time for fourteen hours. The same rule applies to farm servants. The extreme length of the hours of daily labor is indeed one of the dark phases of the condition of the working classes in Prussia, and generally throughout Germany."—"*Labor in Europe and America,*" 1875, p. 573.

† Reduced to fifty-six hours per week in 1874, which has been the general law and practice ever since.

day less) labor than those in France, and fifty-six cents a week more, with nearly three hours a day less than those in Germany.

If we compare the variation of prices in those countries, which it is necessary to do in order to know how much wealth or real social well-being this rise of wages represents, we shall see the difference is still greater in favor of England. I have been unable to obtain anything like full returns of prices for the whole of the period since 1850, but, such as there are, they all clearly point in that direction. The price of wheat, for example, in England, has fallen from one dollar and sixty cents a bushel in 1850 to one dollar and sixteen cents a bushel in 1881; while in France during the same period it actually rose from one dollar and fifty-six cents to one dollar and sixty cents a bushel. And taking a given quantity of wheat, potatoes, meat, eggs, butter, and sugar, which in France in 1850 cost ninety-four dollars and twenty-four cents, in 1880 cost one hundred and six dollars and eight cents, showing an actual increase of eleven dollars and eighty-four cents, or over twelve and one-half per cent; while the same quantity of the same articles in England in 1850 cost eighty-six dollars and eight cents, and in 1881 only sixty-six dollars and forty cents, showing an actual fall of nineteen dollars and sixty-eight cents, or about twenty-three per cent.*

The same is true to even a greater extent of manufactured articles. This is shown by the fact that, in spite of high tariffs, England can compete with, and, in

---

* These prices are taken from Tooke and Mulhall's "Histories of Prices," the former of which comes down to 1855, and the latter to 1885.

many branches of industry can undersell, continental countries in their own markets, although she pays from thirty to eighty per cent higher wages than they do. While the statistics of prices on the continent are not complete for the whole of the period from 1850, they are quite ample for the last quarter of a century, sufficiently so to enable approximately correct general price levels to be obtained in the leading countries. According to Mulhall's tables, the price level of 1881–83, as compared with that of 1863–70, fell in the different countries as follows : England, twenty-eight per cent ; France, twenty-one per cent ; Italy, twenty-one per cent ; and Belgium, six per cent. Germany is not given, but assuming the fall of prices to have been as great there as in France, it will be seen that since 1870 the price level has fallen—*i.e.*, the purchasing capacity of a dollar has increased nine cents more in England than in France or Germany, and nearly ten cents more than the average of the four most advanced continental countries. As a general fall of prices is an actual addition to real wages, if we add this to the amount of the rise in nominal wages already referred to, we shall have an approximately correct statement of the actual and relative increase in the material well-being of the laboring classes in those countries.

Now, assuming that the general movement of prices from 1850 to 1870 was as great in France and Germany as it was in England—which we have every reason for believing it was not—the actual increase in real wages since the adoption of the ten-hour and half-time working system in England stands as follows :

        Germany........................ .... $1.62 per week.
        France .... 1.72   "
        England.. .... 2.40   "

Thus showing that the real wages of every laboring man, woman, and child have increased since 1850 sixty-eight cents a week more for two hours a day less labor in England than they have in France, and seventy-eight cents a week more for nearly three hours less labor a day than they have in Germany.

That this greater rise in real wages in England is due to the increased social opportunities afforded by short-hour legislation, is clearly shown by the fact that the wages of the agricultural laborers—to whom it did not apply, except indirectly through their contact with the towns—have only risen in about the same ratio as those of the same class on the continent, as will be seen by the following table of daily wages of agricultural laborers in the various European countries in 1835 and 1884.*

Countries.	1835.	1834.	Increase.
England	$0.32	$0.56	$0.24
France	.30	.50	.20
Germany	.16	.36	.20
Austria	.20	.40	.20
Holland and Belgium	.18	.40	.22
Russia	.12	.24	.12
Italy	.10	.24	.14
Scandinavia	.16	.28	.12

This is inconsistent with the theory that high wages increase prices, but it is in full accord with the principle we have maintained throughout this work, that high wages in the long run mean cheap things, and low wages mean dear things. This is so, for the simple reason that high wages mean large consumption,

---

* Mulhall's "History of Prices," p. 125.

which in turn means the more extensive use of capital and improved methods of production, and, as a consequence, always reduces prices. Accordingly, we find the use of natural forces is the greatest, and hence motive power is the cheapest, in those countries where wages are the highest, as will be seen from the following table :*

Countries.	Percentage of Steam Power Used.	Cost per 1000 Foot Tons of Energy in Cents.	Weekly Wages Paid to the Laborers.
Russia	10	25.20	$3.60
Austria	29	32.20	3.84
Italy	34	35.60	3.60
Portugal	34	42.40	3.60
Scandinavia	34	20.40	3.66
Spain	41	27.60	3.84
Holland	45	29.40	4.80
France	58	28.40	5.04
Germany	60	23.20	3.84
Switzerland	71	22.40	4.80
Belgium	73	20.20	4.80
Great Britain	78	16.80	7.44
Average for Europe	45	24.20	$4.40
Average for the Continent	36	26.60	$4.12

It will be seen from the above, that wages are eighty-four per cent higher, the use of steam is one hundred and seventeen per cent greater, and the cost of productive power thirty-seven per cent less in England than is the average in continental countries.

---

* These tables are condensed from those given by Mulhall in his "History of Prices," 1885.

To state the same fact another way: Through the larger consumption and consequent improved methods of production, the productive capacity of ten laborers in England (assuming their skill and dexterity to be the same) is equal to twenty in France, twenty-six in Germany, twenty-seven in Austria, forty-three in Spain, sixty-one in Italy, and seventy in Portugal.

This explains why, with a greater rise of wages, there has been simultaneously a greater fall of prices in England than on the continent since 1850. Hence, the great English statistician proudly and truly exclaims:* "This advantage enables us (England), as far as labor is concerned, to undersell continental nations by twelve per cent, although our workmen's wages are almost double."

The degree of progress in the material well-being in any country is also clearly indicated by the actual income per capita of the population. Measured by this standard, the actual progress in the different countries in Europe, from 1870 to 1880, was as shown in table on next page.

From this table it will be learned that four important facts are established: (1) That since 1870 the gross income per capita of the population has increased in every country in Europe except Turkey. (2) That in Russia, Italy, Portugal, and Germany taxation per capita has increased in a greater ratio than the earnings. Hence, the net income (free of taxes) in those countries was actually one dollar and ten cents per capita less in 1880 than in 1870. (3) That in England the increase in the gross income per capita

---

* Mulhall's "History of Prices," p. 57.

THE INCOME AND TAXATION PER CAPITA OF THE POPULATION OF THE DIFFERENT COUNTRIES IN EUROPE FOR 1870 AND 1880.

Countries.	Gross Income per Capita of the Population for 1870.	Gross Income per Capita of the Population for 1880.	Increase or Decrease in the Gross Income per Capita of the Population.	Taxation per Capita of the Population for 1870.	Taxation per Capita of the Population for 1880.	Increase or Decrease of Taxation per Capita of Population. Increase.	Increase or Decrease of Taxation per Capita of Population. Decrease.	Increase or Decrease of the Actual Income per Capita of the Population Free of Taxes. Increase.	Increase or Decrease of the Actual Income per Capita of the Population Free of Taxes. Decrease.
Turkey	$20.40	$19.20	−$1.20	$2.88	$2.64	....	$0.24	....	$0.96
Russia	36.84	37.92	+1.08	4.80	6.00	$1.20	....	....	0.12
Italy	42.28	42.64	+0.36	12.00	13.20	1.20	....	....	0.84
Portugal	38.48	38.56	+0.08	7.20	9.12	1.92	....	....	1.84
Spain	46.26	54.12	+7.86	10.08	10.80	0.72	....	$7.14	....
Austria	53.72	56.56	+2.84	8.88	9.84	0.96	....	1.88	....
Norway and Sweden	71.20	77.54	+6.34	4.80	6.48	1.68	....	4.66	....
Denmark	101.34	105.96	+4.62	10.56	10.32	....	0.24	4.86	....
Germany	88.84	89.88	+1.04	8.16	10.80	2.64	....	....	1.60
France	99.52	110.64	+11.12	15.12	21.12	6.00	....	5.12	....
Belgium	96.48	101.60	+5.12	10.56	12.72	2.16	....	2.96	....
Holland	122.02	125.08	+3.06	15.84	16.80	0.96	....	2.10	....
Great Britain	146.52	160.88	+14.36	17.52	18.96	1.44	....	12.92	....
Average for Europe	$74.14	$79.26	$4.34	$9.87	$11.44	$1.56		$2.79	
Average for the Continent	68.78	71.57	3.52	9.22	10.82	1.58		1.94	

during that period was ten times as great as that of taxation, and four times as much as the continental average. (4) That in England the actual increase in the income per capita, free of taxes, was five dollars and seventy-eight cents per annum more, or nearly double, that of any other European country, more than four times that of the European average, and over six times as large as that in continental countries.

It will thus be seen that in whatever way we consider the question, we find that the actual increase in the consumable wealth per capita (real well-being) has not only been nearly twice as great in England as that of any other country, but, taking them altogether, the increase per head subject to taxation has been four times as great, and that, after deducting taxes, has been six times as great as that of countries which have not adopted a similar industrial policy. Again, if we compare the present actual condition of the masses in England with that of those in continental countries, the difference is equally pronounced.

One of the best indications of the social condition of any people is the extent to which their energies are absorbed in providing food, clothes, and shelter. Whatever the nominal rate of wages may be, the social condition is the highest where these physical necessities can be obtained with the fewest days' labor, and where the largest proportion of the laborer's time and energies is devoted to the gratification of the higher social wants, and *vice versâ*.

The average number of days' labor per year required to furnish the laborer with food, clothing, house-rent, and taxes, and those remaining to be applied to the satisfaction of the higher social wants in the various European countries, are as follows :

Countries.	Food.	Clothes.	House Rent.	Taxes.	Higher Social Wants.
Great Britain...	114	34	29	32	91
France...	120	36	30	45	69
Germany...	155	40	27	38	40
Italy...	162	44	24	60	10
Belgium...	133	40	20	33	74
Russia...	180	49	20	37	14
Austria...	159	43	22	34	42
Spain...	164	41	24	56	15
Scandinavia...	147	40	23	30	60
European average...	148	40	24	40	46
Continental average...	152	41	23	41	40

From these facts it will be seen that the English laborer, poor as he is, after supplying himself and family with food, clothes, and shelter (all of which are better than those of his continental brother), and paying his quota of taxation, has left to be devoted to his higher social wants the income from ninety-one days' labor a year; or that of twenty-two days more than the Frenchman, forty-nine more than the Austrian, fifty-one more than the German, seventy-six more than the Spaniard, seventy-seven more than the Russian, and eighty-one more than the Italian.

In other words, the average Englishman is seventeen days' labor a year better off than the best, eighty-one days better than the worst, and fifty-one days better than the average laborer on the continent. Or, stated in money, the Englishman, after paying for his food, clothes, house-rent, and taxes, has one hundred and twelve dollars and eighty-four cents a year to devote to his higher wants, as against fifty-seven dollars and ninety-six cents for the Frenchman, twenty-five dollars and sixty cents for the German, eight dollars

and forty cents for the Russian, and only six dollars a year for the Italian. Nor has the intellectual progress of the masses in England during the period under consideration, as compared with that of those on the continent, been any less pronounced than that of their material prosperity. Take the matter of education, for instance. The number of children in proportion to population who attended school in England before the passage of the half-time school and ten-hour laws was one fourth less than in the low countries, one third less than in Switzerland and Scandinavia, and nearly one half less than in Germany; and in 1878 it was equal to that of Germany, greater than that of any other country in Europe, and about seventy per cent above the continental average, having increased about eighty per cent.

Another evidence of the greater progress in the general intelligence of the masses in England, as compared with other countries, is shown by the greater increase in the number of letters sent through the mails per capita of the population, as will be seen by the following post-office returns for 1867 and 1877:

Countries.	1867.	1877.	Actual Increase per Capita.
Great Britain	27	35	8
France	10	10	0
Germany	9	15	6
Switzerland	24	30	6
Low Countries	9	14	5
Scandinavia	7	9	2
Austria	6	8	2
Spain and Portugal	4	5	1
Italy	3	4	1
Greece	$1\frac{1}{2}$	2	$\frac{1}{2}$
Russia	$\frac{3}{4}$	1	$\frac{1}{4}$

Thus it will be seen that letter-writing, which is one of the best evidences of intelligence and general culture, has not only increased during the decade referred to thirty per cent per capita more in England than in any other country in Europe, and two hundred and fifty per cent more than the average on the continent, and, with the exception of Switzerland, it has more than doubled that of any other country in Europe.

Poverty, ignorance, and immorality being the natural accompaniments of each other (which all statisticians now admit), a permanent improvement in the material conditions and an advance in the general intelligence may be taken as implying higher morality.* Accordingly, we find that crime in proportion to population has diminished seventy-eight per cent in England since 1850,† only a little over thirty per cent in France, and twenty-five in Germany during the same period; while in Italy there has been no perceptible decrease of crime during that time. And, as we have seen in the last chapter, the number of paupers, as compared with population, has decreased sixty-one per cent since 1850, while in France they have slightly increased (one fourth of one per cent).‡

Although the number of paupers has not been diminished in France during the last thirty years, it is lower there than in any other country except England. This shows that the number of paupers was much

---

* "That public morality has risen in every country in the same degree as instruction is fully proved by the statistics of crime. In Great Britain, for example, the annual convictions compared to population have fallen sixty per cent in the last forty years."—*Mulhall's* " *Progress of the World*," p. 102.

† Chapter VII., Part III., p. 319.

‡ Mulhall's " Progress of the World," p. 546.

smaller prior to 1850 in the former than in the latter country. Through the influences to which we have referred, since that time they have been so greatly reduced in England, while remaining stationary in France, that to-day, although England keeps a more complete registry of her needy poor, she has a smaller number of paupers per hundred of the population than any other European country, as the following official statement for 1880 clearly shows :

Countries.	Total Number of Paupers.	No. per 1000 of the Population.
Great Britain	1.037,000	30*
France	1,151,000	32
Austria	1,220,000	35
Italy	1,365,000	48
Prussia	1,310,000	50
Switzerland	140,000	54
Scandinavia	301,000	38
Low Countries	1,010,000	105
Average		49
For the Continent		51

From this it will be seen that there has not only been a greater diminution of pauperism in England than in any other country since 1850, but that in 1880 it was actually seven per cent less than the lowest, and forty-two per cent less than the average in continental countries, and in 1885 the difference was still greater.

Evidence of this kind could be almost indefinitely increased, but enough has been produced to clearly establish the truth of our claim that every phase of

---

* In 1885 there were only a little over twenty-one paupers to the thousand of the population in Great Britain.

social progress—material, intellectual, and moral—has been strikingly greater in England since the adoption of the half-time and ten-hour working system than in any other country in Europe which has not adopted that industrial policy.

If we compare the progress of the political freedom of the British laborer with that of those in other European countries, the difference is equally marked in favor of England.

Section II.—*Industrial Progress in England and the United States Compared.*

In view of the higher wages and superior social and political condition of the masses in this country, we have come to habitually regard republican institutions as proof against the influence of economic conditions. Accordingly, while we have looked with some degree of sympathy not unmixed with self-conceit upon the industrial condition of the European laborer, we have persistently—though, perhaps, to a large extent unconsciously—adopted the same industrial policy, as though the same causes would not produce the same effects here as in Europe. Under the spell of this optimistic blindness, we have accepted England's economic doctrine, and ignored her industrial reforms. The consequence is, that the same industrial and social evils which we have vainly endeavored to believe were peculiar to Old World monarchies have become a permanent feature of our social life under democratic institutions.

Industrial depressions and enforced idleness, with all their evil consequences, are now as frequent

here as in Europe, as the following table clearly shows :

Great Britain.	France.	United States.	Germany.	Belgium.
1803	1804	....	....	....
1810	1810	....	....	....
1815	1813	1814	....	....
1818	1818	1818	....	....
1826	1826	1826	....	....
1830	1830	....	....	....
1837	1837	1837	1837	1837
1847	1847	1847	1847	1848
1857	1856	1857	1855	1855
1866	1866	1867	....	1864
1873	1873	1873	1873	1873
1883	1882	1882	1882	1882
1885	1885	1885	1885	1885

The pernicious industrial policy pursued in this country, which recognizes the laborer only as a physical factor in production, while ignoring him as a social factor in consumption, forcing him to accept long hours of exhaustive labor, with its socially degrading belongings, has greatly neutralized the social advantage of our republican institutions. As a consequence, we are to-day brought face to face with the startling fact, which every American statesman and citizen may well take seriously to heart, that during the last thirty-five years the laboring classes in this country have actually made less progress in social well-being than those of monarchical England.

We must not be understood as saying the laborer in England is better off to-day than the laborer in this country, nor as saying that the economic condition of the American laborer is now worse than it was in 1850. What we affirm, and what the facts prove, is that the progress in the social well-being of the masses since

that date has been less in this country than it has been in England.

If we compare the real wages — the amount of wealth obtainable for a day's labor—in this country and England in 1850 and at the present time, we shall find not merely that wages have risen a greater per cent, but that the absolute increase has been greater in England than here.

In the last chapter (page 246), it will be remembered we found that the rate of wages in England (exclusive of agriculture) from 1850 to 1880–83, taking the most moderate estimates, has risen two dollars and ten cents per week, and that during the same period the general price level has fallen—the purchasing capacity of the dollar has increased—about fourteen per cent, making a net increase in real wages of sixty-five per cent, or two dollars and forty cents a week. According to the returns given in the general census for 1850, 1860, 1870, and 1880, the average wages in this country rose during that period about twenty-nine per cent, or one dollar and ninety-nine cents a week.* Mulhall estimates that at two dollars and four cents a week. If we examine the elaborate returns given in the twentieth volume of the United States Census for 1880, which is specially devoted to wages and prices in this country from 1850 to 1880,† and in which five

---

* This is based upon the returns for three hundred and thirty-two industries or branches of industries, exclusive of agriculture. See volume on Manufactures of United States, Census for 1880 ; Table I. on Manufactures, pp. 5–8, and general remarks on manufactures, pp. 12–20.

† Speaking of the tables contained in the above volume of the Census Reports, Professor Francis A. Walker says : " The tables which are embraced in the following report of Special Agent Weeks constitute, it is believed, the largest magazine of statistics relating to the

hundred and sixty-three pages are devoted to tables of wages, embracing every occupation (outside of agriculture) in all the States, we find the average wages in those industries which existed at both dates have increased two dollars and twenty-four cents a week.

But in order to understand the amount of social well-being represented in this rise of wages, we must ascertain the movement of prices during the same period. From the price tables given by Mulhall * for each decade from 1825–30 to 1881–83, the average price of a given quantity of sixteen principal articles, including flour, meat, groceries, dairy products, cotton, wool, leather, coal, iron, etc., rose from 1841–50 to 1881–83 twenty-nine per cent, while that of clothing and furniture fell nearly thirty per cent. Assuming this to constitute ten per cent of the laborer's expenditure (which is a very liberal estimate †), it would make a rise in the general price level of twenty-six per cent during that period. According to the very extensive investigation of prices in Massachusetts made by the Bureau of Statistics of Labor, the general price level in that State, from 1830 to 1860, rose 12.70 per cent,‡ and from 1860 to 1878 it rose 14.50 per cent,§

---

wages of labor to be found in any single publication. . . . While no large body of statistics can be assumed to be free from error, the following collection of statistical data relating to the wages of labor in the United States is believed to have been as thoroughly tested and as carefully purged as it is reasonable to expect in the case of any statistical work whatsoever. All the virtue there is in frequent revision has been imparted to these tables."

* "History of Prices," pp. 183, 184.

† See Report of Bureau of Statistics of Labor, 1879, p. 89; also Engel's "Law of Consumption," *ibid.*, 1885, p. 152.

‡ Report of the Bureau of Statistics of Labor (Massachusetts), 1885, p. 466.

§ *Ibid.*, 1879. Tables VII., VIII., IX., and X., pp. 87–89.

making a rise for the whole period of 27.20 per cent. And from the returns of the Census Bureau, given in the report already referred to,* the price of a given quantity of forty articles of food, clothes, and fuel in the leading cities and States of the Union from 1850 to 1880 rose a little over twenty per cent.

Thus it will be seen that Mulhall's investigations, covering the forty-three years from 1840 to 1883, show a rise of prices of twenty-six per cent; that of Colonel Wright, embracing the forty-eight years from 1830 to 1878, shows a rise of 27.20 per cent in the price level; and that of the United States Census Bureau for the thirty years from 1850 to 1880 shows a rise of 20.17 per cent.

Now, assuming that half the rise which Colonel Wright found to have taken place between 1830 and 1860 to have occurred before 1850 (which is about what is indicated by Mulhall's tables for 1825–30 and 1841–50), and allowing the same ratio for the ten years covered by Mulhall prior to 1850, the result of these three distinct investigations of the movement of the general price level in this country from 1850 to 1880 will stand as follows:

	Percentage of Increase.
Mulhall (1850–1883)	23.00
Colonel Wright (1850–1878)	20.85
United States Census (1850–1880)	20.17

While none of these results may be literally true, their close similarity affords indisputable evidence of their approximate correctness.

Taking the most favorable estimate (which is probably the nearest correct), the price level has risen—

---

* Twentieth volume of United States Census, 1880, special report on wages and prices.

the purchasing capacity of the dollar has fallen—since 1850 in this country, twenty per cent. If we deduct this from the rise of two dollars and twenty-four cents in nominal wages, it leaves a net increase of real wages in this country since 1850 of one dollar and seventy-nine cents a week, as compared with two dollars and forty-three cents a week in England.* In other words, notwithstanding our political and natural advantages, the material well-being of the average artisan in monarchical England has actually increased sixty-four cents a week more since 1850 than that of the laborer in republican America.

If we consider the social well-being of the people as indicated by the national income, either inclusive or exclusive of taxation, instead of by wages, we shall find the facts all point to the same result—*viz.*, that the increase in wealth in proportion to the population has been greater in England than in this country. There are few questions of fact upon which the general public are more misled by our public men than upon this. The advocates of high tariff (miscalled protection), both of the press and the forum, are never tired of citing almost bewildering statistics showing the enormous increase of wealth in this country, which they falsely ascribe to tariff legislation.

They may show us—as Mr. Blaine frequently did during the presidential canvass in 1884—that from 1870 to 1880 the annual income of the people of the United States rose in round numbers from five billion and ninety-eight million to six billion seven hundred

---

* The change in house rent in the two countries has been about the same. In England in 1880 house rent took the earnings of twenty-nine days a year, and in this country it required about thirty.

and forty-nine million dollars, an actual increase of one billion six hundred and fifty-one million dollars a year; while in England, where the income is the next greatest in the world, it only rose during the same period from four billion six hundred and thirteen million to five billion five hundred and forty-nine million dollars, or nine hundred and thirty-six million dollars a year. Thus showing that the actual increase in the annual earnings of the people of Great Britain during the decade from 1870 to 1880 was seventy-six per cent less than that of those in the United States.

These facts are presented to prove, and are generally accepted as proving, that the well-being of the masses in this country had increased during that decade seventy-six per cent more than that of those in England. This conclusion, however, as we shall soon see, is as false as the figures are correct. The error is not in the facts, but in the half use made of them. As a measure of the progress in the material well-being of the masses, the increase in the aggregate national income, taken alone, is even more misleading than is the percentage of increase in wages before referred to. Any percentage of increase, however small, in the real wages of the laborer indicates some progress in his material well-being, but the aggregate income of a nation may double without any improvement; nay, even with a deterioration in the well-being of the people. The wealth or poverty of the people in any community does not depend upon the actual amount of the aggregate income of the nation, but upon the ratio between that income and the population. For example, the aggregate income of Russia is four times that of Holland, but the population is more than twenty times that of Holland. Consequently, the in-

come per capita (real well-being) in the latter is nearly three times as great as that of the former, being one hundred and twenty-four dollars and eighty-six cents in Holland as against forty-eight dollars and forty-eight cents in Russia. If we consider the increase in the annual income of England and this country from 1870 to 1880 in this light, which is the only sense in which it can be taken, as indicating the economic well-being of the people, we find the charm of these seemingly optimistic aggregates is greatly modified. For while it is true that the annual income during that decade increased one billion six hundred and fifty-one million dollars in this country as against nine hundred and thirty-six million dollars in Great Britain, the increase in our population was more than three times as great as that of England. The consequence is that the large aggregate in this country only yields an actual increase of about two dollars and sixteen cents per capita of the population, while that of England gave an increase of about fourteen dollars and thirty-six cents per capita.

There is one circumstance, however, which will be commonly regarded as greatly modifying the above result in favor of the United States. It is the fact that taxation in this country during the period referred to has been reduced five dollars and twenty-eight cents per capita, while that of Great Britain has been increased one dollar and forty-four cents per capita. If we assume that the whole amount taken in taxes is wasted, and recognize only that portion of the income as representing real well-being which is over and above taxation,* the facts would

---

* This would be a mistake, however, for while, perhaps, a larger per cent of the wealth taken by taxation is unwisely spent, a considerable

still show that the net increase was greatly in favor of England.

By adding the five dollars and twenty-eight cents per capita saved by reduced taxation to the one dollar and sixty cents gross increase in this country, and deducting the one dollar and forty-four cents per capita of increased taxation from the fourteen dollars and thirty-six cents increase in the gross income in England, the net increase in the annual income per capita of the population (free of taxes) in the two countries stand : United States, six dollars and eighty-eight cents ; Great Britain, twelve dollars and ninety-two cents.

It will thus be seen that, viewing the facts from the most favorable standpoint possible for this country (even unfairly so), we find that instead of the progress in the well-being of the masses having been seventy-six per cent greater here than in England (as indicated by the aggregate national income), the actual increase per capita has been over eighty per cent greater in England than in the United States.

If we compare the progress in the general intelligence, morality, and freedom in the two countries, we shall find the facts are equally in favor of England. The number of children attending school, as compared to population, since 1850, has increased forty-two per cent in England, and less than twenty-five per cent in the United States.* The same fact is further indi-

---

portion of all taxes are used for purposes which really represent social well-being. For example, all wealth devoted to public improvements, education, administration of justice, protection of life and property, etc., tend to increase the value of wealth and the social safety and comfort of the community.

* Not that the attendance in proportion to the population is actually greater in England than in this country, but that the increase during

cated by the proportion of the population who write letters. According to the post-office returns for the two countries, we find that the number of letters sent through the mails per head of the population from 1867 to 1877 increased eight in England as against four in the United States.

The criminal calendar shows that the number of convictions are (1878) as 1 in 900 of the population in this country, as against 1 in every 1880 of the population in Great Britain. In 1885* they had fallen to 1 in 3272 in England, while in this country they have remained practically unchanged, being in 1887 † still 1 in every 930 of the population.

It is a notorious fact that during the last quarter of a century the social and political institutions in England have constantly tended toward greater democracy for the masses, while in this country, as elsewhere shown,‡ the tendency has been increasingly in the direction of contracting the democratic principle in our government. This movement to limit instead of to extend the social influence and political power of the masses has become strikingly pronounced in municipal and state governments, and is now beginning to show itself in our national institutions. All this does not mean that the laborer in England to-day is economically better off or politically freer than the laborer

---

the last thirty-five years has been greater there than here. In 1830 it was forty per cent less there than here, and in 1880 it was only ten per cent less. To-day it is probably about the same.

* First Report of the United States Commissioner of Labor, 1886, p. 431; also Sir John Lubbock's "Digest of Statistical Report for 1885."

† Second Report of the United States Commissioner of Labor—"Convict Labor," 1887, p. 288.

‡ See next chapter.

in this country, but it does most emphatically mean that he is making greater progress in that country.

Therefore, despite the depressive influence of an odious land system, a privileged aristocracy, a state church, an obstructive House of Lords, and an opulent and obdurate monarchy, it is manifest that the economic, social, and political progress of the masses under the short-hour and half-time *régime* in England has not only been greater than that of any other country in Europe, but even greater than that of this republic during the same period.

CHAPTER IX.

THE SOCIAL AND POLITICAL NECESSITY OF AN EIGHT-HOUR AND HALF-TIME SYSTEM.

IT is now clear that the proposition for a general reduction of the hours of labor and the adoption of half-time schools for working children is not only theoretically sound and practically feasible, but as an effectual means for increasing the social opportunities and promoting industrial progress, it is more potent than are ideal political institutions.

This is shown by the fact that during the last thirty-five years the laboring classes have made more real progress with short hours under a monarchy in England than with long hours under a republic in America. Nor is this due to our political institutions, but, on the contrary, it affords a striking confirmation of the principle we have so frequently affirmed, that political institutions are not the cause but the consequence of the industrial conditions and social character of the masses. Hence, instead of regarding our social evils as the result of our political institutions, it is only by improving the industrial conditions and elevating the social character of the masses that we can maintain the integrity of our democratic institutions.

The fact that the general adoption of an eight-hour and half-time system would be an economic advantage, as we have seen, to all classes of the community—to

say nothing of the humane and moral effects—is sufficient to warrant the demand for its immediate adoption. But its social and political necessity is more imperative than its most sanguine friends have hitherto appeared to realize, or its opponents have ever been able to understand. As we have so often remarked—and it can hardly be repeated too often ; at least, until it is much better understood—the true barometer of human progress is the social character of the people. That is the dial upon which the true state of civilization, in all ages and countries, and under all conditions, is most correctly registered. While it is futile to endeavor to promote intellectual and moral development and social and political freedom without industrial prosperity, it is equally impossible to permanently accelerate industrial progress by any means which are inimical to the social and political development of the masses. Yet this is what the modern industrial policy of long hours of exhausting, unwholesome labor would seem to be specially designed to undertake.

As the complexity of productive methods has increased and the factory system has extended, an industrial policy has gradually come into vogue, the evil social effects of which the employing class have no adequate conception. Nor is this a necessary feature of the present industrial system, as is generally assumed. There is no economic or social reason why the use of improved methods of production should be inimical to social progress. Indeed, from the very nature of things, it should be the reverse. There is nothing in the division and concentration of labor and the use of machinery that necessarily involves the physical deterioration or moral and social degradation

of the laborer. Nor do we think it would be just to assert that conditions which lead to these results are due to special meanness on the part of the employing class. Employers, as a rule, would gladly do anything in their power to improve the condition of the laboring classes, if they only knew what to do without injury to themselves. If the present social evils were a necessary part of the wages system or of the natural depravity of the employing class, reform would be possible only by the entire overthrow of existing institutions, and a radical change in human nature, which might fairly be regarded as a hopeless task.

But, fortunately for civilization, such is not the case. The mere fact of working for wages does not necessarily involve either industrial hardship or social disadvantage. The laborer is not rich or poor by virtue of the particular means by which he obtains his wealth, but according to the amount of wealth he receives. Wages, as already explained,* are simply stipulated, as distinguished from contingent incomes. When the laborer worked for himself, his income was contingent upon the immediate results of his labor. When he works for another, it is stipulated in advance. And there is nothing inherent in this economic relation to make the stipulated income less than the contingent. Indeed, it is under the *régime* of stipulated incomes (wages) that the laboring classes—and all other classes — have made their greatest progress. The stipulated income of the laborer to-day is many times greater than it was when it was contingent—*i.e.*, when he worked for himself and owned all the product.†

---

* See Chapter II., Part II., pp. 73, 74.
† See Chapter I., Part I., pp. 19-21.

Indeed, all industrial differentiation tends to the specialization of labor, and all specialization of labor tends to the stipulation of incomes. Accordingly, in the most civilized countries we find the largest per cent of wage and salary receivers, and uniformly the highest incomes. In short, there is nothing in the wages or stipulated income system, *per se*, to prevent wages from rising from five hundred to five thousand or to ten thousand dollars a year, any more than there was to prevent them from rising from fifty dollars a year in the fourteenth century to five hundred dollars at the present time.

No ; the trouble is not due to any inherent principle in the existing industrial system or in human nature, but to mistaken conceptions of the law of economic relations. The employing classes have been taught to believe that profit is the centre around which all economic and social interests revolve ; that the prosperity of the community depends upon that of the employing class ; "*that profits rise as wages fall;*" * and therefore that the interests of the employing class—and hence of the whole community—are best promoted by keeping down wages.

These inverted notions of economic movement, due mainly to a misconception of the law of wages, have naturally led to a mistaken and most uneconomic industrial policy. Viewing the laborer simply as so much productive force—failing entirely to recognize his importance as a consumer—how to make labor cheap has been the important object. Accordingly, everything which tended to promote this object has

---

* See Ricardo's Works, pp. 63–75 ; also Mill's " Political Economy," Vol. II., p. 512.

been uniformly encouraged, and whatever seemed inimical to it has been vigorously opposed by the employing class.

In pursuing this policy they have constantly endeavored not only to give the laborer the minimum amount of wages, but also to procure the maximum amount of labor for it. To accomplish this, the working day has invariably been made as long as possible, being in many cases twelve and thirteen, and in the Southern States and in many countries in Europe fourteen and fifteen hours a day, including women and children, and this very often under the most unwholesome and degrading conditions.

In proportion as the use of improved machinery is extended, and the specialization of labor is increased, does this labor become physically and nervously more exhausting ; and in proportion as this pressure increases, unless the working time is correspondingly reduced, the laborer's susceptibility to the refining and elevating influences of his social environment is lessened, and his leisure moments find him dull and indifferent to all moral and political influences.

The inevitable tendency of these conditions is to cause the laborer to gravitate toward the saloon rather than to the reading-room, lecture hall, museum, and theatre for his instruction and entertainment. Persons who have to be subject to such long hours of continued toil from childhood, amid the foul air of mines and the sweltering heat and stifling atmosphere of mills and factories for a poor existence, cannot be expected to develop the ambition and force of character necessary to inspire and elevate their domestic and social relations.

And the effect of these conditions upon the women

and children is even worse. The forcing of women, especially wives and mothers, into the factory, tends directly to sap the very source from whence the springs of character arise. Just in proportion as woman is transferred from the home to the workshop, is her inspiring and refining influence in the domestic circle destroyed; and hence the social environment, and therefore the character of the children, the family, and ultimately that of the whole industrial community, is thereby lowered.

The tendency of the modern industrial policy to thus limit the social opportunity of the masses is necessarily inimical to progress; but in no country is its evil influence so dangerous as in this; and while we, of all nations, can least afford to lower the social character of our laboring classes, we are more exposed than any other country in the world to the causes which naturally tend to produce that result. Nor do our common schools afford us any adequate protection against the evils to which we refer. It is true that our schools, to which all are freely admitted, afford a considerable degree of opportunity for intellectual and social development; but a very large portion of the laboring class does not, except to a very slight extent, go through the schools. In the first place, a very large and increasing proportion of our laboring population, through industrial conditions over which they have no control, are practically outside the pale of our social and educational institutions. Were the laboring classes in this country wholly composed of our native population, reared under the influence of republican institutions, we might witness a different state of things.

In this we are unlike any other country. One of the

characteristic features of our phenomenal growth in wealth and population is that a large per cent of the laboring classes, and especially those employed in the industries where the worst conditions most prevail, are foreigners or born of foreign parents, whose social characters have been moulded by Old World conditions. To these the common school constitutes but a very small factor in their social environment. For the most part, those who are born in foreign countries do not reach our common schools at all. They go directly into our mines, factories, and workshops, where, together with the tenement hovels and their surroundings, they spend their lives amid an industrial and social environment which is seldom very little better and sometimes even worse than that of the Old World.

Nor does the common school form a much greater proportion of the environment at least of a very large per cent, of those born here of foreign parents. Indeed, it cannot reasonably be expected to be so. Parents into whose lives the refining and elevating influence of education and social culture never entered cannot be expected to have any due appreciation of the importance of education for their children.

The consequence is, as all investigation into the condition of the schooling and employment of working children shows, that through the indifference of the parents to the importance of education, and the need they have through their poverty for the few cents a day the little ones can obtain for working, combined with the insatiable desire of the employers to obtain cheap labor, children are forced into factories and workshops at seven and eight years of age. Although in many states the law forbids the employment of chil-

dren under ten years of age, yet through the causes to which we have referred, aided by ignorance of our language, and the indifference of the authorities, it is flagrantly evaded by a wilful misrepresentation of the children's ages, in order to get them out of the school and into the workshop. This is done to an extent wholly incredible to those unacquainted with factory life and practices in this country.

Indeed, the extent to which this occurs, even in New England, especially among the non-English-speaking operatives, is positively appalling. I have myself known parents who actually changed the ages of all their children in the register in their family Bible, dating their births uniformly two years earlier, in order to evade the law and get their children into the mill two years earlier; and this solely for the sake of the twenty to twenty-five cents a day they would obtain by their labor in the factory.

Manifestly, therefore, that portion of our laboring population which is of foreign birth or parentage may properly be regarded, for all general, social, and economic purposes, as outside the influence of our common schools. Hence, to the extent that our laboring classes are composed of persons of foreign birth or parentage are they, for the most part, deprived of the social opportunities indispensable to the development of the mental, moral, and social character necessary to the safe citizenship of a republic.

It is only necessary to realize the extent to which the wage-workers of this country are composed of persons of foreign birth or parentage, to show that the question of the social opportunities of the laboring classes is assuming a degree of social and political, as well as economic, importance which we cannot much

longer afford to ignore with safety to republican institutions.

Out of the 17,392,099 persons engaged in the various industries in 1880, 3,494,647 were born in foreign countries, 4,368,309 were born here of one or both foreign parents, and 3,474,344 were women and children under fifteen years of age. In other words, 45.20 per cent of all who pursued gainful occupations were of foreign birth or parentage, and 19.98 per cent were women and children under fifteen years of age.

If we examine the proportion in which these are distributed among the various industries, the importance of the point to which we have referred will at once be apparent. Taking the ratio of persons born in this country having one or both parents of foreign birth, as $1\frac{1}{4}$ to 1, which is about the proportion they sustain to each other in the whole population, we shall find that, taking employers and employed together, the per cent of those engaged in the various occupations in 1880 who were of foreign birth or parentage was as follows :

> All occupations...................... 45 20 per cent.
> Agriculture........................... 23.65   "
> Professional and personal service....... 55.08   "
> Trade and transportation............. 56.99   "
> Manufacturing, mining and mechanical 71.88   "

If we leave out the profit, rent, and salary-receiving classes, and consider the question solely in relation to those who work for wages, the extent to which our industrial classes are composed of persons of foreign birth or parentage will be more distinctly seen. Out of the 17,392,099 persons engaged in occupations for gain in this country in 1880, there were 10,547,814 working exclusively for wages. These were distributed

among the various industries as follows : Agricultural laborers, 3,323,876 ; domestic servants, 1,075,745 ; transportation, mercantile, and other industries, 2,374,-618 ; manufacturing, mining, and mechanical industries, 3,773,575.

In these industries persons of foreign birth or parentage prevailed in about the following proportions : Agricultural laborers, 23.85 per cent ; domestic servants, 54 per cent ; transportation, mercantile, and other industries, 67.33 per cent ; manufacturing, mercantile, and mining industries, 72.63 per cent. Taking fifty of the principal cities, over ninety-three per cent of those engaged in the last-named industries are of foreign birth or parentage.

It will thus be seen that of the nearly seven million of laborers employed in productive industries, outside of agriculture, about seven out of every ten, and in fifty of the principal cities more than nine out of every ten, are of foreign birth or parentage. It should also be remembered that in these industries there is a large proportion of women and children. In 1880, in fifteen important manufacturing industries, including those of cotton, woollen, silk, carpets, hosiery, clothing, tobacco, etc., 67.29 per cent of the employés were women and children under sixteen years of age.*

In view of these facts, it is idle to talk of relying for the remedy of our social evils solely upon the influence of our educational institutions, for the simple reason that, as we have seen, the great mass of our laboring population are, at least until the third generation, practically outside the influence of these institutions.

---

* United States Census, 1880, volume on Manufactures, p. 34.

It must not be inferred from this, however, that I am opposed to unaided immigration. I should just as soon think of opposing the use of improved methods of production. I refer to these facts, not to censure the emigrant or to prevent his immigration, but that we may not lose sight of the true nature of our industrial and social conditions, and in order that we may more fully realize the quality of the social material out of which, as economists and statesmen, we are called upon to make suitable citizens for a progressive republic.

The poverty consequent upon the low industrial and social conditions of Europe has sent millions of her people here to make for themselves homes. They have not come here as beggars, but as producers in search of an opportunity to procure for themselves and their families a living, and to improve their social condition, which privilege was denied them at home. They have ploughed our prairies, dug our mines, built our furnaces, forges and factories, and covered this continent with a network of highways for travel, transportation, and communication, the like of which the world has never seen before. They have given wealth and power to us, and it is our duty to create social opportunity for them. This is not only our duty to them, but it is an imperative necessity—the only means of social and political protection to ourselves.

In this regard we have been very negligent. We have vainly endeavored to both "eat our cake and keep it." Having adopted the European industrial policy, born of a one-eyed political economy, which sees the laborer as a factor in production, but not as a factor in consumption—as the preponderating element in the general market—we have made as much of

him as possible as a producer, and as little as possible of him as a consumer. Under our spread-eagle offering of "an asylum for the oppressed of all lands," we have not only extended a general invitation to the laborers of all countries to come among us, but we have taken special pains to approach the poorest, and hence socially the weakest and least characterful, portion of the laboring classes in Europe and Asia. We have held out startling, and often delusive, inducements for them to come here, sometimes actually importing them as industrial chattel.

By this means, instead of obtaining the most advanced and intelligent element, which unaided emigration would naturally bring, we have obtained the most ignorant and incompetent portion of the social product of European and Asiatic countries.

Indeed, this class has, for the most part, been preferred, because, through the perverted economic estimate of the laborer already referred to, they have been regarded as being *cheap*, which was the only reason for importing them. Then, instead of surrounding them with the best social conditions possible, we have forced them into the very worst that the consensus of the community would tolerate. We have turned them into our factories, mines, and workshops almost without regard to age, sex, or even sanitary conditions. We have put them in contact with the most improved and high-speed machinery eleven, twelve, and sometimes more hours a day, thereby putting them under greater physical and nervous strain than they were used to in some of the countries of the Old World. And we have at the same time crowded them into unwholesome hovels, the social influence of which is of the same degrading character.

THE TRUCK SYSTEM.   367

The pest-breeding and morally degrading conditions of the homes and the social life of the great mass of the laboring population in our industrial centres almost beggars description.

I have long been convinced that if their true condition was fully realized by the great intelligent middle class, they would not long be permitted to be used for human habitation. It is a common thing in the manufacturing centres, even in the Eastern States, to find a large per cent of the laborers practically in a state of pawn to the corporation for which they work. The tenements in which they live, the store at which they trade, as well as the factory in which they work, are all, directly or indirectly, in the hands of the employer.

By this means the store-book and the pay-roll are made to keep pace with each other, and a large per cent of the laborers scarcely ever receive a dollar in money, often being permanently in debt to the corporation, for which the latter holds a mortgage on their household effects. Thus the laborers are tethered to the spot, unless they go forth as tramps, leaving their little furniture behind them, or, as is commonly the case, steal away in the night.*

---

* Of this I can speak of my own knowledge. During the spring and summer of 1875 and the winter of 1875-76 I had occasion to visit nearly all the factory towns and cities in New England, except Vermont. I found the "truck system" was the general rule, especially in the smaller towns. In the spring of 1875 a strike took place in Taftville, which was regarded as one of the best factory villages in Connecticut. I was sent there from Fall River as a representative of the United States Cotton Operatives Association, of which Taftville was a branch, to investigate the case and endeavor to settle the dispute. I found a large number of families who had never been out of debt to the company since they went to the place, and a still larger

The tenements in which the operatives are housed are such as to make physical health and moral character almost impossible. They are generally owned by the corporation and built near the work, without regard to the sanitary condition of the surroundings. Frequently from six to ten or more families are crowded into one building, with but one entrance, and not even having a back door or anything approaching modern conveniences. Often these tenements have but one privy to a whole house of many families, consisting of from thirty to fifty persons.

My vocabulary is wholly inadequate to describe the condition of the tenement-houses I have seen in the factory centres in New England. A faint conception, however, of the condition of the houses of the laboring classes may be drawn from the following official statement in reference to the laborers' homes in Massachusetts, the most advanced State in the Union: "In the cities and manufacturing towns," says the report,* "the herding together of tenants in large numbers and narrow limits has become wofully prevalent. In a single building, in the town of W—, thirty-

---

number who for months together never drew a penny of money for wages. Even rent for a seat in the church was collected in the mill office. Being unable to agree upon any settlement of the dispute, the operatives decided to leave the place and go to work elsewhere. Although the union was ready to pay all the expenses of their moving, a large portion of them were compelled to stay or lose all their furniture, this being in pawn to the corporation store. See Report of Massachusetts Bureau of Statistics of Labor, 1871, pp. 467, 468 ; also *ibid.*, pp. 434-438 ; also Report for 1872, pp. 409-421. Compare Report of Labor Bureau of New Jersey, 1882, pp. 6-8 ; *ibid.*, 1883, p. 126.

* Report of the Massachusetts Bureau of Statistics of Labor for 1874, pp. 33, 34. See also *ibid.*, 1873, p. 379 ; *ibid.*, 1872, pp. 442, 443 ; *ibid.*, 1871, pp. 521-528.

two feet long, twenty feet wide, three stories high, with attics, there habitually *exist thirty-nine* people of all ages. For their use there is one pump and one privy within twenty feet of each other, with the several sink-spouts discharging upon the ground near by. The windows are without weights, and the upper sashes are immovable. No other provision is made for fresh air. Scores of similar overcrowded and uncleanly tenements exist and could be cited. It is well attested," continues the report, "that there commonly exist, in connection with the homes of the laboring classes everywhere, filthy and insufficient privies, with overflowing vaults, unhinged doors, and rotten floors ; cesspools, sink-drains, and sewers, broken or surcharged, the foul discharges permeating the soil in the immediate vicinity of wells and cisterns ; cellars, where dampness and decay are doing a constant work of death, and yet are often inhabited, enclosures made pestilential by the causes mentioned, and pig-pens and garbage-tubs ; while stairs and passage-ways are carpeted and draped with dirt of every nature."

The statements made by the Labor Bureau are fully sustained by the investigations of the Boards of Health and Education, as a most superficial glance at their reports will show.[*]

Nor is Massachusetts referred to because her laborers are worse housed than those of other States. On the contrary, they are, on the whole, socially better conditioned than the same class in any other State. Indeed, it is for this reason that industrial and social

---

[*] See Fourth Report of State Board of Health, p. 396 ; Fifth Report of Board of Health and Works of Local Boards ; Report of State Board of Health for 1872-73. Also Report of Registration, 1870, p. 63.

investigations have been more thorough, and, consequently, reliable data is more abundant there than elsewhere. She was the first to have a Labor Bureau, and its investigations have been more exhaustive and scientific than those of any other, perhaps, in the world ; and she has enacted more industrial legislation than any other State.

Since the Massachusetts Bureau was instituted, in 1869, fifteen other States have followed suit, and a National Labor Bureau has also been organized, and, so far as their investigations have been at all comprehensive, their reports reveal the social condition of the laboring classes to be as bad, and, in many States, worse to-day than they were in Massachusetts ten years ago.*

Moreover, it should be observed that these abominable tenements in which the laboring classes are housed, for the most part, at least, outside of the very large cities, are owned by the corporations, and the laborers are compelled to occupy them, on the corporation's terms, as a condition of employment. Even in so large a city as Fall River, Mass., I have seen operatives discharged for refusing to live in corporation tenements, because they were inferior to those they were occupying.

If we turn to the large cities, we find that, in many respects, the case is even worse. While the truck system, for obvious reasons, does not obtain in the large cities, the tendency to crowd the masses into small,

---

* See Second Report of Bureau of Labor of New York, 1885, pp. 154, 155, 277-286; also Maryland, 1885, p. 61 ; also Michigan, 1885, p. 262 ; also the Report of the Tenement-House Commission of 1885, city of New York, the Annual Report of the Board of Health for the city of Baltimore, etc.

unwholesome dens, where the causes which tend to prevent the development of their social character wholly neutralize the civilizing influences of city life, is appallingly manifest. In New York City alone there are thousands of families, consisting of from four to ten and twelve persons to a family, eating, sleeping, and working in apartments of one and two rooms, which, according to the official statements, are in an indescribably filthy, pest-breeding condition.*

Some idea of the alarming extent to which these conditions prevail may be conceived when it is known that in New York City there are over eight hundred and ninety-seven thousand nine hundred persons living in these tenement-houses, and more than one hundred and seventy-five thousand five hundred families existing in apartments of only three rooms each.† Nor is this state of things confined to New York City, but, unfortunately, it is proportionately prevalent in all the large cities. In Baltimore, for example, according to the latest returns,‡ there are four thousand one hundred and twenty-two families that live in houses or apartments consisting, on the average, of only two and one sixth rooms to a family.

The inevitable effect of such conditions is too obvi-

---

* See account of cigar-making in tenement-houses in the Report of the Bureau of Statistics of Labor, New York, 1884, pp. 143-182; also Report of the Council of Hygiene, pp. 8, 9, 41, 78, 84, 216, 217, 279, 280, 349; also Report of Tenement-House Commission, 1885, pp. 26, 27, 28, 29, 43, 44, 50, 51, 52, 84, 85, 86, 87, etc.

† This is based upon the investigations of the Tenement-House Survey, made by special corps, under the direction of the Sanitary Bureau, in 1879, and the unpublished data obtained by that bureau down to September 1st, 1886. This is further sustained by the returns given in the United States Census for 1880.

‡ Annual Report of the Board of Health for 1884.

ous to need stating. To expect anything better than social depravity from such influences is to expect a miracle. It may be said that we give the foreigner the ballot, which he did not enjoy in the Old World. True, but in so doing, without at the same time furnishing the opportunities necessary to develop the intelligence with which to direct its use, we have simply inflated his conscious importance as a social factor, without improving the quality of his social character. In this way we have supplied an abundance of accessible and cheap material for political and social corruption, which, it is needless to say, is being freely utilized. Forgetting that the most fatal danger to republican institutions is the ballot in the hands of the poor and ignorant masses, we have, in our economic blindness, largely fulfilled Macaulay's prophecy, and within our midst we are permitting, if not promoting, the development of the "Huns and Vandals," which, though unconsciously, none the less surely threaten the very life of the republic.

Nor is this taking an unduly pessimistic view of the situation. The dangers to which we, more than any other people, are exposed from this source are alarmingly manifest in the marked lack of political integrity and industrial and social safety that prevails. If we pause for a moment and consider where anarchy, and the use of dynamite, and other physical-force methods for reforming social evils are the most in general use ; where the lack of confidence and even pronounced distrust between social classes is most prevalent ; where the enmity of the laborers to the successful classes is most fierce and outspoken ; where the hatred of and opposition to established authority is most bitter, persistent, and general, and where all forms of political

corruption—the buying of votes, the selling of charters, the packing of caucuses, the trading of offices, from the presidency down—are the most constant, we shall find that it is in the large cities and industrial centres. It is in these very centres where, as we have seen, the greatest proportion of foreigners exist under the degrading influences of our infamous tenement-house and factory life ; where poverty, ignorance, and vice furnish abundant conditions for low social character, and supply the most inflammatory material for revolution, and the strongest excuse for despotism.

The existence of these evils is painfully recognized, but not so the causes from which they arise and the means by which they can be eliminated. We have observed the fact that the advocates of anarchy, dynamite, and other forceful methods of social disruption, with their ignorant, impulsive, and misguided followers, are mainly persons of foreign birth and characteristics. We have seen that while the foreign-born element constitutes only about fourteen per cent of our total population, it furnishes over thirty per cent of our drunkenness and crime, and a still greater per cent of the corruptible material in politics. But while we have developed a keen perception of these facts, we have shown an utter incapacity to recognize the obvious causes which have produced them. Instead of endeavoring to ascertain and remove the influences which promote this social disease—the influences which prevent the development of the mental, moral, and social character—we have, for the most part, been content with denouncing the victims, and devising, for remedies, measures which tend to their further social degradation.

Among the measures which have been offered, many

of which have been adopted, are propositions for limiting immigration, imposing property, educational, and other qualifications for voting ; lengthening the terms and increasing the appointing power of executive officers ; making popular elections less frequent ; taking the expenditure of public moneys out of the hands of popular elective bodies, and putting it into those of appointed commissioners ; taking public offices out of the reach of politics, etc. Not one of these measures has the slightest causative relation to the social malady for which they are proposed as remedies. Notwithstanding the fact that they have emanated from the journalism and colleges of the cultured classes, they are entitled to be denounced as the merest political quackery.

After having been to Europe and Asia and induced the poorest and, therefore, the lowest class of laborers to come to this country, and then turn them into the mills, mines, and factories to work as hard and as long as their physical energies can endure ; crowding them together in unwholesome tenements, in contrast to which the modern rumshop is a refining luxury; then to denounce them for their lack of intellectual, moral, and social character, is simply to condemn them for not being what we have made it practically impossible for them to be.

Nor would a property or educational qualification for voting in any way tend to remedy the evil. It might disfranchise the poor and ignorant, but it would in no way tend to increase their wealth or intelligence. Thus, having blindly prevented the social development of the masses, their incapacity is made the excuse for their disfranchisement, and, under the pretence of saving civilization, liberty is being destroyed.

The same is true of all attempts to improve our

social conditions by lengthening the terms of public offices, increasing the appointing power of executive officers, reducing the frequency of popular elections, etc. Instead of developing the character of the masses up to the level of sustaining our democratic institutions, these measures are attempts to whittle away our democratic institutions, in order to sustain our blind and pernicious industrial policy. As such measures do not affect the cause of the evil, each step in that direction only tends to make the next more necessary and the ultimate reign of despotism more certain.

Such miscalled statesmanship, whether consciously vicious or ignorantly blind, is the veriest high treason, not only to the republic here, but to human freedom everywhere. Social degradation is not peculiar to nationality, but to character; and if the character of the foreign element in our population is lower than that of the native American, it is for no other reason than that their social environment has been viler.

The social crisis, especially in this country, is increasing in gravity every day. Like all neglected economic questions, it is rapidly assuming a social and political aspect; and unless we abandon our present undemocratic and uneconomic policy of superficial tinkering with our political institutions, to evade the effects of a mistaken industrial policy, and approach the subject on the plane of broad social principles, we shall ere long find ourselves in the terrible dilemma against which Macaulay warned us, of being compelled to choose between " civilization and liberty." Social degradation and democracy are incompatible. *Either the social character of the masses must be elevated to the level of that of the political institutions, or no power on earth can prevent the character of the latter from falling*

to that of the former. This is the verdict of universal social law, from which there is no appeal.

The question, therefore, that most urgently demands the attention of the true statesman to-day, beside which all schemes for mere administrative reform are incomparably insignificant, is that of increasing the opportunities for elevating the social character of the masses. Give us this condition, and all else will be vouchsafed. With a high state of social culture among the people, wise and safe reform of existing institutions would be guaranteed. Vote-buying and ballot-box-stuffing, with their numerous phases of political chicanery, would then be impossible, and hence the many undemocratic schemes for the purification of politics, by removing the government further from the people, which are so assiduously urged by gilt-edged reformers, would become obviously inexcusable.

Such questions as tariff, finance, taxation, etc., would then be intelligently considered by the masses and scientifically settled by their chosen representatives, instead of being manipulated by superficial politicians, as is always the case with an ignorant and incapable voting constituency. Then the empty eloquence of earnest but ill-informed enthusiasts, who substitute their assumed knowledge of God's intentions for that of economic law, would exercise a less dangerous influence over the masses. The various socialistic propositions for revolutionizing existing institutions would also be estimated nearer their true social worth, and their final adoption or rejection would be determined by the intelligent judgment of the masses, rather than by the sympathetic eloquence and magnetic personal influence of a few individual leaders. The power of

personal leadership always diminishes as the general intelligence of the masses increases.

Manifestly, therefore, in view of the cosmopolitan character of our population, the increasing complexity of our industrial methods, and the democratic character of our public institutions, the maintenance of the influence and integrity of the republic makes the increased social opportunities of the masses—which a reduction of the hours of labor and half time schools alone can adequately supply—not only an economic, but also an imperative social and political necessity.

SUMMARY AND CONCLUSION.

IN the foregoing pages we have taken particular pains to avoid all appeals to sympathy or sentiment. We have asked the reader to take nothing for granted, but have endeavored to establish inductively every foot of the ground we occupy.

The principles established and propositions presented in this volume may be briefly summarized as follows :

First. That the natural order of social progress is from the material to the social, intellectual, and moral, making economics the basis of ethics, and not ethics the basis of economics. In short, that the industrial condition of the masses is the subsoil for all social, political, and moral institutions. That poverty, ignorance, and vice give despotism, while wealth, intelligence, and morality give freedom. Therefore, social progress depends upon improving the material conditions of the masses.

Second. That the wealth of the laboring classes cannot be increased by lessening that of any other class, nor by any method of redistribution whatsoever, but only by increasing the aggregate wealth produced. That no distribution of wealth can be equitable or economic which does not take place as an inseparable part of the process of production.

Third. That the only way of increasing the income

and improving the material conditions of the laboring classes is through a natural and permanent advance of real wages.

Fourth. That a natural rise of wages does not tend to increase prices, diminish profits, or to reduce rents.

Fifth. That the rate of wages is not governed by supply and demand, nor by the amount or value of the product, nor by the skill of the laborer or the caprice of the employer, but that the price of labor is governed by the same economic law as that of everything else which is subject to the conditions of exchange—viz., the cost of production.

Sixth. That the cost of producing labor is governed by the standard of the laborer's living. In other words, *the standard of living is the law of wages.*

Seventh. That the standard of living is determined by the social character of the people. Thus wages, like social and political institutions, finally depend upon the social character of the masses.

Eighth. That the character of any people or class is mainly determined by the social environment, being low or high in proportion to the simplicity or complexity of their social relations—*i.e.*, according to the *extent of their social opportunities.* Hence, social opportunity, or, in other words, contact with an increasing variety of social influences, is the natural foundation for all industrial, political, and moral reform. Therefore, no proposed change can, in any permanent sense, improve the material and moral well-being of the masses which does not tend to *increase their social opportunities.*

Ninth. That under wage-conditions, and especially under the factory system, the most, if not the only,

feasible means for enlarging the social opportunities of the masses is *a general reduction of the hours of labor*.

Tenth. That this can be effectually accomplished by the general adoption of two simple propositions :

(1) A uniform eight-hour system and (2) a half-time school system for all working children under sixteen years of age.

We do not present these propositions as a panacea for all the ills known to society, but we present them as the natural and necessary first step toward increasing the wants, developing the character, and advancing the wages of the laboring classes, and by this means lay the natural economic and social foundation for permanently sustaining democratic institutions here and promoting the progress of social and political freedom everywhere.

In saying this, we do not underrate the importance of reforming our system of finance, taxation, civil service, etc. All such reforms, however, are of a secondary character, because they do not sustain any fundamental relation to the influences which directly impel social progress. They are administrative rather than creative in their character. They relate only to the wise adjustment and regulation of the wealth, institutions, and social relations that now exist, and not to the development or the creation of new. The existing wealth might be as equally or as equitably distributed among all classes as the most ideal Communist could desire ; and the money system, the taxation system, the land system, the judiciary system, railroad, telegraph, postal, and civil service systems might be absolutely perfect without materially changing the economic and social condition of the masses. None of these things, were they possible, would increase

the general production of wealth, increase the wages, or raise the social state of the masses.

But however important these reforms may be, they are impossible until the industrial conditions and social character of the masses are elevated. Public honor and capable and wise administration of affairs are impossible, especially under democratic institutions, without a high level of general intelligence and character among the great mass by whom the legislative and executive officers are to be elected and sustained. Therefore the greater the importance of these reforms, the more imperative becomes the necessity for increasing the opportunities for developing the social character of the masses upon which they depend.

The true philosophic policy for the wage-receiving classes to pursue is not to form new political parties with long platforms and many platitudes, but to concentrate all their political and social influence upon the single issue of securing *a general reduction of the hours of labor*.

Nor should the movement be limited to any industry, or state, or to this country; it should be purely social in its character and international in its operations.

The times are ripe for such a movement. In England, where they have had more advantages from short-hour legislation than in any other country, the Trades-Union Congress now in session has taken the first step, by instructing its parliamentary committee to consider the subject, and has decided to call an International Labor Congress in London in 1888.

Such a movement, based upon the principles of sound economic philosophy and broad, comprehensive statesmanship, should receive the hearty co-operation

and support not only of workingmen, but of statesmen, moralists, philanthropists, and social reformers of all kinds whatsoever, and, above all, it should receive the support of the employing class. If an eight-hour system for adults and half-time system for all working children under sixteen years of age could be uniformly adopted in this country, England, France, Germany, Belgium, and Switzerland, its effect upon emigration, enforced idleness, business depressions, and upon real wages, together with the growth of intelligence and social character, would in twenty-five years change the face of the industrial and social institutions of Christendom.

Soc
HD
8072
G95
1990